THE IRISH BOXING REVIEW

2015 EDITION

STEVE WELLINGS

In memory of

Paddy Hyland

and

Eamonn Magee Jnr

.

CONTENTS

INTRODUCTION

Hello and welcome to the latest instalment of the Irish Boxing Review. It's hard to believe that we have reached number five already! No wonder I have got little else done over the last few years.

This year's cover star is unbeaten Belfast boxer Dee Walsh. Following in the footsteps of previous cover stars: Andy Lee, Carl Frampton, Tyson Fury and Phil Sutcliffe Jnr, I believe Walsh has the talent to go far in this sport. Dee has long possessed the skills but now with trainer Gerard McCafferty and promoter Mark Dunlop at the heart of his development I maintain that he has a team behind him necessary to reach the top. Promoter Mark Dunlop's influence on boxing in Belfast and Ireland as a whole cannot be underestimated. Mark has built up a solid stable of local talented boxers who can shift a few tickets and duly turned them into a niche attraction. His shows are the lifeblood of the sport and alongside the likes of Alan Wilton and Pat Magee keeps the pulse of boxing ticking in small halls across the country.

I think the domestic scene, particularly in the Republic, still misses Brian Peters. I remember Peters receiving criticism online (which comes with the territory I suppose) whenever he was promoting and he rightly stated at the time that he would be missed whenever he was gone from the scene. This has proven very much to be the case. His quality shows in Dublin, Limerick, Castlebar and Letterkenny, as well as in Belfast, kept the scene thriving but it was understandable that as soon as national broadcaster RTE ended its commitment to professional boxing that he would also step away.

There were as always plenty of highs this past year but also some terrible lows to hit the boxing community. The passing of Eamonn Magee Jnr and then Paddy Hyland, both within such a short space of time from one another, was particularly difficult to take. I interviewed Eamonn shortly before he made his professional debut and found an amiable young man ready to step up and follow in the footsteps of his illustrious father by winning titles. I have no doubt that Eamonn Jnr would've won at least the British title (he modestly stated this was aim when I asked).

On a personal level I was extremely saddened to hear the news that Paddy Hyland was no longer with us. I had not spoken to Paddy for a while, apart from a few Facebook messages here and there, but I briefly caught up with him at the 3Arena Dublin last November. Sitting in the corner, tying his shoelaces as son Patrick warmed down after a points win, I went over and chatted with Paddy. Regrettably this would turn out to be the final time.

I started writing about boxing in 2005 but really got involved in the Irish scene in 2007 and Paddy Hyland was a constant presence throughout these early stages of my development. He promoted one of the best fights I have ever been ringside for, when son Eddie Hyland went toe-to-toe with Oisin Fagan in the Tallaght Basketball Arena in 2009. He also promoted the first Dublin show I ever reported on, in April 2008, when all three of his sons boxed in the National Stadium. I recall him ringing me up after Paul won the EU belt in Italy, full of enthusiasm about the performance and where it would lead. Ultimately it led the younger Hyland to a European super-bantamweight title fight with Willie Casey in Limerick when Paul stepped in at short notice for his shot at glory. When BUI president Mel Christle invited me down to Dublin to attend a European Boxing Union dinner, Paddy Hyland was on the same table regaling us with many tales from his years within the sport. Like Eamonn Magee Jnr, he will be greatly missed.

On a lighter note, I remain a huge fan of boxing podcasts which appear to be going from strength to strength. I still regularly appear on the Boxing Asylum panel every Sunday evening and occasionally guest host the show when required. I also enjoy listening to the Boxing Coalition, the HBO Boxing podcast, Boxing News' weekly offering, The Boxing Rant and TKO Radio. In early February of this year I embarked on a new podcasting adventure alongside Irish-boxing.com duo Jonny Stapleton and Derek McKenna and Niall Doran of Boxing News and Views. Unfortunately personal circumstances got in the way and I was forced to shelve this venture but I hope to recommence at some point in the future. I think there is definitely room for an Irish boxing podcast as the popular 4thumps show proved. My good friends Kevin Byrne and Ciaran Gallagher joined amateur boxer Eric Donovan for an eight-part series at the end of the 2014 and have plans to return in the future.

As usual I will give a mention to the fellow boxing writers who do an excellent job covering the Irish boxing scene, many of whom are members of the Irish Boxing Writers' Association (visit ibwa.ie for more information).

Gerry Callan (Irish Daily Star), Cormac Campbell (The Detail), Ciarán

Gallagher (Irish Daily Mail), David Mohan (Andersonstown News), Kevin Byrne (Irish Sun, treasurer), Martin Breheny (Irish Independent, honorary), Jonny Stapleton (irish-boxing.com), Nicky Fullerton (Belfast Newsletter), Éamon Carr (Evening Herald), Vincent Hogan (Irish Independent), Darragh Maloney (RTE), Barry Flynn (author), Barry Fitzgerald (Setanta Sports), Declan O'Kelly (Irish Voice), Andy Watters (Irish News), Seán McGoldrick (Sunday World), Paul Gibson (Guardian).

Special mentions go to boxing historian Brian Madden and Mel Christle, the President of the Boxing Union of Ireland, as well as Brendan Galbraith, Leonard Gunning of Boxing Ireland, David Kelly of the Belfast Telegraph, Derek McKenna of Irish-boxing.com and Niall Doran from Boxing News and Views. Thanks to Odhran Crumley for contributing to the book and supporting us. I always give a shout out to the guys at Boxing News who gave me a big break into this journalism lark all those years ago. Also a mention for a bunch of dedicated boxing supporters over on Facebook who are busy running the 'Belfast Boxers Old and New' group led by Hugh O'Halloran and Eamonn Magill. Special thanks goes to Gerry Callan as always for providing results, records and statistics.

Finally, if you enjoy this book and get a spare minute then a quick rating and review on Amazon or a 'like' on our Facebook page would be very much appreciated. You can follow all of our activities via Twitter @irishboxreview, or over at facebook.com/irishboxingreview and Google Plus. Thanks to Sarah Michelle Lynch of SML Publishing (@SarahMichelleLy) for once again doing an excellent job formatting the Review and to Mark Dunlop for providing the cover image.

Don't forget to follow on Twitter: @BelfastBoxing - @boxing_belfast - @Dublin_Boxing - @LoveIrishBoxing - @Irishboxingcom - @Greenjab - @boxingNAV - @belfastboxers and many more. Enjoy the latest version of the Irish Boxing Review.

Best wishes, Steve Wellings

Photograph: Steve with Nicky Fullerton (Belfast Newsletter) and Eamon Carr (Irish Independent)

Is Carl Frampton Set to Bring Irish Boxing to Heights Never Reached?

By Jonny Stapleton

'We've been here before' quipped respected Belfast-based boxing scribe Steve Wellings with a smile sent in my direction as Carl Frampton strutted through a wall of sound en route to the ring.

Myself, Steve, his customary packet of Werthers Originals and the mini army of Irish boxing press had occupied ringside at Frampton fights going back to the Ulster Hall days. We had been in the Odyssey Arena, the venue for that night's Frampton-Martinez I bout, and at McCloskey and Rogan clashes too.

However, Boxing News's Irish go-to man wasn't talking about the arena that was quickly becoming known as 'The Jackal's lair', nor was he indicating that we had previous live fight night Frampton experience. What Mr Wellings was suggesting was we were not raucous atmosphere virgins.

We had been immersed in that hairs-on-the-back-of-the-neck atmosphere before. The collective excitement that makes you want to ditch your pen and note pad, grab a ticket and join the fanatical, vocal and often tipsy punters further away from ringside wasn't completely new to us. It's passionate, partisan and let's party! It's a unique sporting experience that only boxing in Ireland can generate. Forget raising the roof, 'The Jackal Army' where threatening to launch the Odyssey cap into orbit and, yes, we had been there before!

Apart from the flashing of camera phones it was identical to the atmosphere created by one Bernard Dunne back in what up until Frampton's arrival were known as the 'good old days'. That blue European super-bantamweight title and a pacing Kiko Martinez added to the familiarity.

Wellings was talking about the call to arms of the Jackal Army.

You watch with pride as the foreign media sit stunned as cheesy wedding DJ classics such as 'Alice' and 'Sweet Caroline' are belted out like they were national anthems. The 9,000 in attendance warm up their vocal cords, readying themselves to further raise the decibel levels when their man makes his way to the ring.

If you're feeling proud you wonder what the fighter must be feeling as the noise travels down the corridor and into his dressing room. Come ring walk time you stand up, you soak it in, you smile in the knowledge that you are experiencing a special sporting moment. Yes we had been there before, yes we were there again, but in terms of Frampton you get the feeling he could take the modern day Irish fight fraternity to places we have never been.

Like Dunne, the Belfast star has captured the hearts of his home town. The Cyclone Promotions' fighter also boasts that elusive and much-desired 'crossover' appeal and has created a storm among casual fans. Again, similar to Dunne in Dublin, a Frampton fight is massive news in Belfast. He jumps from the back to the front page, is the apple of terrestrial news' eye, celebrities decorate ringside at his bouts and even his lovely wife Christine is in media demand.

It's all reminiscent of the much-mourned Dunne era. Any objections along the lines of "Frampton hasn't emulated Dunne's world title winning achievements" wouldn't be overruled, but whilst he hasn't claimed a world strap he has claimed ticket selling bragging rights.

Frampton's rematch with our old pal Kiko Martinez will be played out in front of 16,000 fight fans while Dunne's fight of the year contender with Ricardo Cordoba tested the hearts of 9,000. And you always got the feeling that historic and unforgettable night in 2009 was going to be the pinnacle of Dunne's career; the end to of an emotional and exciting journey. On the other hand, a win on September 6 could prove the beginning of one of the most exciting chapters in Frampton's career and Irish sport.

The super-bantamweight division is hot at the moment. There are high-profile fights with the likes of Scott Quigg, Leo Santa Cruz and the fighter no one wants a piece of, Guillermo Rigondeaux, all available to Frampton. Unlike Dunne, Frampton is also known outside of Ireland and is a name American and British boxing scribes often type on the keyboards. A bout with Quigg would be massive and given the Sky Sports News treatment, could be a Stadium sell out.

Santa Cruz, who fights as chief support to Mayweather next time out, would provide a passage to the American big time. He has already expressed a desire to trade leather with Frampton and a fight with the Mexican Showtime regular could provide the Cyclone Promotions puncher with the chance to take America by storm. He could certainly do a Ricky Hatton and bring an invading Jackal Army to the States. The Belfast lilt might fill the New York air or drown out the sound of Vegas slot machines as Frampton becomes an American fixture.

Cork-managed Cuban fight legend 'Rigo' provides a potential passage to the pound-for-pound rankings. Although most would urge Frampton to steer clear for now. Regardless, there is a real air of optimism about the Martinez repeat. Not just because Frampton could join names such as Barry McGuigan, Wayne McCullough, Steve Collins, Bernard Dunne, Brian Magee and others on the list of Irish world champions, but rather an IBF super-bantamweight world title win could lead to mega fights.

There are those who will rightly argue that Irish fighters have been involved in fights of the massive, mega and money-spinning kind already. However, modern era-wise there is a unique feel to what Frampton could do. Only recently Matthew Macklin shared a ring with Sergio Martinez and Andy Lee with Julio Cesar Chavez Jr, but at the time neither fighter had a solid base of support in Ireland. Nor did either have the option of winning a world title on home soil or, unless they fought each other, of selling out a 16,000 venue at home.

They both entered those fights as underdogs and as challengers. If Frampton claims the IBF strap he will go into mega-fight negotiations as a champion and with the bargaining chip selling out stadiums brings. Without winning a world title 'The hardest punching super-bantamweight in the world' is already bringing Belfast, the boxing capital of Ireland, the biggest boxing show it has ever seen. Indeed such is his talent and such is the hype, he has ensured Ireland's biggest fight night since Steve Collins challenged Chris Eubank twice in 1995.

All this and he is only 27 and with his peak years ahead. Sunday, September 7 might be the first step in a journey the likes we have never been on before.

Jonny Stapleton is the current editor at Irish-boxing.com.

Jones Backs Frampton to Beat Kiko and Earn World Strap
– 5th August 2014

Boxing pundit Ingram Jones has thrown his weight behind Carl Frampton's world title challenge in early September. Speaking in a special interview conducted for the 2014 edition of the Irish Boxing Review the head of BaylorIC TV explained what he thinks of Frampton's chances and the Belfast man's future prospects.

"I think Carl Frampton could go on to become a great Irish fighter in the future if he is managed carefully. What I mean by this is taking the right fights at the right time," said Jones.

"He has all the talent in the world but that doesn't mean we should throw him to the lions but rather get him in fights that are testing but not fights each and every fight is be a war. [This] causes burnout and his career therefore is shortened. I'm sure his management team are doing a fine job and can appreciate my thoughts."

Ingram also revealed that he is fully aware of the Irish boxing circuit, its history and its current goings on. Jones has interviewed Tyson Fury and his team and counts himself as a fan of their fighting style.

"My knowledge of Irish boxing isn't that bad, Dave McAuley I would watch box on BBC Television with Harry Carpenter. Steve Collins when he challenged Chris Eubank for his title. Matthew Macklin, Andy Lee and of course Barry McGuigan. I wished the fight between McGuigan and Azumah Nelson had happened, that would have been a superfight. Sadly I caught the tail end of Barry's career - he fight with Steve Cruz and his fight with Jim McDonnell. Wayne McCullough was another fighter I watched not only win the world title but fight in some fantastic matchups. Wayne was so durable and a talented boxer, if only he was a power puncher. His fight against Prince Naseem Hamed is still memorable."

Could the Weather KO Frampton's Open Arena Plans?
– 6th August 2014

Frank Brownlow, Belfast Telegraph: "An outdoor arena could of course present weather issue – what the event's promoter, and boxing legend, Barry McGuigan wouldn't give for our sun-kissed spell. The time of year and the exposed and often windy location down on Belfast Lough means it is very possible the weather could turn nasty. [McGuigan] said wind or rain will not halt what is one of the most ambitious sporting events ever staged in Northern Ireland."

Matt Christie, Boxing News: "Boxing has received a massive boost going into 2015 with the news that Carl Frampton's February 28th IBF super-bantamweight title defence will be broadcast live on ITV1. The contest is the first UK-staged world title scrap to be shown live on terrestrial television since Carl Froch beat Jean Pascal in 2008, and will be hosted at the Odyssey Arena in Belfast. Four other parties were interested in broadcasting Frampton's first fight since September, but Barry McGuigan - who heads Cyclone Promotions - wanted it on ITV."

Frampton Reveals He Was Unhappy with First Martinez Performance – 13ᵗʰ August 2014

The clock is ticking down on Carl Frampton's highly-anticipated rematch with Kiko Martinez on September 6 as both men prepare for their crossroads fight. Even though the first Martinez encounter was seen in many quarters as Frampton's finest performance to date, he is not a fan of reliving that glorious February evening.

"Although I won the first fight and people see it as one of my better performances, I don't like watching that fight back. I made so many mistakes in that fight but I've learned from them," assured 'The Jackal'.

"The first fight was a great fight but a close fight before I came on top. I have to give Kiko a lot of credit for coming back to Belfast. We've been chasing a lot of champions, Leo Santa Cruz included, who didn't want to fight me. I'm showing Kiko a lot of respect here and I won't be taking anything for granted. This is a fight that I'm going to win because I feel it's my time to become a world champion. I've been ready for a long time and I'm more than ready now."

Fights with the likes of Leo Santa Cruz, Scott Quigg and Guillermo Rigondeaux have been debated for a while but as yet nothing has been set in stone. If arranged, any one of those bouts on home soil would represent a huge night in the history of Irish boxing. Carl, meanwhile, extended praise to the diminutive Spaniard for not only winning the IBF world crown but also successfully defending it on the road.

"Kiko beat Jhonatan Romero and he beat him well but Romero was one of the weakest champions in the history of the super-bantamweight division. Mathebula was a good fighter but over the hill and the exact same with Hasegawa. He's looked good but against fighters who are past it. I'm better than we fought the first time and I knocked him out so take what you want from that.

"Everything is falling into place for me and it's my time to take the title and keep it here in Belfast for a long time to come," said Frampton.

Chris Avalos: 'I Will Beat the Winner of Martinez-Frampton II' – 27th August 2014

When Carl Frampton and Kiko Martinez clash for the Spaniard's portion of world honours next week there will be one interested spectator across the pond tuning in to see who prevails in the big Belfast blockbuster. California's Chris Avalos, a 24-year-old with a 24-2 (18 KOs) record, sits as IBF super-bantamweight No.1 and will be patiently waiting in line for the winner.

"The IBF have said for whoever wins it's mandatory that within 90 days we have to put a fight together so of course I'll be watching this bout," said Avalos who is reluctant to make a definitive call on who he believes will emerge victorious.

"I don't really want to predict who is going to win or lose this fight because there's a lot at stake. I heard that before the first fight Martinez was going through a lot of issues and problems with his personal life and things. I personally don't want to call anybody out but it could go to a draw maybe."

Chris insists that he should be the one taking aim at champion Kiko, either on September 6 or whenever manager Mike Criscio negotiated had the American's title shot been secured. Avalos, however, has taken solace in the response of the IBF after the governing body stipulated that the winner is automatically required to defend against him within the next three months.

"Yes, me and Martinez were supposed to fight," he continued. "This Frampton fight that's going on was a secret fight. No one knew that it was happening and the only people that knew were in Belfast and some over here [in the United States] so the fight was secretly made. I was supposed to be fighting on a card against Martinez but Frampton paid to get the fight because they put up the money. Myself and Frampton were supposed to box in an elimination for Martinez but we didn't because he pulled out."

When asked if he would be willing to travel across the water to fight Frampton in Belfast -should the Northern Irishman prevail- Avalos's response was emphatic. He cited that in his last contest he travelled to Macao, China to box Japan's Yasutaka Ishimoto on the Donaire-Vetyeka undercard in a bout that served as an IBF eliminator. The corner of 32-

year-old Ishimoto pulled their man out after a sustained beating and Avalos returned home with an eighth-round knockout victory on his record.

"I wouldn't mind going to Belfast but I'll go anywhere. I would be willing to travel to China to fight him and in fact I actually went to fight in China. I just asked where the next fight was and they said China and I didn't care, wherever it's going to be at is OK. It doesn't matter where it happens, the only thing that's going to change is that you are going to have a loss on your record because whoever wants to get in the ring with me I'm going to whoop their ass! Martinez or Frampton, it doesn't matter if we fight two miles away or whatever. The only thing that matters is who they put in front of me and what it's for. I don't care if it's in their backyard or their kitchen, we can fight."

That was a rare moment of frustration slipping through as for the most part Chris Avalos was still as polite and considered as the undefeated prospect, then just 19, that I first spoke to back in 2009. Times have changed and regardless of the two losses he has since suffered the Lancaster resident appears to be a more mature product both in and out of the ring. 'The Hitman' holds a strong belief that the lengthy wait for a world title will only be sweeter when his big chance finally arrives.

"For Frampton and Martinez I just say good luck for the fight and good luck because when you step into the ring with me I will win," he affirmed.

Chris Avalos Says He's Being Avoided and Calls On Rivals to Face Him – 29th August 2014

Super-bantamweight contender Chris Avalos reckons that he is one of the most avoided boxers in the 122lb weight class. Highly-ranked with both the IBF and WBO the 24-year-old fancies a crack at the best and gives short shrift to any suggestion that pound-for-pound talent Guillermo Rigondeaux has no willing and able competition.

"Rigondeaux is a chump. I've been ranked in the WBO number one spot for the world title and it was supposed to be mandatory that we fight," scathed Avalos.

"It's been over a year already but he's been ducking and dodging me. The WBO ordered Rigondeaux to fight me but once again he's not going to. He's just going to vacate the titles and move on to 126lb so that's what I think about Rigondeaux. He's a chump, he's f*****g scared and he doesn't want to fight me."

The 24-2 (18 KOs) talent is instead aiming to fight the winner of the upcoming Frampton-Martinez IBF title contest in Belfast and believes that he has the beating of both men. The IBF's No.1 contender also revealed that he would like a crack at his old sparring partner Leo Santa Cruz but he is not that well acquainted with the work of another super-bantamweight rival in the form of Bury's Scott Quigg.

"I really don't know about Quigg, he's just another fighter to me. I was sparring in the Wild Card one day and he was there and I pointed out to him and said "you're next". He looked really shook up and kind of laughed at me. After that I've never seen him again.

"I've grown up fighting with Leo Santa Cruz. We grew up fighting in the amateurs and we were actually sparring partners as amateurs. He was good competition and a good fighter but I know that he is a "baby" fighter. They take really good care of him. They wouldn't put him in the ring with me.

"I don't care if I'm in the ring with Rigondeaux or Santa Cruz. Anyone who is supposedly big time today, to me they're nothing. I know for a fact that if I get in the ring with them it would be done - no contest for me. I thought that in order to be the best you have to fight the best but it seems nowadays that the best are fighting chumps, people they know they can beat. To me that's not called being the best, that's called cherry-picking."

The self-styled 'Hitman' reckons his 2012 10-round points win over Yenifel Vicente represents the best performance of his career. Puerto Rican Vicente was unbeaten in 25 at the time (with two draws) and the third consecutive undefeated fighter that Avalos had faced when the pair clashed on an ESPN Friday Night Fights affair. Chris also credits Drian Francisco of the Philippines as a tough operator and he took great satisfaction from his most recent win - an eight-round beatdown of Japanese veteran Yasutaka Ishimoto. Avalos lost a 10-round split decision to brief IBF world title holder Jhonatan Romero in 2011 but the Californian disputes that loss and has been doing things the hard way ever since in a bid to restore any career momentum he parted with that night.

"I don't think I lost that fight [with Romero]," he said. "Look at him now, he held the title and lost it in his first challenge. That shows it all right there. That was God saying that it wasn't your time to win the title, it was mine, and that's why I am now mandatory for the IBF world title shot and the WBO. This has been a long time coming and a lot of people underestimate me and think that I'm some random fighter that's just out there but I'm not. I've been fighting since I was 10 years old and I love fighting."

Avalos is now unconcerned with his defeat to Romero. As he alluded to the Colombian went on to hand over his title at the first time of asking, via a heavy six-round knockout defeat to voluntary contender Kiko Martinez. Chris, on the other hand, admits that he enjoyed the experience of boxing in Macao (on the Donaire-Vetyeka undercard) and points to his win over Ishimoto as a clear indication of career progression. He believes that boxing could quickly grow in China as the fledgling nation hosts more big shows.

"The experience in China was really good, and I liked it there. I even told my father [and trainer] that I really like it over there. We stayed over for a whole week and I noticed that I was the only fighter to wake up every single morning to go run and jog. I wasn't on no treadmill either I was outside, running stairs and mountains right up until the last day of the weigh-in.

"I was talking to some guy who said they were barely starting but I think in the future there will be a lot more fights out there," he added.

Big Time Boxing Returns to Dublin at the Red Cow Hotel
Venue – 2nd September 2014

Dublin fight fans should've been enjoying the exciting "Return of the Mack" show on August 30 featuring Matthew Macklin, Anthony Joshua and an enticing Gary O'Sullivan-Anthony Fitzgerald grudge match. That was postponed, however, when Macklin's trainer Jamie Moore suffered an attack in Marbella and is due to be rescheduled for November. Filling the void is this latest card with undefeated middleweight Luke Keeler serving as the headline attraction.

Heavyweight prospect Sean 'Big Sexy' Turner is also ready to rumble for the second time. Turner recorded what is believed to be the fastest knockout in Irish boxing history when he dispatched hapless Hungarian Zoltan Elekes in just 8 seconds of his professional debut. After a few false starts enigmatic Turner finally entered a professional ring for the first time on June 14 in Belfast's Holiday Inn. Sean operates under the guidance of manager Alan Wilton, a highly-respected face on the Northern Irish fight circuit.

Alan's son Matthew is also scheduled to appear at the Red Cow despite being recently added to the "Titanic Showdown" a week earlier. The Titanic event takes place on September 6 and sees Belfast hero Carl Frampton attempt to wrestle the IBF super-bantamweight title from big-punching Spaniard Kiko Martinez in a rematch.

Further down the Dublin bill former Irish cruiserweight champion and EU title challenger Ian 'The Tank' Tims makes a welcome return to the ring alongside lightweight Ciaran Bates who enjoyed an emphatic first-round knockout win on his debut in June.

A Tale of Two Trainers: McGuigan vs. Sarmiento
– 3rd September 2014

The time for talking is almost over and one thing is for sure, when Carl Frampton and Kiko Martinez enter the ring at around 10.30pm this evening both men will be in superb condition. While the physical battle takes place within the ring there will also be a battle of wits and strategies going on outside the ropes as trainers Shane McGuigan and Gabriel Sarmiento attempt to ease their respective boxers to victory. At the final pre-fight press conference both were invited to deliberate over the big fight outcome and each man had their say.

"My assessment is that it will be exactly like the first fight. I don't see Kiko Martinez being able to get up on his toes and box like Sugar Ray Leonard on the back foot," said Shane McGuigan.

"He is what he is, a hard puncher with good head movement and he fights at a high pace but that's something Carl dealt with the first time. He says it was a bad night the first time but let's see how he does this time. Carl's the better fighter and 10 days out of 10 he'll win. That's just my opinion."

McGuigan's candid viewpoint has not changed since he spoke at the initial press conference in early June that was organised to confirm the fight would indeed take place in Belfast.

"I don't think he has improved. I think the best Kiko Martinez has been beaten by us and that just shows Carl's level that night," said McGuigan at the Europa Hotel presser.

"He has tweaked a few things. He doesn't rush in as much and doesn't get hit as much. He has a good tight defence but Carl is so accurate with his punching and has such good distance control. He is getting better and that's why Santa Cruz didn't want to come over. The Mexicans don't take note unless you beat a Mexican. When he knocked out Kiko Martinez they just thought it was any old opponent but when he fought Cazares they stood back and took note. Carl is feared now in the super-bantamweight division but once we get that title he is in a much better driving position."

On the opposite side of the squared circle will be Gabriel Sarmiento, a grizzled Argentine who took over training duties from Pablo Sarmiento at the turn of the year. Gabriel, for his part, was more laconic and measured in his assessment of the IBF title contest. Opting to let the fighters decide their fates rather than speculating on a victor.

"We've been working really hard for this fight and my prediction for Saturday is just that it is all going to take place in the ring as we are here to fight not to talk. What we have been working for will be shown in the ring," he said.

Sergio Martinez: 'Kiko Will Knock Out Carl Frampton This Time' – 4th September 2014

Former middleweight champion Sergio Martinez is confidently backing his namesake Kiko Martinez to retain the IBF super-bantamweight title on Saturday night. Speaking in Belfast ahead of Kiko's defence against local favourite Carl Frampton at the Titanic Quarter, Sergio reckons his charge can end the fight inside the distance.

"I think that Kiko will put on a great show, keep the title and win by knockout," said the head of Maravilla Box.

"I've fought in Belfast before and it is always a great atmosphere here. Both Kiko and Frampton are very experienced boxers and I don't believe they will be disturbed by that pressure."

Sergio boxed at Belfast's King's Hall in 2004 beating Richard Williams in a defence of the IBO light-middleweight title that he had taken from Williams two fights earlier. The 39-year-old now resides in Spain and says that 'La Sensacion' was beset by personal issues in the lead-up to his ninth-round stoppage loss to "The Jackal" in February 2013.

"It was great work by Frampton last time but Kiko is just not the same boxer these days. Kiko is high on confidence after just knocking out three world champions. That brings him more drive to throw lots of punches. We are friends and big fans of each other and we do business together so it's a complete relationship that works well."

Martinez now believes that Kiko will be more accustomed to life under new trainer Gabriel Sarmiento and prove that the form displayed against the likes of Romero, Mathebula and Hasegawa is the result of an athlete reinvigorated.

"Both brothers [Gabriel and Pablo Sarmiento] do very similar work as they work with world champions and today Kiko feels much more comfortable with Gabriel and it's important for a boxer to feel comfortable with his trainer."

Sergio later reinforced the point that even though he respects the talents of 122lb rivals Guillermo Rigondeaux and Leo Santa Cruz he is only focusing on the threat of Belfast's Frampton in the short term.

"I respect them a lot and they are great fighters but for now in my mind it is about Carl Frampton and once that stage is done then we can think about somebody else," concluded Martinez.

Barry McGuigan: 'Kiko Return Will Be Better Than the First Fight' – 4th September 2014

The first fight was an intriguing clash of styles. Kiko Martinez swaggered in to Belfast with his European super-bantamweight title but left empty handed after being comprehensively knocked out by Carl Frampton on a cold February evening at the Odyssey Arena. Now they will do it all again, in an impressively constructed outdoor venue on the Titanic Slipways in early September. This time Kiko arrives with a world title and promoter Barry McGuigan reckons that his man will once again strip the Spaniard of his prize asset. The Cyclone Promotions head man is expecting the fight to be even better than the first and a scrap befitting of the fantastic 16,000 capacity venue.

"The last one was a sensational fight but I believe that this one will be even better," predicted McGuigan.

"Carl has trained terrifically hard. This is an incredible fight and occasion for Northern Ireland boxing. Everything that is Belfast is in this arena out there. The stands are very close together and it's a bit claustrophobic and will be very atmospheric."

One element that could play a part in the mindset of the travelling champion is the fact that he has already been stopped by the man he faces tonight. Kiko was doing well in the first fight and margins on the cards, both amongst TV observers and the judges at ringside, were tight. However, Frampton's equaliser, the big overhand right, that removed Martinez from his senses must surely be in the back of his mind. Barry sees the finish of the first bout as a significant factor in their return but is also at pains to point out that Kiko has improved as a fighter since their first meeting.

"It is significant but just like our opponent I am not going to talk out of turn. I've got great respect for Kiko, we know that he's improved and has more confidence. He's won the title and we believe he got the shot that Carl should've got. This kid [Frampton] is in great condition and I know that Kiko thinks he hasn't improved but we know he has and we will see what happens on Saturday night."

If the first fight was bothering him Kiko did not let it show at Thursday's press conference in the Titanic Centre. Donning an oversized pair of shades, he looked lean and tight in the face as expected, but cool and relatively unflappable. It was a stark contrast to the tetchy, antagonistic visitor that appeared last time and had to be restrained by promoter Eddie Hearn as things got heated. 'La Sensacion' and his team point to out-of-the-ring complications being the reason behind his performance in that first scrap and Kiko himself claims that there was some divine intervention behind the way things have transpired.

"I have no doubt that this will be on the best fights that has ever taken place in this country. The last fight was a learning experience and sometimes God takes something out of you to give you something better and God gave me the world title," mused Martinez.

"It's not about underestimating him or being overconfident, it was just a bad night and that's the way boxing goes."

Jamie Conlan Boxes Estrella and Closes In On World Top Five Spot – 5th September 2014

Jamie Conlan may have been overlooked for a British title shot but the unbeaten super-flyweight is unconcerned as he continues to climb the world rankings. Victory over Jose Estrella on the Titanic Showdown undercard should secure the 27-year-old a top five spot with the WBO as well as their inter-continental crown and a route into world class.

"The lads are telling me I'm not far off that sort of level and the WBO are really impressed with me, that's why I'm being pushed on quickly and fighting for more belts," said Conlan.

"Carl Frampton's a local lad and he's an inspiration for everybody. I've been dreaming about this. Last year I was thinking about not boxing anymore, we were hitting dead ends and my career didn't seem to be going anywhere. I needed to step up a level and since I've got my break these last four fights have been knockouts."

This is tough Estrella's first fight outside of his native Mexico. The visitor has invited Conlan to turn the 12-rounder into an all-action brawl.

"He says he wants me to fight like a Mexican and stand and trade but I'm not stupid," countered Conlan. "I know when to box and when to fight and if I feel I have to fight him then I will but I think he only has one way of boxing and I can exploit that. The fans have paid a lot of hard-earned money to see this and I think it could be one of the fights of the night."

Dungiven middleweight Eamonn O'Kane is hopeful that a victory over dangerous Lithuanian Virgilijus Stapulionis will propel him into a world title shot. Eamonn has completed 135 rounds of sparring under the supervision of trainer Bernardo Checa and defends his IBF inter-continental middleweight strap.

"I'm ranked No. 10 with the IBF and this will push me up even higher with them. Sam Soliman's the champion so we'll do this job on Saturday night and give him a shout out," said O'Kane.

"We know this guy [Stapulionis] likes his right hand and he's a puncher with a good workrate. Nobody loves a workout more than me so it should be a really interesting fight. That's what you want because you'd expect to be fighting good boys at this level."

Marc McCullough gets a tough test in Russia's former world title holder

Dmitry Kirillov. Marc is on an excellent winning run but will have his hands full with veteran Kirillov who once boxed out of Freddie Roach's gym and has mixed in good company.

"He's no mug and I'll have to listen more to my trainer John Breen to avoid getting into a fight so easily," said McCullough.

The most recent addition to the Cyclone stable, super-featherweight Anthony Cacace, gets a rust-shedding exercise against Poland's Dawid Knade. Cacace has described linking up with new trainer Shane McGuigan as a positive step and is aiming for a British title shot.

"Seeing what Carl has grown in to gives me confidence. He's absolutely brilliant but once he was on the same level as myself. With the McGuigans there's no reason I can't do that," said Cacace.

Coalisland middleweight Conrad Cummings meets Poland's Robert Talarek in a six-rounder. Belfast light-welterweight Matthew Wilton boxes Adam Cieslak over four rounds and Limerick's Willie Casey tackles George Gachechiladze.

The Waiting Is Over: Frampton's Fit, Focused and Ready to Fight – 5th September 2014

The intense training camps are over, the talking has been done and the pushing and shoving at the weigh-in concluded. No more time for hype, just action. The main event kicks off at around 10.30pm this evening (GMT) and with 16,000 fervent fans packing in to a specially made structure -including tightly stacked stands for added atmosphere according to promoter Barry McGuigan- it is destined to be an awesome event. Looking trim and confident at the pre-fight press conference Frampton explained how he has ended up fighting Kiko Martinez in a world title rematch and what he will do to the Spaniard when the real business starts later this evening.

"We were hoping to fight Leo Santa Cruz originally but he didn't want to fight me," said Frampton as the Belfastman relayed his road the IBF showdown.

"Other fighters all over the world didn't want to fight me but Kiko Martinez did. He's the champion and a proud man coming for revenge. I dealt with him the first time and I'm a much better fighter than before. Whatever he brings to the table I will be able to deal with it. 14 weeks' preparation mentally and physically, 200 rounds sparring, the easiest I've ever made the weight and the title's staying in Belfast."

After the first fight despite being laid bare in the ninth round Kiko apparently took great pleasure in the fact that he perforated Frampton's ear drum. The challenger jokingly explained how a medical professional told him that a "clip round the ear 'ole from your ma" could also produce the same damage and it was not indicative of a heavy-hitter. 'The Jackal' pointed to the well-publicised split with Matchroom boxing as the main reason behind his untimely ring hiatus.

"I was out of the ring for eight months because of a promotional dispute where we changed channels and started our own promotional company, moving away from the old promotional outfit that we were with," he said.

"That's the reason we were out of the ring. Kiko takes a lot out of the fact that he perforated my ear drum but that has nothing to do with power. I didn't want to be out of the ring, I want to be fighting four times a year.

I'm not overlooking Kiko but when we win this fight I want to be out in December again and boxing regularly. People in Belfast know boxing and they obviously believe in me and see a future world champion. They've got behind me from the very start.

"I think that he is an emotional person which is what we saw at the last fight and what happened at the weigh-in. He's calm and relaxed and he's come over with a different approach but it will still be the same as the last fight. I believe that he's probably improved but in the 35 or 36 fights he's had he's relentless, aggressive and comes forward trying to knock people out. That's his style so I don't expect him to do anything different but he'll be a bit tougher than the first fight."

The Kiko that has landed in Northern Ireland this time around seems altogether more composed and relaxed. There is a comfortable air around the Spanish puncher that did not exist in the build-up to the previous encounter. Frampton senses there is a simple explanation behind the champion's calm demeanour.

"He's come over more humble because he got dealt with the last time and he doesn't want to be embarrassed again," opined the challenger.

Anthony Cacace Aims High After Signing with Cyclone – 5th September 2014

Belfast super-featherweight Anthony Cacace has spoken of how a chance encounter with Barry McGuigan led to him signing with Cyclone Promotions and landing a spot on the Titanic Showdown undercard. Despite a promising start Anthony's pro career stalled after a move to Philadelphia failed to work out. Now he's training with the McGuigans and hoping to bag a British title shot after tonight's rust-shedding fight with Poland's Dawid Knade.

"I was walking through town to meet with my manager and I ran into Barry and we exchanged numbers then a couple of weeks later I was staying in London working towards this next fight," buzzed Cacace.

"It's amazing working alongside Barry, Shane and Carl and it's a positive step. As a trainer Shane's only 25 like myself but he's the best in Britain and he's going to be even better in time. I'm loving working alongside him, his nutrition and all of his advice is working for me. I haven't been in the ring in 10 months so I'd like to just get this fight out of the way and move towards the British title."

Anthony recalls the time he first met his new trainer, back in 2008, when the pair shared a dressing room at the Ulster Seniors. Shane was busy preparing for his fight and had to deal with Cacace and his entourage celebrating in the other corner.

"That was back in the day and I did things wrong," he concedes. "Now I'm more mature and I've wised up. I'm a father and I have a family to look after. Philadelphia was too far away, it wasn't working out for me. I only had one fight in nine months and that wasn't good enough. Everyone in London is very professional and I intend to do everything they ask of me.

"I definitely want to be British champion. Obviously a world title's the dream and if they can take me anywhere near that it would be lovely. I've got the tools but I just need to develop in other aspects of my career."

Cacace draws inspiration from the rise of Carl Frampton and hopes to follow in his new team mate's footsteps

"Seeing what Carl has grown in to gives me confidence. He's absolutely brilliant but once he was on the same level as myself. With the McGuigans there's no reason I can't do that," he said.

O'Kane Ready to Dish the Pain On "Dangerman" Stapulionis – 6th September 2014

Dungiven middleweight Eamonn O'Kane is hopeful that a victory over dangerous Lithuanian Virgilijus Stapulionis will propel him into a world title shot. Eamonn has completed 135 rounds of sparring under the supervision of trainer Bernardo Checa and defends his IBF inter-continental middleweight strap.

"I'm ranked No. 10 with the IBF and this will push me up even higher with them. Sam Soliman's the champion so we'll do this job on Saturday night and give him a shout out," said O'Kane.

"We know this guy [Stapulionis] likes his right hand and he's a puncher with a good workrate. Nobody loves a workout more than me so it should be a really interesting fight. That's what you want because you'd expect to be fighting good boys at this level."

The former Prizefighter champion defends his IBF inter-continental belt against 28-year-old Stapulionis who arrives in Belfast sporting a 23-3 record with 16 knockouts.

"Whenever I beat this guy on Saturday night it will be a good scalp on my record. I've done it as an amateur and I'm doing it as a pro now. I'm starting to box instead of street fighting if you want to call it that. I was trying to put guys under as much pressure as possible but now I'm trying to think and box and land the good shots. I got rid of [Alvaro Gaona] last time in a round so I'm starting to get it all together and I'm hoping to put in a good performance.

"It's great that it's on BoxNation and so many nations across the word are showing the fights and they'll get a chance to see us in action," he said.

Estrella Ready to Put in a Star Performance Against Conlan
– 6th September 2014

Mexican super-flyweight Jose Estrella has landed in Belfast and is itching for a good scrap. The Tijuana boxer quickly accepted the call to face local favourite Jamie Conlan on Saturday's 'Titanic Showdown' extravaganza and the Latino slugger has been swotting up on his opponent in the meantime.

"I've watched his last couple of fights and that has been enough but I'll know a bit more about him in the ring on Saturday," said Estrella.

"This is my first time in Belfast and I'm finding the city very nice and beautiful. The people are very welcoming and I've been treated well."

Conlan was originally scheduled to box Daryl Basadre but when the Filipino failed to shake off a sparring injury Mexico's Estrella was drafted in, having been alerted of the potential opportunity while Cyclone sweated on Basadre's fitness.

"I haven't known about this for too long but I've been fighting a lot lately anyway so I come here well prepared even at short notice. I've fought a lot in Tijuana so I'm ready," added Jose who says that his record may not be littered with familiar names but all of his previous foes could fight a bit.

"In Mexico everybody that you fight is very tough but I can't give names that you would recognise. I know I can create a surprise because the level in Mexico is different."

Estrella boasts a 14-5-1 (10 KOs) record and has his eyes on the prize of a WBO Inter-Continental belt that the winner will take home. The man who calls himself 'Hollywood' has called upon Conlan to live up to his 'Mexican' ring moniker and meet in the trenches on fight night. Jamie is too smart to be drawn by those tactics though and knows as well as Estrella that the Tijuana man needs plenty of close-quarter warfare to win the contest.

"A win for me will be very important because better things will come afterwards. The goal is a win and then we'll see. It is a privilege for me to be here and thanks to Cyclone Promotions for bringing me over for this fight," said Estrella.

Note: Since this article was written Estrella could not make the championship limit of 8 stone, 3 pounds, weighing in 5 ounces over. Subsequently the title will be on the line for Conlan only tomorrow night when these two square off in an exciting 10-round championship contest.

Lewkovicz Labels Titanic Clash "Most Intriguing Fight of the Year" – 6th September 2014

Kiko Martinez has arrived in Belfast with quite the managerial entourage looking out for his interests. The Spaniard was flanked by business manager Miguel De Pablos and Sergio Martinez of Maravilla Promotions. Kiko's promotional activities are also handled by Gary Shaw and Sampson Lewkovicz with the latter present in Belfast to oversee the diminutive puncher's comings and goings. A jovial character, Lewkovicz had plenty to say at Thursday's Titanic Centre press conference. He is banking on Martinez avenging his loss to Frampton and revealed that Kiko has been waiting patiently for a second crack at the Northern Irishman.

"After the first defeat Kiko Martinez has revenge and a rematch in mind so this fight was made with logic and friendship," said Lewkovicz.

"This is the most intriguing fight of the year. When Kiko first fought Frampton he did not know what was going on with his life. Boxing is all about mental preparation and Kiko was not ready. Now Carl has a fight on his hands. The welcome we have had will make the fight even bigger. I have known [Kiko's latest trainer] Gabriel Sarmiento for eight years ever since I started working with Sergio."

Originally from Uruguay, Lewkovicz was the man responsible for introducing Sergio Martinez to the American market. He has gone on to handle the likes of Celestino Caballero, Chris John and Anselmo Moreno during a long and successful career in boxing. Lewkowicz now works closely with US promotional player Gary Shaw and envisages a third contest if his man wins tonight.

"We want to thank my partner Gary Shaw for his involvement in this fight," he added.

Cyclone representative Jake McGuigan also attested to Sampson's skills as a fair and balanced negotiator.

"I spoke with Sampson back in early May and the process was very easy. We made the fight in a week," said Jake.

Rejuvenated Cacace Moving Forward with Fond Memories – 6th September 2014

On the eve of his comeback fight against Poland's Dawid Knade we grabbed a quick word with west Belfast boxer Anthony Cacace to talk about his career so far, amateur memories and signing with Cyclone Promotions.

How was the overall experience of fighting and training in the United States and what ultimately went wrong?

"There was a lot of stuff happening with the promotional team and a lot of complications that I wouldn't be involved in. I thought going to the States would've been a positive move and fresh start but I'm back now. The sparring was unbelievable, I went in with some undefeated names and Philly brought me on and made me see things in a different light."

How did the Cyclone link-up come about?

"I knew Barry but I'd never known Shane. I remember them getting the limelight even though he hadn't boxed much but I shared a changing room with him and realised that he's a really good guy."

You now look back fondly on your amateur days boxing under the Hawkins brothers at the Holy Trinity and Patsy McAllister's Oliver Plunkett club. Would you say this helped shape you into the fighter you are today?

"The Holy Trinity is a great club and my biggest regret about the amateurs was not putting the work in. I started off at Oliver Plunkett as well in the good old days. I messed about a lot as an amateur, I didn't have the right attitude or dedicate myself the way I should have. I believe I had the skill to go to the Olympics but I was a different guy back then."

Hopefully you'll get a bit of airtime on BoxNation TV. It's fair to say that your last outing on the channel was a forgettable and lacklustre affair!

"That was a desperate fight. I never did get rounds and the plan was to get the rounds and I could've stepped it up and stop him but I want to build the engine. I expect my next opponent [on the Titanic show] to be a tough guy and it's all about shedding the rust."

Frampton: 'I Intend to Keep This Belt for a Long Time' – 7th September 2014

Carl Frampton is the new IBF super-bantamweight champion of the world after defeating **Kiko Martinez** in Belfast. 'The Jackal' had already knocked out Martinez when the pair met last year but he settled for dishing out a comprehensive boxing lesson this time round, dropping Kiko en route to a dominating points' verdict. 16,000 fans packed in to a specially-made venue at the Titanic Quarter and each and every one roared their man to victory.

Frampton started out behind a strong jab while Kiko was more reserved than last time, boxing on the back foot and targetting the body. The early rounds were close but Frampton appeared to be taking them. I gave the champion a share of the second session but nothing else until the seventh. Despite a tentative start Martinez tried to engage more after the fourth but Frampton's superior movement and ring generalship were earning him the tight rounds.

Kiko found Frampton's body more frequently in the opening seconds of the fifth but Carl's footwork was making it hard for the Spaniard to pin him down without tasting spiteful counter punches. Midway through the fifth a frustrated Martinez hit Frampton after a slip. The Belfast boxer was unfazed and responded later in the round by dropping his man with a perfect counter right hand at the end of the round. Dazed, confused and cut over the left eye it was becoming an increasingly futile task for the visitor.

The knockdown only served to further demoralise the champion who spent the sixth round following Frampton around the ring. Carl's sharp jab and slick upper body movement was proving too much. Frampton did, however, take his foot slightly off the gas in the seventh which allowed Kiko to cut the distance quicker. 'La Sensacion' once again found a home for the left hook.

Martinez's body work was going well in the eighth and Frampton needed the use of his jab and shoulder rolls to avoid the bombs. Sensing a potential shift in momentum the crowd rallied their man at the end. Kiko continued to motor forward in the ninth but all the quality came from Frampton who planted his feet, landed the shots and slid away effortlessly to the safety of centre ring.

Through the 10th and 11th Frampton moved side-to-side, using the full perimeter of the ring to befuddle his man. Martinez cut a disconsolate figure in his corner as the champion's threat slowly diminished. He was getting dangerously close to being fully neutralised. Bloodied and weary Martinez shipped a classy flurry of Frampton blows. The crowd rose for the final round, eager to help push their hero over the line.

Frampton dominated the final round, piling on the pressure as a sagging Martinez suddenly looked like he might be stopped. Carl eased off and cruised home to the world title. Referee Steve Gray said later that he was not seriously considering stopping Martinez, pointing to the Spaniard's vast experience in title fights.

The judges' Scorecards read 119-108, 119-108 and 118-111 all in favour of the new IBF super-bantamweight champion Carl Frampton. I totalled 118-110 to the Tigers Bay boxer.

"We've done it!" laughed Barry McGuigan at the post-fight press conference. "I said a long time ago that this guy was going to be the world champion and people laughed at me. We are thrilled. The night couldn't have been better; the weather could've been better though. This was the biggest audience that Northern Ireland boxing has ever seen."

The new champion entered the press conference wearing a Santa Claus suit, looking understandably beaten-up around the facial area but even that could not hide his beaming smile.

"What a night. It hasn't really sunk in yet. My head's still a bit sore and my hands are still a bit sore," said Carl Frampton.

"I was a tough fight but I'm world champion now and it's a long time coming. I haven't had the time to sit down and think about it yet but I intend to hold on to this for a very long time. I'm relieved because that was a tough fight even though I always felt in control."

So, what's next? Abner Mares and Leo Santa Cruz's names were both mentioned but Frampton said that he wants Scott Quigg. Mandatory contender Chris Avalos is also floating around in the background. Carl technically has 90 days to defend against the California boxer, who recently hooked up with Eddie Hearn, but rumour has it that Avalos is currently nursing a hand injury.

Eamonn O'Kane's big show opportunity ended in an unsatisfactory manner when the bout was ruled a technical draw. 'King Kane' and

Lithuanian opponent **Virgilijus Stapulionis** engaged in four rounds of bloody warfare before a gash on Stapulionis's right eye was deemed too extreme to allow the bout to continue.

Eamonn was bang in trouble as early as the first round when repeated right hands to the ear splayed his senses and the Dungiven middleweight was handed a count by referee Marcus McDonnell.

Indeed, McDonnell toiled all night to keep both men in check and Stapulionis was bizarrely deducted a point in the second round for "illegal use of Vaseline" when his corner worked on a cut during a mid-round intervention. O'Kane neglected his jab for long periods and leaned in with a whipping right hook too often as things descended into a scrappy mess. Stapulionis was wild in his approach and showed why he was an avoided dangerman leading up to this bout. Eamonn needed every ounce of his fitness and resolve to take the right hands.

The bout was curtailed due to a severe cut as Mr McDonnell stopped it at 2:47 of round four. Luckily for O'Kane the ending means that he keeps his IBF inter-continental title and still has a fight with world champion Sam Soliman in his sights.

"I need to be boxing better than that but it's a learning curve even at 32 years old," said O'Kane post-fight. "He was coming in with the head a bit and turning, so it was awkward. I should've boxed a bit more than I did. I want to be fighting again before the end of the year certainly."

Marc McCullough was handed a stiff test in the form of experienced Russian **Dmitry Kirillov** but came through with relative ease. The visitor was retired by his corner at the end of the eighth. Marc put another notch on his WBO European featherweight crown and is showing sufficient maturity in his work to suggest a step up to the next level is imminent.

Kirillov entered the ring with an impressive resume that included an IBF world title back in the day. That was down at super-flyweight, however, and the size difference showed as McCullough kept the smaller man at bay with his jab.

Kirillov worked behind a lazy jab of his own and threw plenty of left hooks but offered little else. His head movement was good but McCullough landed a solid right hand early on that bloodied his nose. Dmitry was enjoying himself by the fourth round and even though he wasn't throwing or landing an awful lot more he implemented a backward shuffle. McCullough was unperturbed and kept ramming the jabs home.

Kirillov was holding and hitting in the fifth session, using his veteran smarts to avoid McCullough's heavy artillery. The Russian sneaked in a few right hands at the end of each round to try and steal the points but McCullough was bossing every three minutes. Referee Steve Gray admonished Kirillov for a low blow in round eight. Marco coasted down the stretch even though he could've upped the pace and finally his opponent looked troubled. The scorecards were ultimately not needed as Kirillov's corner withdrew their charge from further punishment and McCullough claimed a deserved victory.

The Shankill Road boxer, who is trained by John Breen and Eamonn Magee, improves his record to 11-1 with six stoppages while 35-year-old Kirillov fall to 31-5-1.

"I'm delighted with the win and a patient performance," said McCullough after the contest. "He's a former world champion and very tricky so I had to throw the combinations. Every shot I threw he was gone by the second one. John was screaming at me from the corner to use the jab."

Conrad Cummings registered a 60-54 victory over **Robert Talarek** at middleweight. Cummings' movement was crisp early but he pushed his punches a little from the second round. The left hook was working well but Talarek showed commendable resilience and threw back some meaty counters. Bossing the middle rounds Cummings was making use of his workrate, trying new angles.

Talarek came into it in the fourth and by the fifth Conrad initiated a few more clinches. Talarek had a bloodied nose by the final round and spat his gumshield out to gain a few seconds' rest. Referee Hugh Russell Jnr had a little more to do as the bout wore on but Cummings was well worth his win, moving the slate to 4-0 (2 KOs).

"That guy's tough and has some good wins on the record and his record doesn't do him justice," said Cummings. "I want another couple before the year's out. I was starting to box a bit more and I enjoyed it. I could've done more than six rounds. He caught me with a few shots, it was a learning curve."

Anthony Cacace got the evening off to a flying start with a comprehensive second-round knockout win over **Dawid Knade**. The Polish visitor came out with reasonable intent but was soon squirming under the pressure of Cacace's quality work. The hometown boxer's jab was functioning well and started clipping in a right hand as the opening round neared its conclusion. Early in the second of this four-rounder Cacace dug in a prime body shot followed by an overhand right that saw Knade crumble. He rose and tried to continue but was counted out at 2:09 by referee Hugh Russell Jnr. Joined in the ring post-fight by a smiling Shane McGuigan, who recently took over his training duties. Anthony showed the skills that saw him win a string of amateur trophies.

Cacace improved his record to 9-0 with four knockouts and is now chasing a crack at the British title. After spending a frustrating 10 months out of the ring while pursuing his dream in Philadelphia Cacace is now signed with Cyclone Promotions and expects bigger opportunities to come his way.

Jamie Conlan added the WBO Inter-Continental title to his collection after a 10-round points victory over **Jose Estrella**. Conlan took a unanimous decision by scores of 97-93, 97-93, 99-92 on the judges' reckoning.

Willie Casey also won his clash when **George Gachechiladze** was stopped in the sixth round.

Matthew Wilton was given the unenviable task of boxing after the main event. Wilton recorded a commendable shutout over **Adam Cieslak**, 40-36 on John Lowey's scorecard.

Frampton Oozes Class from the First Bell
– 7th September 2014

Back in 2009 when Carl Frampton turned professional Barry McGuigan was keen to tell anyone who would listen that his new signing would one day become a world champion. As a stellar amateur with title-winning pedigree it did not seem too far-fetched an assertion but McGuigan claims he was laughed at for making such a bold claim. Now five years' later his 27-year-old star is packing out arenas at home and creating plenty of interest across the water. As McGuigan himself was quick to point out last night, nobody is laughing at him now.

Frampton was certainly favourite to take the world crown from Kiko Martinez. After all, he'd already beaten the Spaniard via a comprehensive knockout. But plenty of water had passed under the bridge since the first encounter in February 2013. Martinez had gone on to win a portion of the global belts and opinion was divided between the "Kiko has improved" camp and the "he's been flattered by weaker opposition" argument. As it transpired even the motivated, physically strong specimen that arrived in Belfast earlier this week was unable to exercise a game plan worthy of pushing back a relentless challenger who refused to be denied in front of his hometown faithful.

The outdoor setting, as impressive as it was, didn't manage to recreate the intensely forbidding atmosphere generated inside the Odyssey Arena. Without a roof to capture the chants and sounds of a capacity crowd the noise simply floated off into the night's sky and proved difficult to sustain.

Inside the ring we witnessed a mature, methodical boxer at the peak of his powers. Carl Frampton oozed class from the first bell and barring a couple of slightly sleepy rounds half way through the contest 'The Jackal' bossed matters. The new look Kiko opted to box off the back foot in the opening round, allowing Frampton time and space to dictate behind his underrated jab. Kiko did enjoy a modicum of success in the second but Carl was still finding the target with calculated combinations.

The noise levels rose in the third round as Frampton landed a left hook, and shortly after a right hand, to bring the 16,000-strong crowd to their feet. Martinez's left hooks to the body were landing a little more in the fourth but Frampton's slick movement was still making all the difference.

Kiko introduced some nefarious tactics early into the fifth but Carl remained unimpressed and responded by dropping the Spaniard with a counter right hand reminiscent of their previous meeting.

By this point I had given Martinez only a share of the second and throw in a 10-8 in the fifth and it was starting to look a touch desperate for the Alicante bomber. Martinez began stalking the challenger more frequently but was failing to effectively cut off the ring. Whenever he reached Frampton and unloaded he got punished in return.

The Spaniard's strategy finally started to bear a little more fruit as Carl took the seventh off. It was still relatively close but Kiko stole the session. Same again in the eighth as Martinez finished stronger, landing some meaty left hooks to Frampton's torso and prompting the Belfast crowd to respond with an increase in sound levels to rally their hero.

With that temporary blip over Frampton was back in business by the ninth, controlling from the middle behind his ramrod jab, forcing Kiko back. Carl's greater quality of output once again shone through. Martinez was even starting to look battle weary as Frampton glided around the ring, stopping only to pick his man off with ease. Chants started up in the 11th as the crowd began to realise that their man was boxing his way to a world title. Martinez remained resolute but outclassed. Midway through the final round Kiko was quickly backed up by Frampton's spiteful combinations and referee Steve Gray began to hover. Carl retreated and the soon to be ex-champion managed to hear the bell.

I scored it 118-110 to the new IBF super-bantamweight champion. Motivated and revelling in the moment Carl was busy calling out domestic rival Scott Quigg while his young daughter Carla slept soundly at ringside amidst the cheers and adulation that her father was busy receiving.

After the bout Frampton mused over his future options:

"I think I'm a level above most of these guys [potential rivals]. I'm happy to fight anyone. We're going to have to sit down and discuss things. Chris Avalos is the mandatory now and my mate Eddie Hearn has teamed up with him. I don't know what he's playing at, he's like an old girlfriend that won't go away. We've options now, loads of options. Abner Mares says he wants to fight me as well as Leo Santa Cruz. Obviously Quigg is the fight that I want, but every fight from here on in is huge."

"Carl's the best at distance and he's the hardest super-bantamweight out there," added trainer Shane McGuigan. "He showed today that he's comfortable at distance and when he got inside he fought him there as well."

Ringside Scorecard: How I Scored It Round-By-Round
– 7th September 2014

Round 1:
Frampton starts strong behind the jab. Kiko more reserved than last time, boxing on the back foot and targetting the body.
Martinez 9-10 Frampton

Round 2:
Closer round as Martinez tries to engage more. Frampton's superior movement and ring generalship ends a tight session.
Martinez 10-10 Frampton

Round 3:
'The Jackal' every inch the boss in this round as Kiko struggles to find punching range. A solid left hook and right hand have the crowd excited,
Martinez 9-10 Frampton

Round 4:
Kiko finds Frampton's body more frequently but Carl's footwork is making hard for the Spaniard to pin him down without tasting spiteful counter punches.
Martinez 9-10 Frampton

Round 5:
A frustrated Martinez hits Frampton after a slip. Kiko dropped by a perfect counter right hand at the end of the round. Dropped and cut over the left eye.
Martinez 8-10 Frampton

Round 6:
Martinez looks thoroughly demoralised and is just following Frampton around the ring. Carl's sharp jab and slick upper body movement is proving too much.
Martinez 9-10 Frampton

Round 7:
Frampton takes his foot off the gas a little and allows Kiko to close the distance quicker. 'La Sensacion' finds a home for the left hook.
Martinez 10-9 Frampton

Round 8:
Martinez's body work is going well and Frampton has to use his jab and shoulder rolls to avoid the bombs. The crowd try to rally their man at the end.
Martinez 10-9 Frampton

Round 9:
Kiko motors forward but all the quality comes from Frampton who plants his feet, lands the shots and slides away effortlessly to the safety of centre ring.
Martinez 9-10 Frampton

Round 10:
Frampton goes side-to-side, using the full perimeter of the ring to befuddle his man. Martinez cuts a disconsolate figure in his corner.
Martinez 9-10 Frampton

Round 11:
The champion's threat is close to being neutralised as a weary Martinez ships a classy flurry of Frampton blows. The crowd rise for the final round.
Martinez 9-10 Frampton

Round 12:
Frampton dominates the final round, piling on the pressure as a sagging Martinez looks like he might be stopped. Carl eases off and cruises home to the world title.
Score Total: Kiko Martinez 110-118 Carl Frampton

Judges' Scorecards: 119-108, 119-108 and 118-111 all in favour of the new IBF super-bantamweight champion Carl Frampton.

View from Press Row: How the Boxing Media Called Frampton vs. Martinez II – 10th September 2014

"Strip away the hyperbole and even the spine-tingling occasion at Titanic Quarter on Saturday night, here was an insight into what it must have been like to be Mozart, Beethoven, Van Gogh, Picasso and every other master in their craft. Carl Frampton and the noble art were as one.

"Back in his dressing room for the night, the trailer used for making Game of Thrones, Frampton sipped water and glanced at the inspiration for his night's work – wife Christine and daughter Carla, who slept through the whole 12 rounds – sitting on a sofa and pinned up on the wall the order of service from his grandfather's funeral….."

David Kelly, Belfast Telegraph

"Carl Frampton's head was hurting and his hand was stinging, but his heart was pumping with pride and joy. It was 1.30am on Sunday morning after the exhilarating Saturday night before and in a second floor room in the Titanic building, Northern Ireland's newest world champion was reflecting on his stirring contest with Spain's Kiko Martinez in the post-fight press conference. The 27-year-old's face was bruised and battered, but hey...you should've seen the other guy!

"On Saturday evening, the Lagan lookout bridge took a pounding like never before with thousands of excited fans walking from Belfast city centre towards the Titanic slipways, some not wanting to risk trying to find a car parking space (wise choice for anyone arriving after 8pm), other having enjoyed themselves in nearby bars. The volume was well and truly cranked up when Sweet Caroline had the spectators bouncing in the stand with Frampton's entrance, just after 10.30pm, moments away."

Steven Beacom, Belfast Telegraph

"Carl Frampton kept his footing on the slipway down which the Titanic slid towards disaster and brought his first world title home to Belfast. The Jackal's speed of hand as well as movement overwhelmed Kiko Martinez's defence of his IBF super-bantamweight title. Ulster, reconciled behind its new standard bearer for an improved present and a better future, rejoiced. The setting, a pop-up arena for 16,000 in the historic Titanic

Quarter, made its own statement about the growing prosperity of a city trying to leave its Troubles behind."

Jeff Powell, Daily Mail

Matthew Wilton Impresses After Frampton World Title Win – 13th September 2014

Carl Frampton comprehensively outpoints Kiko Martinez for the world title in front of 16,000 delirious supporters and cements his name into Irish boxing history. Follow that. One man who had to try was Belfast light-welterweight Matthew Wilton who came on in a four-rounder after the main event. To his credit Matthew not only kept his cool and motivation but posted one of his most impressive boxing performances to date en route to a 40-36 shutout of Poland's Adam Cieslak.

"It was a good performance and I caught him with every jab, near enough, that I threw," smiled Wilton. "There are still some learning points but that's all part of it really. It was hard getting motivated there for the last 15 minutes. It sort of took forever. We were meant to be on before Eamonn, then it was after Eamonn and then it was before McCullough."

Matthew reckons that his increased sparring and gym work with Bernardo Checa is beginning to bear fruit. The young slickster nicknamed 'Speedy' has amassed a solid record boxing on the thriving Irish boxing scene.

"I've been sparring a lot lately and I was sparring Eamonn in the build-up to tonight before I actually got the call in for the fight so I was motivated anyway. I was trying to watch Frampton over a wall but I didn't get to see much so I'll have to go home and watch it.

"He [Cieslak] was a boy with a winning record so we can't really ask for much more. I came in late, at three weeks' notice, and sold over 500 tickets so I hope they'll have me back anyway."

Matthew is not sure what will come next. He was seated ringside in the Red Cow Moran Hotel on Friday night to see Dublin's rising stars duke it out. Wilton had been hoping to get on that show himself but being staged on the Friday night meant he was unable to take part due to BBBofC regulations.

"If it had been on the Saturday then I would've been fighting on it but you have to have seven days in between. I'm very pleased though, no cuts either," he added.

Titanic Showdown Undercard: McCullough Leads the Way
– 14th September 2014

Marc McCullough posted his most impressive victory to date when the Belfast featherweight forced Dmitry Kirillov's corner to retire their man after eight punishing rounds. Marc made a successful defence of his WBO European title in the scheduled 10-rounder.

Even though he was not made to work as intensely as in his last bout against Martin Parlagi, the way Marc dominated and demoralised a seasoned former world champion shows that he is ready for the next level. 24-year-old McCullough was too big and strong for his 35-year-old opponent who once held the IBF belt at super-flyweight.

The Russian bobbed and weaved to try and avoid Marc's laser jab but his nose was bleeding from the early stages. Kirillov did offer some sporadic left hooks to keep McCullough focused but the Shankill Road man stayed on task and started planting his feet more from the fifth round onwards. Referee Steve Gray was starting to take a closer look at the veteran in the eighth session but it was soon academic as Kirillov failed to come out for the ninth round and left the ring holding his left arm in discomfort.

McCullough is now turning his attention to a crack at the British and Commonwealth titles.

"He was very tricky and a bit frustrating," said McCullough. "Kirillov's a former world champion and John Breen was shouting at me from the corner to use the jab so that's what I was trying to do. At times I just wanted to stand and fight with him and I ended up chasing him around the ring.

"Coming out in front of all those people was brilliant," he added.

Conrad Cummings was made to work for his 60-54 win over Poland's Robert Talarek. Appearing on the first televised bout of the evening gave Cummings the opportunity to show what he was all about and plenty of grit and resolve were needed as Talarek pushed hard.

Cummings has been involved in some high-quality sparring sessions of late and is visibly improving under the tutelage of Shane McGuigan. The jab and left hook were landing crisply in the opener but as the bout wore on Conrad looked to hold more as his opponent's output increased. High on confidence after defeating an 11-0 prospect in his last contest Talarek started tagging the Coalisland middleweight. Cummings' fitness was the key in the final session as Talarek started to feel the pace and was looking for breathers. Promoter Blaine McGuigan said they are aiming to get Cummings out again a couple of times before the end of the year.

"It was a night to impress but I realised that he was here to stay and I showed my class," said Cummings. "I wouldn't call him a journeyman. He was a game guy coming here to win this and hearing of his reputation motivated me. He caught me with a couple of wee shots and it was a welcome to professional boxing. When I've got 10 fights I won't be making those mistakes."

Going on after the main event was no easy task but light-welterweight Matthew Wilton stayed focused to defeat Poland's Adam Cieslak. 'Speedy' Wilton earned a 40-36 on referee John Lowey's scorecard.

Limerick's Willie Casey stopped George Gachechiladze in the sixth and final round of their featherweight bout.

Titanic Showdown Undercard: Conlan and O'Kane Win – 14th September 2014

Jamie Conlan had his hands full with sprightly Mexican Jose Estrella on the Titanic Showdown undercard but managed to eke out a unanimous victory. Scores of 97-93 (twice) and 99-92 enabled the Belfast super-flyweight to take away the WBO inter-continental belt. Estrella pressed the action throughout and was not easily deterred, making it a tough night's work for Conlan who also suffered a cut.

After a promising start rounds four and five were difficult for Conlan who was forced to dig deep into his reserves to repel the Mexican's advances. Having battled through the rough spots he finished strongly to take a clear and deserved points win.

The WBO later told Jamie that he had made a "statement performance" and he could expect a lofty world ranking for his efforts. With the experienced heads of John Breen and Eamonn Magee in the corner, Conlan's nasty cut was never allowed to become an issue. However, this was a bruising introduction to the upper echelons of the 115lb division that is dominated by Latin American and Asian boxers.

"When I got the cut I couldn't see a thing for the whole round but as usual Eamonn Magee told me to stop whining," said Conlan.

"I hit him with some cracking right hands that I even felt but he just nodded back at me and smiled. That's good though, you don't want someone who's going to fall down."

Eamonn O'Kane had to make do with a technical draw after an untidy brawl with Lithuania's Virgilijus Stapulionis. Eamonn dispensed with the jab and was dragged into the trenches by Stapulionis who came out swinging. O'Kane got caught towards the end of the opening round with a right hand behind the ear and was stretched across the ropes receiving punishment before Marcus McDonnell administered a count. O'Kane's legs were unsteady but he managed to fiddle his way to the bell. Stapulionis ended the round with a cut to his right eye (from an accidental clash of heads) which would play a key role in the fight's conclusion.

In the second round the visitor was deducted a point by Mr McDonnell for "illegal use of Vaseline" as the corner tried to work on his cut during a mid-round inspection. The laceration was visibly worsening and an unstoppable stream of blood prompted the officials to call a halt midway through the fourth. Under IBF rules it was ruled a technical draw as four rounds had not been completed.

"He was an awkward guy but I'm defending this IBF title and if I'm going to be looking to fight for world titles then I have to be boxing better than I did," said O'Kane.

"We knew this guy was dangerous and had a good right hand," added coach Bernardo Checa.

Unbeaten Anthony Cacace opened the show with an impressive second-round dismissal of Dawid Knade in a four-rounder. Laying in to Knade from the opening bell and working behind a stiff jab the Belfast super-featherweight showed just why Cyclone Promotions plucked him from a period of obscurity.

Cacace landed a body shot and fizzed over a right hand to the head that dropped Knade heavily. The Polish boxer rose and tried to continue but was counted out at 2-09 by referee Hugh Russell Jnr.

Red Cow Round-Up: Full Dublin Show Report
– 15th September 2014

Luke Keeler tucked a solid six rounds under his belt at Dublin's Red Cow Moran Hotel on Friday night. The middleweight outpointed **Laszlo Kovacs** 59-55 on referee Emile Tiedt's scorecard. Keeler was guilty of overreaching in the first two rounds and throwing a few too many heavy, looping blows. Luke's aim was to blast Kovacs out of there and send his legion of supporters home happy but the Hungarian visitor was made of sterner stuff. Trainer Paschal Collins implored Luke to throw the jab and indeed the 27-year-old looked every inch the boss when he did let the rangefinder go first. Kovacs offered little in an offensive capacity early on but upped his game in the third round, landing more than his fair share of scything hooks. Keeler worked the body well in the fourth round and Kovacs finally began to show signs of fatigue in the fifth.

The Hungarian's corner clearly fancied the job and urged their man on in the initial stages of the sixth and final session. Kovacs dropped in a couple of tasty swipes when Keeler dropped his hands but this was the visitor's last stand as he began wilting from that point onwards. The final two minutes were a race against time as Keeler poked and prodded away at his rapidly tiring foe, trying to grab a knockout. Kovacs made it to the final bell and can be pleased with his efforts throughout an honest 18 minutes of endeavour.

"I didn't give him much respect going in there, I wasn't really up for it even warming up," admitted Keeler backstage. "He was durable and awkward, moving back, hooking and bending down so I couldn't really catch him clean."

Paschal Collins' latest recruit, London middleweight Frank Buglioni, was in attendance at ringside alongside another product of the Celtic Warriors gym, Stephen Ormond. Alan and Jane Wilton's first foray into the Dublin boxing scene can be deemed a success as the hall was packed out from start of the evening and the passionate crowd created a raucous atmosphere throughout.

Sean Turner is making a habit of removing Hungarian heavyweights. Not content blasting away Zoltan Elekes in record time, 'Big Sexy' uncorked a thumping left hook to emphatically disconnect **Istvan**

Ruszinsky from his senses in the fourth and final round of their meeting here. Turner found Ruszinsky's wobbly midriff the perfect spot to repeatedly hammer in left hooks but to the Hungarian's credit he dutifully soaked them up and continued to motor forward until the finisher.

Sean's weight will certainly continue to drop and more four-round workouts of this nature will do his lung capacity no harm at all. The former Drimnagh BC clubman clearly has the skills and power to make a dent in fighters at a decent level once he gains the type of experience that comes only from regular ring time.

Philip Sutcliffe Jnr dropped Scotland's **Martin McCord** three times but rather than pushing his foot all the way down and getting his man out of there, Phil settled for a 40-33 win on Mr Tiedt's card. Plucky southpaw McCord circled the ring throughout this light-welterweight four-rounder and found the switch-hitting Dubliner too hot to handle. McCord hit the canvas in the opening round from a combination of shots that included right hands to head and body. He was down from a similar burst in the second and a right hand brought about a delayed reaction knockdown in the third as the Ayr man slumped to the deck. Referee Tiedt was considering a termination but the away man convinced him to let it continue.

McCord will wake up in the morning with a couple of shiners on each eye as Sutcliffe continued to bash him around for the remainder of the contest. One of the highlights outside the ring came from the charismatic instructions of coach Phil Sutcliffe Snr who was joined by Bernardo Checa in the corner as manager Pat Magee looked on. Cries of "do the bumble bee", "Rigondeaux, Phil, Rigondeaux" and "throw the Russian" could all be heard at various stages. Whatever those various instructions meant they certainly did the trick as young Sutcliffe responded accordingly.

Sutcliffe Jnr improves his record to 6-0 (5 KOs) with the first distance win of his career. McCord falls to 1-4-1 (1 KO).

Ian Tims opened the evening with a resounding 40-36 victory over Hungary's **Tamas Danko**. The visitor took a barrage of blows in each round but hung in there when others may have folded. Paschal Collins repeatedly screamed "use the jabs Timsy and take the rounds" as Tims huffed and puffed in search of a stoppage. Left hooks to the head and right hands to the body reddened Danko's torso and forehead but he refused to buckle. Emile Tiedt handled the contest.

Declan Geraghty defeated **Ignac Kassai** 40-35 in their super-featherweight four-rounder. The 34-year-old Hungarian looked close to being stopped in the opener following some bruising combinations and the ignominy of a count. He sucked it up and took his punishment with little complaint for the remainder of the contest, even landing some cheeky left hands much to "Pretty Boy's" chagrin. Geraghty whipped in hooks and uppercuts from a variety of angles as the two southpaws willingly engaged in the final round. Kassai's ill-fitting gum shield came out twice during the bout.

Ciaran Bates wasted little time in decimating the threat of Hungary's **Miklos Szilagyi** at 1-35 of the first round. Emile Tiedt did not like what he saw from Szilagyi after the referee asked him if he was OK in the corner. Szilagyi looked stunned and Tiedt duly called the bout off. Miklos had been battered from the start, shipping solid left hooks and jabs before a left hook high on the head finished him off. Bates made it two wins from two.

'Big Sexy' Looking Good As Turner Blasts Away Another Opponent – 16th September 2014

Sean Turner certainly knows how to work a crowd. Just moments after registering his second pro knockout 'Big Sexy' was off celebrating with his Dublin faithful, packed inside the Red Cow hotel. While Turner's debut opponent, Hungary's Zoltan Elekes, lasted a mere eight seconds his compatriot Istvan Ruzsinszky did at least manage to reach the fourth and final round. His efforts were rewarded with a spiteful left hook that landed with such devastating finality that referee Emile Tiedt waved it off without counting.

"It was great, I'm delighted with that. I got the three rounds in and then took him out in the last," buzzed Turner minutes after the destruction.

"It just goes to show now that the fitness is getting there and I was still working hard in the last round. He was tough and I was hitting him with some shots to the body and I was losing a lot of energy because I was putting them in harder and then I realised that it wasn't hurting him too much."

Turner switched codes off the back of a successful amateur career and agreed professional terms with Belfast's Alan 'Alio' Wilton. He's wasted little time acquainting himself with the pro game and clearly possesses the type of punching power to frighten potential future rivals.

"I'm a good body puncher but he was taking some of them on the gloves but then he just dropped his hands and went for me. I leaned back and caught him with the left hook and that was it, sparked," surmised Sean.

"As I said, once I catch you clean there's no one going to stand in my way or stay up, they're going to sleep. Whoever. I want some big fights and some big money but it's only my second fight so a few more to go yet."

New Champ Frampton Could Become Greatest Irish Fighter of All Time – 18th September 2014

The questions at the post-fight press conference were firing back and forth, thick and fast, as journalists and Team Cyclone collectively came down from the world title-winning high that had finished just minutes earlier. On more than one occasion Barry McGuigan was quizzed on how far his young charge could go. The former world champion has always said that 'The Jackal' had the potential to surpass his own ring achievements and then some. This, he said, was the first step on that road. There were strong suggestions that Frampton could go down as the greatest Irish boxer of all time.

"I don't know who the greatest Irish fighter is but I wouldn't suggest for one minute it was me. If he's handled correctly and gets the right fights he can really go as far as he wants to go," said Barry.

Another part of the promotional outfit is Barry's son Blaine McGuigan who was not so keen to discuss future options with the more persistent members of the English media. Rather than speculate over mega fights with the likes of Scott Quigg, Guillermo Rigondeaux or Leo Santa Cruz, Blaine was looking to bask in the glow for a while.

"Yeah let's not talk about fights," he reasoned. "I think we should just savour the moment a little bit rather than talk about what's going to go on next. That's one of the biggest nights that Northern Irish boxing's ever had."

His plea fell on deaf ears as the likes of Gareth A. Davies, Ron Lewis and Jeff Powell -as well as their Irish-based counterparts, myself included- preferred to eagerly anticipate Frampton's next move on the increasingly intriguing 122lb chess board. After all, now that Carl has secured his place in the record books where will our next big moment come from?

"There are loads of fights out there," agreed Barry McGuigan, getting into the spirit of things. "We'll speak to the IBF and look at the injuries. This kid could end up as the best Irish fighter there has ever been. He can go to featherweight and super-featherweight. He knocks out lightweights in the gym. He can move through the weight divisions."

Kiko's team were also clearly impressed with what they witnessed on the night. Sergio Martinez had predicted a Martinez knockout win beforehand

and even though he would not be drawn on the specifics, manager Sampson Lewkowicz was confident that his man would prevail. He didn't, of course, and is now left to pick up the pieces of a long and successful career. Make no mistake there will be further opportunities for a fighter like Martinez. The heavy-handed super-bantamweight has shown that he has no issues travelling abroad and remains a good, solid name at the weight class.

"After the fight Sergio Martinez said that he [Carl] is one of the most exciting fighters in the world today. Sampson said he was absolutely fantastic and a great fighter. They got straight up and said he is tremendous," grinned McGuigan.

McGuigan Commends Kiko Performance and Lauds Frampton – 20th September 2014

Barry McGuigan has paid tribute to the bravery and toughness of Kiko Martinez. The Spaniard willingly travelled to Belfast to face IBF title challenger Carl Frampton on September 6 but left the isle without his coveted strap. Following 12 hard rounds of action Frampton quite literally boxed rings around his demoralised foe but Barry was full of praise for the ex-champion.

"Kiko was phenomenally brave and his face is twice the size it normally is," he said post-fight.

"His head movement was better but he was dropped in the fifth round. Kiko Martinez is every bit as tough, if not tougher, than Leo Santa Cruz. He's a heavier puncher too, he's relentless, like perpetual motion. It was a different Kiko, his head was almost parallel with the floor and he was hard to hit on the chin."

An elated McGuigan went on to thank IBF supervisor Lindsay Tucker and referee Steve Gray for their respective roles in the big fight, staged at what he described as "an iconic venue." Even though Barry has been involved in huge events both as a fighter and promoter he sees no parallels to the 'Titanic Showdown' that saw some 16,000 fight fans descend on Belfast's Titanic Quarter.

"Tonight was different because there were so many people involved with this. We took such risks to get this fight here, financially and emotionally, but it's just great. He's an exceptional kid. I want to thank my sons Blaine, Jake and particularly Shane who's done the one-to-one stuff with Carl for the last three or four years.

"You can see the fighter that he [Frampton] is. We believe that we are just at the bottom of the ladder now. You have to win a world title before you get real traction in your career. We had to do it the hard way. We paid a lot of money to get Kiko here and took a lot of chances," said McGuigan.

'Titanic Showdown' Undercard Boxers' Summary
– 21st September 2014

Super-flyweight Jamie Conlan was made to work for the full 10-round duration by Mexico's Jose Estrella. Conlan prevailed on points but this was the perfect bout for his progression. On the negative side Jamie suffered a cut but on the plus side he has boosted his position within the WBO.

"When I got the cut I couldn't see a thing for the whole round but as usual Eamonn Magee told me stop whining so I didn't mention it when I got back and it was fine from then. I dealt with a few different obstacles here tonight and I think I did alright. I sort of doubted myself a bit and John and the lads got back into my head with the confidence. I felt great after the ninth, amazing, then I did a wee bit in the last and tired then he came on and it made for a bit of an entertaining last round. I enjoyed it and he said I was a warrior.

"I hit him with some cracking right hands there and I felt them but he just nodded back at me and smiled. That's what you want, you don't want someone who's going to fall down. I don't have an ego and I don't need an ego massage. I want someone who can hit me back and test me mentally and physically in the same way that I pushed myself for 10 weeks there. The WBO said afterwards that they think they are going to rank me pretty high now. They saw it as a statement performance. The fight didn't go as I expected because I actually thought I'd hit him and he would go over. I felt so strong in training camp and I'm glad I got tested like that from a guy who hits hard and pressurises. We thought his footwork was terrible in his previous fights but he found the range for his right hands and it was a good testing fight."

Eamonn O'Kane had a tough task on his hands with awkward Lithuanian Virgilijus Stapulionis O'Kane was dropped early but battled back in to the contest before a nasty cut curtailed Stapulionis's evening The bout was ruled a technical draw with four rounds having not been completed.

"The verdict is that I got tagged early around the back of the head and I felt clear but the legs are never always that clear for a round or two. The distance that you like to do your boxing in wasn't there because he just liked to jump in and close it, then it got messy. He either caught you with that right hand or he missed you and it was hard to get the timing on him. He was an awkward guy but I still like to think that I could've boxed better than that but I'm still learning at 32 and it's a kick up the backside. I still think that I was trying to do the cleaner boxing.

"We knew he came for it. He missed with his right hand and I was going to try and throw my right hand and he hit me on the side of the head with his momentum. He's getting the blame! Whatever the team decides next. I need to get out a bit quicker next time as April's too long. Sometimes you get a bit stale. One of the fights I did watch he got robbed blind in it. I'm defending this IBF title and if I'm going to be looking to fight for world titles then I have to be boxing better than I did. Rematch? Definitely, if I have to fight these boys again then I will. They can all punch at world level. It was very hard to time him. I better get back in the ring before the end of the year."

Marc McCullough eased through his toughest test to date when Russian opponent Dmitry Kirillov retired after eight punishing rounds. McCullough is now aiming for a crack at the British title.

"He was very tricky and a bit frustrating. I could only hit him with single shots not combinations because every time I landed a shot and I went or the second one he was away. Kirillov's a former world champion and John was shouting at me from the corner to use the jab so that's what I was trying to do. At times I just wanted to stand and fight with him and I ended up chasing him around the ring. John told me to just keep on boxing him. Coming out into the ring in front of all those people was brilliant."

East Belfast light-welterweight Matthew Wilton had the unenviable task of trying to follow on from the main event. He outpointed Adam Cieslak and looked comfortable throughout.

"It was alright, a good performance. I caught him with near enough every jab I threw but still some learning points. It was hard getting motivated for the last 15 minutes. We were meant to be going on before Eamonn and then it was after Eamonn and we got out last. I've been sparring a lot lately and I was even sparring Eamonn before I got the call to fight so I'm fit anyway.

"He was a boy with a winning record, coming in late at three weeks' notice and selling 500 tickets was all god so hopefully they'll have me back anyway. There's a show next week but it's on the Friday and I can't fight because you need seven days between fights."

Conrad Cummings endured some uncomfortable middleweight

moments against Robert Talarek. Cummings is constantly improving and is looking to keep busy for the remainder of 2014.

"Big step up and that guy's record doesn't tell you how good he is. It was a night to impress but I realised that he was here to stay and I showed my class. I enjoyed it and I wanted to force an impression and I boxed the head off him. I looked my best when I boxed him. He caught me with a couple of wee shots and it was a welcome to pro boxing. When I've got 10 fights I won't be making these mistakes. I'm really pleased with my growing fanbase and I'm learning every day. I get world-class sparring and Shane trains me hard. I want another couple before the end of the year. My fitness is amazing. It motivated to her of his reputation and he was coming to win this he was a game guy. I wouldn't call him a journeyman."

Frampton's Jab the Key to World Title Victory
– 22nd September 2014

If Showtime's Al Bernstein had set out his keys to victory before the 'Titanic Showdown' main event there is a good chance he would've picked out the exact strategy employed by Carl Frampton on the night. Side-to-side movement, exchange and move and, most importantly, work behind a hard, accurate jab could all have found a place on Al's list. Frampton's use of the jab and domineering sense of ring generalship were indicative of the 27-year-old's newfound maturity.

"I think I controlled it better this time [than in the first fight] although I've got lumps all over my head," admitted Frampton. "I was clever when winning the rounds and I hurt him a few times and then dropped him. I felt fresh in there, even in the 12th round. I don't know whether it was the cool air or what but I could've done 15 rounds tonight."

Carl relayed his view of the fight to the assembled press following a bruising world title encounter that saw the Tigers Bay man enter the Titanic Quarter conference room sporting a variety of bashes and bruises across the face. Frampton said that his main responsibility was to listen to the instructions of head cornerman Shane McGuigan and "be smart" especially after knocking Martinez down in the fifth round.

"I just kept on with what I had been doing," 'The Jackal' continued," and I caught him a few more times and had him on the ropes in the 11th and 12th. After I hurt him I thought to myself I've only got a couple of rounds to go so don't be getting stupid. He's a worthy champion as well but I have a good jab for such a small guy and my jab, when I get it going, is very strong. I think it probably was [my best "jabbing performance"] and I was hitting him on the top of the head and that hurt my hands a bit. It was all working well so I gritted that out and kept doing what I was doing."

Carl adopted an "if it ain't broke, don't fix it" approach to the remainder of the fight and diligently persisted with a disciplined approach. It was basically a shrewd box-and-move policy devised to nullify Kiko's ability to land flush and potentially cause an upset similar to the 2007 surprise blitz of Bernard Dunne in Dublin.

"He's one of the toughest guys around, honestly. A fight like this will benefit my career. Being involved in a war with such a proud man will help me. That was the performance of my life," concluded Frampton.

Philip Sutcliffe's Back in Business and Ready for a Title Assault – 22nd September 2014

Philip Sutcliffe Jnr made a welcome return to the ring recently and manager Pat Magee has big plans for his young charge. The veteran Belfast manager who guided Brian Magee to world-level success and also handled Kiko Martinez at a time is using his expertise to handle the careers of Sutcliffe Jnr and cruiserweight Tommy McCarthy. Sutcliffe enjoyed a one-sided four-round points win over gallant Scottish southpaw Martin McCord in Dublin's Red Cow venue on September 12 and was delighted to be back in business following a layoff.

"Considering it was nearly 11 months out of the ring it all went well," said Sutcliffe. "I felt that I needed the rounds with it being my first fight back but I could've stopped the lad in the first, second or third. I waited to put the pressure on and enjoyed myself. I just wanted to get the hang of things again as I've only sparred a handful of times so the rounds did me good. The lad took a few hard shots and I wouldn't say that I put too much pressure on him either."

Phil also dabbled with the southpaw stance in a bid to rediscover the flexibility that only good quality ring time can provide.

"I was getting loose again and getting used to being back in the ring - the whole lot," he said. "Considering the class of my opponent I was just trying to watch his head. He hung in there and took three counts. The first one was a bit soft but he hung in and showed that he's a tough lad. Pat has me down for October on a show in London somewhere but it doesn't matter, I'll fight anywhere and I just want to keep busy and active."

One issue that could cause concern was Sutcliffe wincing in discomfort as his gloves were being removed. Hopefully it was nothing more than a hazard of the job and not a recurrence of the hand problems that have previously threatened to derail his progress.

Top boxing journalist Kevin Byrne of the Irish Sun later tweeted:

(@KevooByrne) "Sutcliffe Jnr visits specialist tomorrow for more on latest hand injury. Wish him well."

Keeler Can't KO Kovacs but Grabs a Points Victory – 25th September 2014

Middleweight prospect Luke Keeler improved his record to 6-0 (4 KOs) on Friday, September 12 but the 27-year-old disclosed afterwards that he was not overly impressed with his own performance. Despite tucking a rigid six-round workout under his belt, via a 59-55 victory over Laszlo Kovacs, Luke revealed that he was much to learn before he can consider moving up in levels.

"I was disappointed with it to be honest, I didn't feel great, even warming up I didn't feel great," he said. "I'm glad I got the six rounds and it's a good learning fight. I was rushing a bit as well but still I can just learn from that. I didn't give him much respect going in there, I wasn't really up for it even warming up. He was durable and awkward, moving back hooking and bending down so I couldn't really catch him clean.

"I was a bit anxious. When I first saw him I thought I'd blow him out in a round or two because he was a bit smaller but in fairness to him he was tough and took the shots. I landed four or five clean shots and he took them."

Keeler will now switch his attention to potential title opportunities. Belfast talent Alfredo Meli has been whispered as a possible Irish title opponent but Luke is keen to grab his place on Matchroom's rescheduled Dublin show that is being mooted for mid-November in the O2. Irish boxing is blessed with plenty of middleweight talent right up to the very top with Matt Macklin and Andy Lee flirting with world class honours.

"There's a Celtic Nations title I could go for and hopefully this Matchroom show goes ahead in November and I could step-up and fight for that. I've been doing very well [sparring with the likes of Frank Buglioni] and feeling relaxed. Hopefully the Macklin show goes ahead but either way I'll be out again in November."

Kassai Gets Six of the Best As Exciting Geraghty Wins Again – 27th September 2014

Declan Geraghty is making waves and gathering interest with his fan-friendly style. The MGM stable in Marbella that Declan trains in currently boasts a rich variety of talent on its books. The quality of sparring is currently at a premium with many fighters travelling over to reap the benefits. The Irish boxing scene may be experiencing a slight lull at the moment but this does not mean that the talent is not out there. Geraghty enjoyed a four-round points victory over Ignac Kassai in Dublin on September 12 to improve his record to 6-0 (1 KO).

After placing Kassai on the seat of his pants in the opening stanza it looked for all the world that the Hungarian would fold. Despite shipping continual bombardments of heavy punches pelting in from all angles the away man fidgeted his way through the first two and to his credit was even firing back in the third round, occasionally tagging the hometown boxer.

"Yeah I'm happy. I put him down in the first round and to be honest with you I thought he was just going to be one of those journeymen looking to get out of there," said Geraghty. "I'll give him credit where credit's due, he stuck it out and I gave him good punishment. I didn't want to blow myself out.

Even though Declan's work was slightly ragged at times he did show the rough diamond qualities that have led some revered observers to suggest he may go far in the game.

"I honestly thought he was going to go but he bit deep and got down to it. I didnt want to hurt my hands or get a stupid cut because I'm boxing again in two and a half weeks' time in a six-rounder so I didn't want to do too much damage to myself. Shea [Macklin, trainer] just said to take it easy. I'm happy with the rounds I'm getting in and I'm only a super-feather boxing at lightweight. It's another win under my belt and on to bigger and better things now.

"If I thought I knew it all I'd pack the game in now. I'll just keep learning off Shea and do what he tells me. It seems to be paying off," said Geraghty.

Trainer Macklin was indeed pleased with his man's work: "He boxed well, yes. He loaded up a bit but loads to learn and we'll start stepping it up now."

Dee Walsh Ready for War with Tough Pole Grabiec
– 3rd October 2014

Belfast light-middleweight Dee Walsh is aiming for his eighth win when he boxes at the Devenish Complex on Saturday evening. Poland's Adam Grabiec is the opponent on a nine-fight 'Champions Night' card.

"This guy's tough and he's never been stopped but the weight is coming down nicely and I'll be ready," said Walsh.

"My trainer Gerard McCafferty is always on my back, pushing me to my limits with circuits and sparring."

Dee has been busy sparring former opponent Gerard Healy in preparation and the 24-year-old reckons their tough sessions are of huge benefit to his progression.

"I spar Gerard every day and he always wants more. He brings the best out in me and whenever you hit him hard he comes straight back."

Walsh had been angling for an Irish title shot on the undercard of Carl Frampton's recent world title-winning headliner. The big ticket seller now concedes that it could've been too much too soon.

"I wanted the Irish title shot but it didn't happen and maybe that was a blessing in disguise," he said. "I was out of the ring for a long time and I need to get rounds under my belt. I've sparred Matthew Wilton and Willie Thompson in the past and I handled both OK. Sparring is different from a fight of course and Willie is an experienced boxer who went the distance with Lee Murtagh."

Dee will now leave his future plans to manager Mark Dunlop.

"I'm leaving my destiny in Mark's hands. Sometimes fighters can be too brave for their own good but he has a plan for me and I trust him to deliver."

The 'Champions Night' card also features Belfast cruiserweight Tommy McCarthy alongside Paul Hyland Jnr, Daniel McShane, Gerard Healy, James Fryers and Michael McKinson. Darren Cruise and Alan Donnellan complete the line-up.

Tommy McCarthy Targets Irish Title Showdown
– 4th October 2014

Belfast boxer Tommy McCarthy reckons that it won't be long before he is rumbling with domestic rivals. Tommy is strongly favoured to improve his record to 3-0 at the Devenish Complex tonight when he boxes fellow unbeaten Dimitar Spaiyski of Bulgaria on the 'Champions Night' card.

"I saw a couple of videos of Spaiyski on YouTube and he doesn't look too bad. I never worry about the opponents anyway because I just go in and do what I do," said McCarthy.

"This year is all about building the record, getting some experience and serving my apprenticeship. Next year we're going to start climbing the rankings and getting in the mix. Ian Tims and Michael Sweeney are the two biggest names in cruiserweight boxing in Ireland. They are both good fighters and if you want to be the best you have to beat the best."

Training in the Oliver Plunkett gym under Patsy McAllister alongside Panama's Bernardo Checa has helped Tommy make a smooth transition over to the professional game.

"I'm still a novice pro so I'm soaking up everything. The last year I was amateur, in 2013, the scoring changed and the head guards came off as well. So for the whole of that year our training regime for the High Performance changed. Our styles became geared towards the pro style so I was already adapted when I turned over.

"Everything has gone perfectly. I've been sparring with Dee Ramsey and Steven Ward. Big Steven's only back from the Commonwealth Games so he's in great shape and giving me brilliant spars," added McCarthy.

The fighter managed by Pat Magee is anticipating a raucous atmosphere inside the Devenish with plenty of crossover support for their local heroes.

"I'm expecting good support even though I only got put on the show at the last minute. Gerard Healy is on and he's from the same area as me and there are a couple of other fellas on the bill that I know. Dee Walsh always brings a good crowd and hopefully they'll all get behind me anyway because we are all from west Belfast."

Dee Walsh is in action against Adam Grabiec while James Fryers meets Lewis O'Mara, Daniel McShane faces Qasim Hussain and Paul Hyland Jnr boxes Andy Harris. Michael McKinson makes his debut against Jan Salamacha while Gerard Healy gets Liam Griffiths. Alan Donnellan and Darren Cruise make up the card.

Classy Walsh Dazzles at the Devenish
– 6th October 2014

Belfast light-middleweight **Dee Walsh** extended his record to 8-0 (3 KOs) with an impressive 40-36 win over Poland's **Adam Grabiec** at the Devenish Complex. Walsh (11st 4lbs 6oz) used the opportunity to showcase his vast array of skills to an appreciative home crowd as referee Hugh Russell Jnr remained a passive observer. Grabiec (11st 2lbs 5oz) offered little more than stubborn resistance. With more experience and activity talented 'Waldo' can start fulfilling his early promise.

"You have to entertain people, keep them happy and wanting to come back next time," said Walsh who has his eye on Peter McDonagh's Irish title. "I'll be back again in November and ready to fight whoever they put in front of me."

Belfast cruiserweight **Tommy McCarthy** (14st 8lbs 5oz) showed glimpses of why manager Pat Magee is labelling him "the best prospect in Ireland" after the former amateur standout bludgeoned Bulgaria's **Dimitar Spaiyski** in the first of a four-rounder. Down twice from spiteful combinations and counted out at 1-07 by referee Paul McCullagh, Spaiyski (14st 8lbs) was quickly out of his depth. Now 3-0 (3 KOs) Tommy has the British title on his radar for 2015 and next fights on Matchroom's November 15 show.

"I've got good amateur experience and I feel that cruiserweight is there for the taking," said McCarthy.

Paul Hyland Jnr earned a lopsided 40-35 win over Gloucester's **Andy Harris**. The Belfast lightweight had Harris stumbling around under severe distress in the third round and the bloodied journeyman was dropped from a heavy flurry in the final session. Harris (9st 9lbs 5oz) survived and John Lowey's verdict pushes Hyland Jnr (9st 10lbs 4oz) to 3-0.

Belfast's **James Fryers** moved to 5-0 after posting a hard-fought 40-36 victory over Portsmouth's **Lewis O'Mara** (9st 12lbs 5oz), 3-3, on Hugh Russell Jnr's reckoning. Now coached by former British champion Martin Lindsay, 21-year-old Fryers (10st 2lbs 5oz) is a neat boxer who is benefitting from increased ring time.

Galway's **Alan Donnellan** (12st 3lbs), 6-3 (2 KOs), dropped Brighton's **Iain Jackson** (12st 8lbs 8oz) in their super-middleweight opener but boxed off the back foot to a 40-35 success on Paul McCullagh's scorecard.

Popular light-middleweight **Gerard Healy** (11st 2lbs 4oz), 3-4-1, sent his fans home happy after Hugh Russell Jnr handed the Belfast man a 40-36 triumph over Bognor Regis southpaw **Liam Griffiths** (11st 6lbs).

Belfast super-featherweight **Daniel McShane** (9st 5lbs 7oz), 9-0 (3 KOs), dominated Sheffield's **Qasim Hussain** (9st 5lbs 2oz) for a 40-36 win on John Lowey's card.

Belfast-based welterweight debutant **Michael McKinson** (10st 9lbs 6oz) outpointed Poland's **Jan Salamacha** (11st 1lb 7oz) 40-36 on Mr. McCullagh's total.

John Lowey granted Roscommon's **Darren Cruise** (12st 5lbs), 4-3, a 40-36 verdict over York's **Harry Matthews** (12st 2lbs 9oz) at super-middleweight.

View from Press Row: How the Boxing Media Called the Devenish Show – 7th October 2014

"Dee Walsh added to his growing reputation with a sublime performance at the Devenish Complex in Belfast on Saturday night. The Belfast light middleweight was just too fast, sharp and good for Adam Grabiec over four rounds and was a runaway 40-36 winner on the referee's scorecard. Walsh always looked comfortable and in control, showing clever boxing skills to outclass his opponent. Walsh landed a number of big shots but the durable Grabiec stayed up to the final bell - but he had been handed a boxing lesson by Walsh - who looks like one for the future."

Nicky Fullerton, Belfast Newsletter

Dee Walsh Wins After Outclassing Plucky Pole Grabiec – 8th October 2014

Dee Walsh produced a boxing masterclass on Saturday evening to repel the threat of Poland's Adam Grabiec over four rounds. Walsh's 40-36 success at Belfast's Devenish Complex was never in doubt but it was the manner of the victory, rather than the cold statistics of a unanimous decision, that impressed ringside observers.

"I wanted to put him to the test at the start to see how he took them and he did take them well," said Walsh. "I had the cold beforehand and I couldn't breathe through my nose from the third round so I took a step back and put on a bit of an exhibition to show that he couldn't hit me. My pride got me through it. There were shots I caught him with tonight that I saw rocking his head and they would've knocked a lot of people out but he's a tough boy."

While Grabiec is clearly no world beater he did arrive with a reputation as a resolute operator who does not get deterred easily. 'Waldo' realised this early on and used the opportunity to showcase an assortment of tricks borrowed from a variety of legends. Over the course of the four rounds we spotted moves from Floyd Mayweather (Dee even sported a cheeky Mayweather-esque beard on the night), Sugar Ray Leonard and Roy Jones Jnr. Was there anybody missed?

"Sugar Ray Robinson and Ali," smiled Walsh, clearly now a fighter at peace with himself both in and out of the ring.

"I enjoyed that fight and I'm enjoying life at the moment, being in a routine and getting up every morning for the running and with the training and sparring it's all good. Watching those boxers and imagining yourself being like them obviously helps and that's what I do."

Walsh admitted pre-fight that the Irish title shot he craves could perhaps be left to simmer while he grabs a couple of tough stamina-building six or eight rounders. However, the 24-year-old is making it clear that a fight with current domestic king Peter McDonagh is something he is aiming for.

"I would love to get the Irish title shot but I took a step back from that after it didn't happen on the Frampton show so I can get the rounds under my belt. I want a six-rounder next that will hopefully go the distance and then maybe go for a 10-round Irish title shot."

Aside from the entertainment factor and abundant talent, Walsh also brings a growing fan base along with him. Possessing the ability to shift a bucket load of tickets is vital to any young boxer looking to gain valuable ring time at smaller venues.

"I sold a load of tickets for a small hall show and it shows that people want to come and watch me. I've got power, I can make people miss and put on a show. You have to entertain people, keep them happy and wanting to come back next time. I'll be back again in November and ready to fight whoever they put in front of me."

Trainer Gerard McCafferty took the final word, reminding assembled members of the press about the sacrifices that this new incarnation of Dee Walsh is willing to make in order to fulfill his title aspirations.

"On Monday the fight was off as he had the flu and wasn't going to be boxing but he's a professional and he did what he had to do," said McCafferty.

Photograph: © Mark Dunlop

Gerard 'Boom Boom' Healy is Back for a Title Shot
– 10th October 2014

Belfast boxer Gerard Healy made a welcome return to the ring on Saturday, October 4 and notched up a deserved points win for his efforts. 'Boom Boom' out thought and outfought Bognor Regis mover Liam Griffiths over four well-contested rounds to take the spoils 40-36. Even though fight source BoxRec.com has Omagh's Dee Taggart listed as Healy's next foe the 31-year-old is hoping to snare a title shot of some description.

"Dee Taggart's name is down on BoxRec but I don't think that's happening now," agreed Gerard. "My plan is to fight for a title. That could be an International Masters or Celtic Nations title which would both be eight rounds."

While Healy was happy with his performance and felt that he boxed well he promises now that a portion of ring rust has been shed he will be better next time. It was an entertaining fight for the most part and Gerard is always keen to give the fans their money's worth.

"I was switching southpaw and leading him on to hooks and uppercuts and the fans love all that. I know I can be better but I've been out for the guts of a year and a half and at the end of the fourth round I felt like I could've done another couple. I caught him with a couple of flash shots and I could've stepped it up but he isn't the kind of guy that gets stopped, even though he told me afterwards that I do hit hard.

"Sparring with Dee Walsh, Joe Hillerby and Frankie Carrothers is bringing me on and our gym has a buzz about it. [Club coaches] Gerard and Sean are brilliant guys and we have a good thing going on."

Healy has endured a chequered career thus far, mostly taking the short end of the stick and going is an unfancied "opponent". This latest win, coupled with the overtly positive response from a ticket-paying public, has rekindled Gerard's enthusiasm for the sport and he is confident that title fights could soon be heading in his direction.

"I would like an Irish title shot next year. Sparring Dee Walsh is bringing me on so much as is the work I'm doing with the coaches, Sean and Gerard McCafferty. People think that Dee is just a brilliant boxer but he can fight too if it comes down to it. Dee Walsh is world class, honestly. The sky's the limit for the two of us; me and Dee are going to the top. Joe

Hillerby as well is so underrated; he's a brilliant talent and he's back in November."

Whenever a possible third fight with John Hutchinson was mentioned Gerard broke into a smile. "John Hutchinson cut me up!" he joked, before qualifying his comment by stating that Hutchinson is a nice guy out of the ring but not so amiable inside of it.

"Definitely it [a Hutchinson rubber match] can happen again and with an Irish title on the line it could sell big tickets," he added. "I'll fight anybody and I've always had the hard end of the stick. I sold 100 tickets and a lot of people couldn't get them so they paid in at the door. I sold over 100 tickets which is good for a small hall show. More performances like tonight will hopefully get me a title shot next time and I can build a fan base.

"My fitness is alright and I'm back out on November 22 so hopefully I can get that title shot," concluded Healy.

Fryers Puts the Heat On O'Mara in Belfast
– 11th October 2014

James Fryers is willing to do whatever it takes to get the victories on his record even if that means stepping into the trenches and winning ugly. The Belfast lightweight was made to work hard for his fifth professional win, achieved in the Devenish Complex last Saturday evening, but he managed to grind out a shutout over Portsmouth southpaw Lewis O'Mara. As the Irish boxing system continues to push out talented fighters from a relentless conveyor belt Fryers could be one to watch in the future.

"I wish I had put in a better showing but winning ugly is just as good," he conceded.

"He [O'Mara] was ducking down every time I threw a punch and I was a bit frustrated. I was trying to throw a jab to the body but he ducked down so I threw it to the side and it worked a few times but I ended up getting too close. I needed to take half a step back and I ended up throwing bombs but it's all experience.

"I'm happy enough with the win which is the important thing. I'm like a snooker player who thinks about the next shot when I should be thinking about my own thing. I'm glad to be getting the rounds in now."

One man who knows a thing or two about the boxing business is former featherweight star Martin Lindsay who has been helping to put Fryers through his paces at the Immaculata club.

"I have been working with him and I have been doing a wee bit of sparring with him," Lindsay told the Belfast Newsletter before this latest contest.

"James is a good boxer - he is cute in the ring - and I believe he will do well. His preparation has gone well with Nugget, Alfredo Meli and myself. Saturday night should be a good test but he will get the job done and move on," Martin added.

Despite taking a few punches (a hazard of the job I'm sure) James said that he felt comfortable throughout the contest. Fryers describes himself as more of an inside fighter who likes a tear-up but claims that he is adaptable enough to change his approach if the situation dictates.

"I can box if I want to but once you get punched you want to get stuck in there and I jumped in a bit and should've boxed a bit more. He was slipping and spinning me but I should've been smarter and stepped off to work the shots a bit more but it's one to look back on and learn from.

"I took a body shot but it was one of those ones that you can breathe out after a few seconds so I'm not worried about my fitness. I haven't seen a mirror yet but I think I came out unscratched. I'm hoping Mark [Dunlop, promoter] will get me out again."

The next Devenish show, scheduled for November 22, will provide Fryers with the perfect opportunity to add another name to his record should he get the chance to appear.

"For the first two years I suffered too much from inactivity and I heard a rumour that Mark's having another one here in November so I want to keep active as much as I can," he said.

McCarthy Delights the Devenish but Tougher Tests Will Come – 13th October 2014

It's fair to say that sparking an overmatched Bulgarian at a small hall show in Belfast may not put the cruiserweight division on red alert. But if Tommy McCarthy progresses as quickly as his team, fight fans, boxing scribes and the man himself all believe then the top cruiserweights in Ireland and the UK will be finding out sooner rather than later. As far as Tommy is concerned speed brings power.

"I always say that if you walk into a wall it won't hurt you but if you drive into a wall you're going to die," was his erudite analogy.

Spaiyski immediately resembled somebody that looked like he'd just walked into a wall. The Bulgarian may not have been the stiffest test ever brought over to these shores but such was the ruthless nature of McCarthy's intent it is unlikely he will be rushing back again in a hurry.

"The speed of my hands and the technique were both there and it's another KO on my record and a step closer to where I want to go," continued McCarthy.

"Training hard every day for these fights means I don't have to be exactly on the weight so I weighed in for this fight at 14st 8lbs and the championship weight is 14st 4lbs so I'm not killing myself to make weight. I'm meant to be boxing in Dublin on November 15 and I'm looking to do a scheduled six-rounder already. Next year I want to be getting in the mix with some names because I feel that with my talent I don't need to do too much learning. I've got good amateur experience and I feel that cruiserweight is there for the taking. Pat's a brilliant manager and everything he said he would do for me he has done so far. I don't there is a better manager in the country than Pat Magee and I feel that he is going to guide me the way he guided Brian [Magee]."

Overall, McCarthy clearly enjoyed his evening's entertainment in the Devenish but admitted he would rather have rumbled with one of his previous opponents (both dispatched soundly over in England but each lasting slightly longer than Spaiyski). Tommy possesses a ruthless desire to not only beat his foes but comprehensively knock them out and if a target presents itself his intentions are always to find a finisher.

"I don't want to say anything but a couple of fights down the line I'd love to get in with [Ian] Tims because he's the number one cruiserweight in Ireland. Well, I'm the number one cruiserweight in Ireland but he's the other one!"

Pat Magee Excited By Big Puncher McCarthy
– 16th October 2014

Belfast manager Pat Magee knows a thing or two about bringing a fighter along the right way. Having guided namesake Brian Magee to the highest level, as well as handling a string of other talented pugilists, Pat is ready to let his latest hope, Tommy McCarthy, off the leash. Speaking shortly after Tommy's first-round destruction of Dimitar Spaiyski in the Devenish Complex Magee discussed his bright prospect's progress so far and where they plan to take the 24-year-old next.

"It's another learning fight for Tommy, his debut in Belfast and he wanted to please people," assessed Magee. "Obviously he achieved that because you saw the reaction from the crowd. I think that's the last time you'll see him in a four-rounder. We can go six in the next fight or maybe even eight. He's fit enough to do six or eight rounds and it's just a question of getting him the right opposition as you don't want him blowing people out in a round all the time.

"He's had three imports, three good wins and now we want to measure him against somebody we know from the UK or Ireland. Let's see who we can get because he's not that easy to match. He could've been on a Matchroom show there last month and there were two cruiserweights on the bill and Matchroom were quite prepared to put one of them in with Tommy but they wouldn't touch him. There are so many young so-called prospects now with five, six wins or a 7-0 record that won't fight anybody but Tommy will fight anyone you put in front of him."

Pat was ringside in Dublin last month to see Ian 'The Tank' Tims return to the ring with a four-round victory on Alan Wilton's Red Cow show. Tims meets fellow cruiserweight Michael Sweeney in an Irish boxing grudge rematch on Matchroom's 3Arena show but Magee insists that he would have issues throwing McCarthy in with Tims anytime soon.

"We wouldn't have any problem taking Tims. That would be a tough one at this stage of Tommy's career and we're not in any hurry but equally we know that he doesn't need 20 fights before he fights for a title.

"I'm every bit as excited as when I started with Brian [Magee] and I thought whenever Brian retired I would retire at the same time but with Tommy and young Phil Sutcliffe there's something about the punchers. In the professional game especially you have to be able to hit and they can both hit. That guy [Spaiyski] wasn't great but he was hurt from the first shot and Tommy wants to knock people out which is a good thing in the boxing game."

Pat believes that with his connections and experience from many years in the fight game he can bring his boxers along quickly. With the likes of Rigondeaux and Lomachenko fighting for titles after a minuscule number of pro bouts the top amateur stars are making the transition to the pro game smoothly.

"We are seeing evidence now of all these great amateurs turning pro and they don't need 20 fights anymore," he said. "You saw [Artur] Beterbiev last week and Tommy knows him because he was in the same tournaments. Beterbiev blew away a former world champion [Tavoris Cloud] in only his sixth fight. I'm not saying we want to move as quickly as that but we are not going through the journeymen scene. Every fight from now on is going to be a fight to test him and see where we are at. I can see Tommy fighting for a British title in 2015. When I look at what's there I don't see anything to be concerned about.

"We are looking for good sparring now and we've been offered the opportunity of sparring with Youri Kalenga the French African and we've also been talking to Nathan Cleverly's people about going over to Wales which we'd love to do. Quality sparring will bring him on because he's got the expert coaching from Patsy [McAllister] and Bernardo [Checa] and all we need him to do is re-produce what he's doing in the gym in the ring and we saw flashes of that tonight.

"His amateur experience is there to be seen and I think he's the best prospect in Ireland," said Pat Magee.

Before we wrapped up for the evening I briefly asked Pat how his big-punching light-welterweight hope Phil Sutcliffe Jnr was progressing.

"We got good news about Phil's hand. It's still painful but there's no damage and he'll be ready to fight again in November after a couple of weeks' rest. He threw a punch that hit the guy [opponent Martin McCord] awkwardly on the top of the head and these things happen," said Pat.

Ryan Burnett Added to 'Back to the Future' Card – 18ᵗʰ October 2014

Ryan Burnett has been added to Mark Dunlop's 'Back to the Future' card on Saturday, November 22 in the Devenish Complex, Finaghy Road North. This latest MHD Promotions card sees the cream of Belfast's young crop of talent enjoying another run-out as they chase title opportunities. In the headline attraction Dee Walsh takes on Terry Maughan for the vacant Irish light-middleweight title and Olympic Youth gold medallist Burnett has bagged a spot on the undercard.

Burnett has amassed a 4-0 (3 KOs) record thus far as a professional and takes part in his first fight of 2014 under the guidance of new trainer and manager Adam Booth who has handled David Haye throughout his long and illustrious career. Often touted as a potential future star of Irish boxing, Burnett is only 22 and still has plenty of time to fulfill his vast potential.

Fresh from a raucous evening on October 4 some familiar faces will be returning to action on the next Devenish show. Paul Hyland Jnr, James Fryers, Gerard Healy, Alan Donnellan, Darren Cruise and Michael McKinson will all feature. James Tennyson and Daniel McShane are not involved and will both box again next year.

In the main event talented Belfast mover Dee Walsh gets a move up in class against Nottingham's Terry Maughan who boxes out of the Carl Greaves stable. Here's how Greaves broke news of the fight on Twitter.

Carl Greaves: "After negotiations with @MARKHDUNLOP I'm pleased to announce @Team_Maughan will be fighting for the Irish title 22.11.14 v dee walsh."

Hyland Jnr to Step Up On 'Back to the Future' Card – 22nd October 2014

Paul Hyland Jnr is stepping up to six rounds on Mark Dunlop's November 22 card as the 24-year-old moves along the professional learning curve. The popular Belfast boxer is fresh off the back of a resounding 40-35 success over Gloucester's Andy Harris on the last Devenish show and will now look to stave off the threat of southpaw mover Lewis O'Mara as part of the 'Back to the Future' event headlined by Dee Walsh. Speaking after the Harris victory Hyland Jnr was generally pleased with his display and whenever the youngster planted his feet and let the punches go it looked increasingly likely that the usually resolute visitor was close to being removed early.

"He was all over the place but held on for dear life there but I just couldn't get the knockout," lamented Paul. "The first round was just about gauging his power and he felt strong enough but he wasn't really hitting me so I upped the pressure and caught him to the body I caught him to head and he was all over the place. I hit him straight on the button."

Hyland's rangy style could be adapted to his advantage then the young boxer could perhaps mould a style form himself similar to the likes of Paul Williams or Celestino Caballero. Paul always looks a more frightening and commanding figure when he operates behind his jab.

"Everyone says that my jab is the key to the door and I want to keep working behind the jab. I cut his eye early from the jab so I knew it was working," he added.

"I'm looking forward to November already. It's all about winning and building the record. He was ranked above me so that will push me up a bit. The calm boxing and control of the fight pleased me. He touched down but didn't get the count for it and he got up but held on and I did what I could to get the clean shots."

Now boasting a 3-0 slate Paul is trained by father and namesake Paul Hyland Senior, an intense coach who admits he demands high standards from his boxers.

"I'm always critical because I want to improve," said Hyland Snr after the bout. "I'll have a good look at the tapes tomorrow but I was pretty happy. There's more in him, he's only tipping the iceberg so far. There's so much more to come. It's hard not to get carried away with the crowd because a lot of people put a lot of time and money into coming to watch the fights so he's under pressure to perform.

"The crowd are cheering and chanting and there's a big following for him. The better he boxes then the more people will come and watch him. It's not just about getting wins but in his and he wants to look good doing it.

"I'm never happy, I always want better!" he said.

Sweeney Saving His Best Performance for Tims Revenge – 27th October 2014

Mayo cruiserweight Michael Sweeney is pumped up and ready to exact revenge on domestic rival Ian Tims in one of the most intriguing fights on the Irish boxing circuit this year. As if tensions between the two were not high enough already, a pre-fight scuffle during a photograph face off has raised the stakes even further.

"I lost to Tims before so I'm after revenge big time. There's no bad feeling on my side, I'm just in to fight," said Sweeney.

The pair first clashed in March 2011 on the undercard of Willie Casey's fight with Guillermo Rigondeaux. An out of shape Sweeney was expected to prevail but solid Dubliner Tims refused to be denied on the night and pushed the fight for every second, claiming a 97-95 success on referee Emile Tiedt's scorecard and bagging an Irish title in the process. Michael has been eager ever since to erase that blemish from his record.

"Training has been going well and I'm in to four weeks now. I've been getting very good sparring with loads of good guys and it's good to be back fighting in Dublin, on a big stage with Sky TV. I'm well prepared and ready to win.

"I've got a new team around me now and I'm managed by Leonard Gunning and trained by Peter Fury in Bolton so things have changed big time. A win here would land a big fight and I'm open to a fight with Conall Carmichael if it comes."

Sweeney had previously been lobbying for a fight with Carmichael in Belfast but the bout never materalised. He still fancies that one if a promoter wishes to make it happen. Recently I was deliberating over Sweeney's best win so far as a professional and I came to the conclusion that his third-round pummelling of Limerick brawler Jamie Power on the Dunne-Kratingdaenggym undercard was probably Mike's most solid win and performance. Sweeney, as always, reckons the best is yet to come.

"My best performance will be my next on November 15," he asserted.

Frampton Believes Belfast Atmosphere the Best Around – 31ˢᵗ October 2014

"Big Tony Bellew over there will tell you that Liverpool fans are the best but they aren't, Belfast fans are!" yelled Carl Frampton shortly after settling down on the ring apron to speak with BoxNation TV. Bellew, commentating at ringside for BBC Five Live, was no doubt grinning away as the diminutive Frampton hollered across the ring. No animosity was intended from the jubilant newly-crowned world champion, still on a high after posting the finest win of his career to date.

Speaking afterwards, once the buzz had slightly died down from his resounding defeat of Kiko Martinez, Carl agreed that he was struggling to come to terms fully with his massive achievement. He was quick to pay tribute to 16,000 fans that turned out to help cheer him on to victory.

"It's not just boxing but any sport, the atmosphere they can create here for local guys doing well is unbelievable. The support Paddy Barnes gets, guys like McIlroy, the Ulster rugby team, the rest of the golfers. If you're doing well then people will come out and support you," he said.

Frampton went on to reinforce his viewpoint that he remains a step or two ahead of domestic rivals like Scott Quigg and Kid Galahad. The latter has been quite vocal himself of late, pining for a chance to engage with his contemporaries (some would say superiors) while Galahad's team have upped the pressure slightly by making a public offer to try and tempt Quigg into a showdown. Carl is willing to face mandatory challenger Chris Avalos next but 'The Jackal' is still nursing sore knuckles that could curtail that bout until next February. On the night Frampton showed how much he has improved since the first Kiko meeting and displayed a set of tools capable of handling any if his 122 lb foes.

"We had a game plan to stamp my authority in the middle rounds. I could've outfought this guy if I'd wanted but I had to be smart and use my jab which was working well.

"We had a plan to plant my feet a bit more in the middle rounds which I think I did. Barry thought I did it a wee bit too much but I was in control for the entire fight," he concluded.

Downpatrick Cricket Club Pro Show Round-Up
– 2nd November 2014

Belfast promoter Alan Wilton and wife Jane continue their unshakeable commitment to professional boxing in Northern Ireland with an eight-fight card in here Downpatrick Cricket Club.

Local hero **Paul Quinn** took his time in wearing down plucky Pole **Dawid Knade** but eventually the visitor crumbled in the sixth and final round of their featherweight encounter. Knade was knocked out in two rounds by Anthony Cacace on the Titanic show in early September.

Exciting Dublin heavyweight **Sean Turner** outpointed Ugandan survivor **Moses Matovu** 40-36 as Turner parades towards an Irish title fight.

Bangor brawler **Casey Blair** is now unbeaten in three after registering a four-round points win over Bognor Regis survivor **Liam Griffiths**. Blair won 40-37 and had already shut out Griffiths at the Holiday Inn in June.

Alfredo Meli kept busy with a 40-36 victory over Brighton's Iain Jackson at middleweight while 20-year-old **Michael McKinson** defeated Pawel Seliga 39-37 at welterweight. **Dee Walsh** went through the motions en route to a four-round shutout over **Dee Taggart**.

Dubliner puncher **Ciaran Bates** was extended into the second round but still removed the threat of slippery southpaw **Lewis O'Mara**. In an all-action affair Gerard Whitehouse knocked out Jakub Czaprowicz.

Tommy McCarthy Stepping Up Levels in Bid for Title Shot – 12ᵗʰ November 2014

Tommy McCarthy is aiming for a fourth professional victory when he boxes in Dublin's 3Arena this Saturday night. The Belfast cruiserweight faces Martin Horak of the Czech Republic over four rounds and is eager to impress. Tommy has been busy preparing with a week sparring Nathan Cleverly as the Welshman limbers up for his grudge rematch against Tony Bellew. The 24-year-old gained good experience in that camp and is now focusing on his weekend assignment.

"Horak is durable and tough and it would be good to get him out of there but I'm looking for a solid win," said McCarthy.

"Boxing in Dublin gives me the chance to impress a wider audience and hopefully get on some more Matchroom shows. After my first bout I was aiming for a six rounder but the opponents have only wanted four."

When Michael Sweeney withdrew from his rematch with Ian Tims, McCarthy's team immediately tried to step in and box the Dubliner but Tims and his trainer decided they would prefer to wait for Sweeney to recover.

"I have no personal beef with these guys but it would've been nice to fight Tims. He's from Dublin and would've had a big crowd supporting him in a bigger fight for me. I don't mind who I fight, it's up to my management."

If Tommy removes Horak, as expected, manager Pat Magee has a date pencilled in at the Ulster Hall on January 24 with a British opponent being targetted.

"Boxing in Belfast would be great as everyone can come down and see me fight. I boxed in the Devenish last time but that was more of a last minute thing and still I got good support," added McCarthy.

Pat Magee views Horak as a step-up in levels from McCarthy's previous three opponents.

"This guy is durable and we cannot underestimate him. Matchroom used their contacts to find an opponent but a plethora of names refused. Tommy needs a challenge and expects to be moved quickly so we plan on accelerating his progress.

"It's difficult to get someone to face him over six rounds. We believe he can move into championship class after nine or ten fights," said Pat.

In the Matchroom main event Matthew Macklin boxes Argentina's Jorge Sebastian Heiland in a WBC world title eliminator at middleweight. 32-year-old Macklin is aiming for a fourth world title shot following three previous failed attempts.

Shane McGuigan: 'Kiko Was Like a Wounded Lion' – 14th November 2014

"A fighter is at his most dangerous when hurt" is an aphorism often trawled out after boxing matches. Trainer Shane McGuigan has seen his own stock rise off the back of Frampton's success, since taking over full training duties from Belfast veteran Gerry Storey. Considered and erudite in his vocal delivery, Shane's record is currently speaking for itself despite the detractors. His direct approach to predictions and assessments of bouts has offered a refreshing change from the standard PR lines and drum-beating hyperbole that members of the press are so often fed in these situations. McGuigan Jnr was spot-on in how he believed the fight would transpire and said that Carl did not finish off Kiko when he had him hurt due to the above maxim of Martinez being dangerous when in trouble.

"A lion's always dangerous when they're hurt. Nigel Benn always got knocked down and he'd be at his most dangerous," said Shane.

"So I said, work off your jab, control it all from the centre of the ring. The first fight he [Frampton] covered a lot of ground and a lot of miles but this time his stamped his authority and every time he took a step back he threw something with venom and it worked. Kiko was so petrified from the last fight that when Carl hit him he gave ground.

"I think in the last fight Carl could outbox Kiko and outfight him as well. There were a few head clashes in there and that was the only worry in my mind. He's a lot stronger than Kiko Martinez. Carl's the best at distance and he's the hardest super-bantamweight out there. He showed today that he's comfortable at distance and then he got inside and fought him in the inside as well," he added.

Frampton himself spoke on the qualities that McGuigan brings to the table as a trainer and friend. Despite the inevitable lamps, bumps and bruising Frampton insists that he was never hurt at any point throughout the fight. He attributes much of the success to the vast worth of his coach.

"I said it on ringside, Shane's the best coach in the UK and Ireland. He knows his stuff and people are going to be knocking his door very soon to start working with him," said Frampton.

Macklin Title Hopes Dissolve After Dublin Beatdown – 16th November 2014

Matthew Macklin's world title aspirations lie in tatters after the heavy pre-fight favourite was ground down and knocked out in the 10th round by Argentina's **Jorge Sebastian Heiland**. Boxing in Dublin for the first time in almost five years Birmingham-born Macklin's strong Irish roots helped gather a large crowd inside the 3Arena to witness this WBC International middleweight scrap.

Despite Macklin's relatively positive start to the contest it soon became obvious that 27-year-old Heiland (11st 4 ½ lbs) was fresh and not easily deterred. Usually so strong in the early rounds Macklin (11st 5 ½ lbs) was visibly forcing his work from the fourth round onwards as his relentless opponent answered every assault with a barrage of his own. Matthew enjoyed a good fifth round but as the sessions flew by he was often fighting hard just to remain competitive.

The Buenos Aires man's work had an awkward efficacy. His style was problematic, from the southpaw jab to the snaking left hand, Macklin was tagged repeatedly from multiple angles. Heiland focused heavily on the body in the seventh and eighth sessions.

Macklin was starting to soak up too many blows early in the 10th and referee Robert Verwijs began to take a closer look. When the finisher arrived it was decisive. Drained of energy and swaying against the ropes Macklin rode a left hand but remained in position to receive a right hook bang on the button. Brave to the last 'Mack the Knife' slumped to the canvas and Mr. Verwijs ended his evening at 0-42 of the round. The unused judges were David Irving, Massimo Barrovecchio and Edgardo Codutti.

After three previous attempts Macklin was hoping to finally win a world title at the fourth time of asking but despite this latest setback the 32-year-old insisted he would not rush into a decision on his future.

"Maybe I burnt up too much energy early on, maybe I'm getting old. I just faded a little bit," explained a disconsolate Macklin.

"Take nothing away from him, he fought a smart fight. I'll have to analyse the performance and see where we go from here. I believe that at my best I'm world class and capable of winning world titles."

Much of the local interest surrounding this monster 13-fight bill lay on a

Gary O'Sullivan-Anthony Fitzgerald fight that ended in spectacular fashion. Cork puncher O'Sullivan (11st 9 ½ lbs) unmistakably settled their "bad blood" feud by starching the fiery Dubliner at 1-15 of the opening round. Fitzgerald (11st 3lbs) bounced into the ring full of confidence but once the 10-rounder commenced 'Spike' O'Sullivan was all business, whipping in hooks from a hands-down stance, oozing confidence.

Midway through the session O'Sullivan flashed in a left hook followed by a right uppercut that caught 'The Pride' flush on the jaw and sent him sprawling to the floor. Anthony, to his credit, attempted to continue but referee Mickey Vann wisely called a halt to proceedings.

Talented Birmingham super-flyweight **Khalid Yafai** successfully defended his IBF Inter-Continental title with a unanimous points win over gutsy Nicaraguan **Everth Briceno**. Yafai (8st 2lbs 10oz) displayed a variety of moves throughout the contest and found a home for his body shots early on - dropping Briceno in the fifth round. The away man had a point deducted by referee Mickey Vann in the sixth for a low blow and was dropped twice in the eighth from further assaults to the ribs. Briceno (8st 4lbs 3oz) hung in against the odds and showed commendable staying power to last the course as Yafai cruised through the latter rounds.

The judges' scorecards read: 120-104 (Emile Tiedt), 119-106 (Toni Tiberi) and 118-105 (Jen Teleki).

"I learned more in that fight than my previous 12," said Yafai who is now seeking a British title shot.

2012 Olympic silver medallist **John Joe Nevin** wasted little time disposing of overmatched Maidenhead man **Jack Heath**. Nevin (9st 5 ½ lbs) loaded up on big shots from the opening bell and Heath (9st 3lbs) received an early count. Two further knockdowns prompted referee Emile Tiedt to wave the six-rounder off at 1-28 of round one.

Anthony Crolla (9st 12lbs) has bagged himself a shot at Richar Abril's WBA lightweight title in January. The Manchester man sharpened up by skillfully outboxing Hungary's former European title challenger **Gyorgy Mizsei Jnr** (9st 12 ½ lbs) to a 60-54 decision on David Irving's scorecard.

Dublin featherweight **Patrick Hyland** dealt sufficiently with late replacement **Oszkar Fiko** (9st 10 ½ lbs) of Romania by claiming an 80-72 shutout on David Irving's reckoning. Hyland (9st 3 ½ lbs) was set for an intriguing bout with John Simpson but the Scotsman withdrew with a back injury.

Sam Eggington (10st 10lbs) made light work of **Sebastien Allais** in their welterweight six-rounder. The 21-year-old Stourbridge boxer landed a peach of a left hook to the body that knocked the stuffing out of the French visitor. Allais (10st 2 ½ lbs) was counted out on his knees by Emile Tiedt at 1-45 of the first round.

Belfast cruiserweight **Tommy McCarthy** had too much in his arsenal for Czech **Martin Horak** in their four-round contest. The shorter southpaw tried to engage with McCarthy (14st 8lbs) but the former amateur talent trapped him in the corner and unloaded on Horak (14st 3lbs) who was rescued at 0-59 of the second round by Emile Tiedt.

When **Michael Sweeney** withdrew from their cruiserweight rematch, Dubliner **Ian Tims** was left with Bolton-based Lithuanian Paul Drago instead over six rounds. Drago (14st 2 ½ lbs) dropped Tims (13st 9lbs) in the first round and Ian suffered an ankle injury from the fall. Referee Emile Tiedt accepted his retirement at 2-57 of the opener.

Local pride was at stake between unbeaten Dublin duo **Declan Geraghty** and **Jono Carroll** at lightweight. Geraghty (9st 5lbs) was disqualified in the fourth and final round by David Irving for illegal use of the head. Declan had a point deducted in the same round for illicit elbow work while Carroll (9st 5 1/2lbs) ended with two nasty cuts.

Clondalkin cruiserweight **David Maguire** (13st 8lbs) bludgeoned Preston's **Paul Morris** (14st 5 ½ lbs) to defeat at 2-28 of the second round. Ref David Irving terminated the four-rounder with Morris under pressure.

Dublin middleweight **Luke Keeler** (11st 10lbs) stopped Shepperton's **Gary Boulden** (11st 8 ½lbs) at 2-17 of the first round. David Irving halted the six-rounder with Boulden struggling to rise from a heavy knockdown.

The corner of Dublin veteran **Oisin Fagan** (10st 2 ½lbs) threw in the towel at 1-23 of the second of a four-rounder with Wythenshawe's **Kofi Yates** (10st 3lbs). Emile Tiedt officiated.

Notes: *Now re-branded as the 3Arena, this same venue was the 02 when it staged Bernard Dunne's remarkable world title winning effort over Ricardo Cordoba and subsequent defeat to Poonsawat Kratingdaenggym in 2009. Dunne also won the European title and sensationally lost it to Kiko Martinez there in its original incarnation as The Point.*

A few rogue elements of the Dublin fight crowd were a little too over excited by the reality of big time boxing returning to the capital. A variety of objects, including plastic bottles and a corner stool, found their way into the ring throughout the evening.

Promoter Eddie Hearn mentioned possible fights with John Ryder and Gary O'Sullivan for Matthew Macklin. Both would be a step down from the world stage he has been accustomed to of late but if Macklin decides to carry on boxing he will need to re-build at this level.

Another Knockout Win for Hot Prospect McCarthy
– 16th November 2014

Tommy McCarthy registered a comprehensive second-round knockout over Martin Horak in Dublin on Saturday night. The Czech visitor had a reputation for durability but once McCarthy landed some heavy leather there was only ever going to be one outcome.

The Belfast cruiserweight was boxing on Matchroom Sport's bumper 13-fight bill and received a warm reception from the 3Arena crowd. After working out the awkward moves of his shorter southpaw foe McCarthy wasted little time pushing Horak on to the back foot with a solid jab and raking right hand.

Horak landed a swiping left hook that caught McCarthy's attention but moments later the 24-year-old was busy punishing the visitor in the corner. Trapped against the ropes Horak shipped a succession of accurate blows that forced referee Emile Tiedt's intervention at 0:59 of the second round. McCarthy is now unbeaten in four, all by knockout.

"I'm delighted because Eddie Hearn came over and complimented me on my work so hopefully he will get me on the up and coming shows in the new year," said McCarthy.

"Everything's going to plan. I'm training hard every day and winning the fights so titles are around the corner if I keep going this way."

"Now's the opportunity to get Tommy into the Ulster Hall because as time goes by it's not big enough for him," added manager Pat Magee.

"I have a date booked for January 24 and that would be next but I'm talking to Matchroom at the moment and if something more attractive comes up we'll take it. At the moment though I'd like Tommy to fight in the Ulster Hall as, believe it or not, he never has before."

There was a shock in the main event as middleweight Matthew Macklin was stopped by Argentine southpaw Jorge Sebastian Heiland in their WBC world title eliminator. Despite a bright start Macklin was listless from the fourth round onwards and a crunching right hook in the 10th dropped the crowd favourite heavily.

"I'll have to analyse the performance and see where we go from here," said Macklin. "Maybe I burnt up too much energy early on or maybe I'm getting old."

Gary O'Sullivan dramatically knocked out Anthony Fitzgerald in the opening round of their middleweight grudge match with a right uppercut.

Tommy McCarthy Excites Dublin Crowd with Fourth Knockout Win – 19th November 2014

Tommy McCarthy made it four wins out of four in Dublin's 3Arena on Saturday evening with yet another foe falling early. Speaking just minutes after starching Martin Horak inside two rounds, Tommy explained to journalists how he had gone about dispatching the Czech boxer on the Macklin-Heiland undercard.

"That's my style, as soon as I get somebody hurt I get the job done. It took a while to get the distance but when I find the target that's it over," he said. "He was shorter than me and he was dipping low and when I jabbed he would come up with the left hook and he caught me with one actually in the first or second so he was awkward enough. Once I figured out the equation it was all good."

McCarthy, one of Irish boxing's most promising boxers, is happy with the varied range of opposition he has been presented with since turning professional. He acknowledges, however, that a solid test from an Irish or UK cruiserweight is needed to advance his progress.

"I've had different kinds of opponents. The first guy was a journeyman type with a tight guard and then the next one was 6"9 so that was awkward enough. This fella here was a shorter southpaw with a bit of power so I'm adjusting to different styles. I've boxed every style there is as an amateur so it's just about adjusting as a pro."

The 24-year-old will now turn his attention to a proposed January 24 show in Belfast's Ulster Hall with a six-round attraction being lined up. Surprisingly, Tommy's veteran coach Patsy McAllister revealed that his charge has never before boxed at the Ulster Hall as an amateur.

"When he won his Senior titles they were all shifted away so he wants the opportunity," said Patsy.

"There are a lot of people who support me in boxing in Belfast and I'm sure they'll all come down and watch me again," agreed McCarthy.

"If that show goes ahead then it will be brilliant. I haven't really got hit that much in my four fights but I'm having brilliant sparring so most of the work is done in the gym. As I say, if you are working hard in the gym then you get an easy night and that's showing in my fights."

Manager Pat Magee was pleased with his man's performance and is hoping that Sky TV and Matchroom were both impressed enough to ask Tommy back for another appearance on their shows.

"The Sky people have to be impressed with that. Once he got the guy going he hit him with some clean punches and the referee was on the job stopping him because at that size and weight guys can get hurt," said Pat.

"As Tommy said himself, we are trying to get him a variety of opponents and you can see the difference because that guy tonight was a grade up from what he's fought before. He caught Tommy with a cracking left hook early on which told Tommy to pay attention. Whenever he got to the corner Patsy said that there's nothing easy in this game and told Tommy to go out and do his business and that's what we did."

Magee envisages big things for McCarthy and his other prospect, Phil Sutcliffe Jnr. The big-punching light-welterweight is edging closer to fight fitness and Pat expects Phil to be ready for late January.

"Obviously I'm going to put the two boys on the show. Phil's hand is improving and I think he's going to start using it next week and we will probably get him out on a six-rounder to get him back. 2015 is going to be a big year for the two of them," Pat added.

Bantamweight Ryan Burnett Aiming to Return with a Bang – 21st November 2014

Ryan Burnett is looking forward to putting a year of inactivity behind him and impressing his fans in the Devenish this Saturday evening. The talented 22-year-old aims to improve his record to 5-0 against Bulgarian survivor Valentin Marinov over six rounds.

"I haven't boxed in a year and it's good to be back boxing, especially in front of my home crowd," said Burnett.

"I've sold plenty of tickets and have lots of people coming down to support me so I'm really looking forward to it."

Burnett has recently hooked up with David Haye's former trainer Adam Booth after initially turning pro with Ricky Hatton. Ryan says that the Hatton partnership ended amicably.

"Things weren't going perfect so I just thought that I had to make the move but we ended on good terms. I'm really glad about the way things have gone since teaming up with Adam and we get on well," said Burnett.

"I've had a great training camp, some great sparring and I feel fit and ready to go. I was sparring with a Danish lad; he was heavier than me and it was tough sparring but I learned a lot."

The Olympic Youth gold medallist is boxing for the third time in Belfast and is eager to progress at bantamweight. He has another fight planned for the end of this month in London.

"Hopefully everything goes well with this fight and then I'll fight again on November 29. If all goes to plan with that one then I'm looking to have a big 2015. Adam believes that we will be able to move quickly through the division if I keep working hard," he added.

Dee Walsh headlines the Devenish show against Terry Maughan for the Irish title. Paddy Gallagher, Paul Hyland and James Fryers also feature.

Walsh Using Irish Title As a Step to the Next Level
– 22nd November 2014

Dee Walsh is ready to push on to the next level when he battles for the vacant Irish light-middleweight title on Saturday night. After a spell away from the sport Walsh's career is now on an upward trajectory. The 24-year-old, unbeaten in nine, reckons that victory over Terry Maughan in the Devenish will only be the start of his success.

"The Irish title does get you up the rankings and all I want to do is climb the ladder," said Walsh.

"I want to be winning titles and hopefully after this, if all goes to plan, I can defend it and move on to maybe a Celtic title shot and then go for a British title. I'm using everything as a stepping stone to keep moving and this is the first step for me but I'm not looking past November 22. This is a 10-rounder against an experienced opponent."

Dee admits that he does not know a great deal about Nottingham's Maughan, who boasts an 8-4-1 record, but sees the fellow challenger as rangy and dangerous.

"He's six foot tall and I'm used to fighting guys smaller than myself. I've been sparring Joe Hillerby to make sure I'm ready for it. I don't like spending a lot of time studying an opponent because you can get dragged in to their game so I just worry about how I am going to perform. He could be very awkward but I feel good and have nothing to worry about.

"I've been sparring with the likes of Joe Hillerby, Gerard Healy and even big super-heavyweight Frankie Carrothers. All of my sparring partners have been chasing me down and going at me. I'm getting a 10-round spar in just for a mental thing. It couldn't be better - no injuries or sickness like the last time so I'm happy enough.

"On the night you never know how you are going to perform so I want to just get past this fight. I'm planning for the distance and I'll be ready," said Walsh.

Welterweight Paddy Gallagher gets his first outing since an appearance in the Prizefighter tournament earlier in the year. Now training with John Breen, Paddy hopes his bout with Liam Griffiths will provide a springboard to bigger opportunities.

"John is training me a lot differently and I'm boxing more but he knows

I can fight a bit too. The Prizefighter helped move me up the rankings and I'm hoping for an Irish or British title next year," said Gallagher.

Elsewhere on the card James Fryers steps up to contest a minor title over eight rounds against Sandor Horvath. Paul Hyland boxes Pepi Perov, Ryan Burnett meets Valentin Marinov and Gerard Healy tackles Yanko Marinov. Darren Cruise, Michael McKinson and Julio Cesar also feature.

Paddy Gallagher's Back and Ready to Rock the Devenish – 22nd November 2014

Paddy Gallagher has been itching to get punching again and the Irish boxing prospect finally gets his wish tonight at the Devenish Complex. Paddy has made some alterations to his background setup and new trainer John Breen has been busy implementing some refinements to the welterweight's game.

"I've changed manager and trainer. I'm with John Breen now and he's training me a lot differently," explained Paddy, speaking at an open workout in the Kennedy Centre.

"No single trainer knows everything and I took different things from Gerard [McManus, former trainer] and now I'm taking things from John. Gerard had me fighting and John has me boxing a lot more."

Paddy recalls a session with Breen and his team a few years' back when he was drafted in to help high-flying light-welterweight Paul McCloskey prepare for a big fight.

"I went to spar with Paul McCloskey a few years ago, before I made my debut, and he was just after fighting for a world title. I boxed very well and John reminded me of that recently. John knows I can hit and fight but he also knows that I'm a better boxer. We've gelled well in two and half months and I'm flying now."

The 25-year-old features on Mark Dunlop's enticing nine-fight show against English southpaw Liam Griffiths in a four-rounder. Gallagher took part in April's welterweight Prizefighter tournament and encountered mixed fortunes on the night. He was, however, just glad to be back in the ring after long spells of inactivity.

"Fights kept falling through but that's part of boxing. I was with John Rooney then and I was inactive for almost a year. I'll get this one out of the way and hopefully win, then in the New Year start moving up the rankings.

"The only thing I did well [in the Prizefighter] was stop a man [Mark Douglas] in the second fight. People were saying I was "chinny" afterwards and I couldn't take a shot but I do have a chin. It was a mad night! Everyone saw it for themselves on TV what happened, there's nothing really to explain. There are some good things that came out of it though. It got me moved up the rankings and I'm hoping for an Irish or British title next year."

Coyle was a reasonable operator but Paddy believes that he played into the Essex man's hands with much of his downfall owing to an intense motivation that left the Belfast slugger caught in a one-dimensional trap.

"I was too pumped up and going for knockouts. Yes Coyle is decent, he's good at what he does, but I played into his hands and gave it him on a plate more or less," he said.

Putting this aside Gallagher has taken the experience and rankings boost as bonuses from a reasonable night's work. He is now looking forward to another local appearance tonight and relishing the opportunity to impress his fans once again.

"This is a good opportunity for me because there are only two shows in town - Mark Dunlop and Barry McGuigan. If you can get on those shows then you're doing alright and there's potential for me to get on one next year. The Devenish is good because I only live five minutes away and I'll get some good support on the night," concluded Gallagher.

Walsh Bashes Maughan in Two and Takes Irish Crown – 23rd November 2014

Dee Walsh moved his career to the next level on Saturday night with a definitive second-round knockout of Terry Maughan. Walsh's win at the Devenish Complex bagged him the vacant Irish light-middleweight title and the Belfast stylist was dominant in victory. Despite Maughan's clear size advantage at the 11 stone weight class, Walsh set about chopping him down with right hands to body and head.

Maughan tried to get his long jab going but midway through the opening session Dee was already landing his shots with alarming regularity. Walsh stunned Maughan in the second with an accurate right uppercut and piled on the pressure, slamming the visitor's head in all directions. Referee David Irving jumped in at 1:08 to no complaint from Maughan or his corner.

Now sporting a 10-0 record Dee's 2015 target includes accumulating more belts and he is happy to accommodate Australian-based Dennis Hogan who is the Irish title mandatory contender.

"Winning the Irish title means everything to me," said Walsh.

"I hear Hogan's ranked highly with the IBF and others so we'll see what happens. Next year I might go for titles like the Celtic or British and get in to the Ulster Hall to keep building my career."

James Fryers registered his first pro stoppage with a second-round demolition of Hungary's Sandor Horvath. Fryers pushed timid southpaw Horvath on to the back foot from the start and raked in body shots and a variety of hooks to the head. Referee Paul McCullagh had seen enough at 2-57 of the session with Horvath backed against the ropes, offering nothing in return.

Ryan Burnett stopped Bulgaria's Valentin Marinov at 3-00 of round one. This scheduled six-rounder never looked like travelling the distance as Burnett landed a perfect right uppercut to floor Marinov. He bravely rose but Ryan's sharper blows, including a quality left hook, invited John Lowey to step in and call a halt. Burnett fights again next week in London.

Paddy Gallagher boxed impressively to a 40-36 decision over Liam Griffiths at welterweight. Paul McCullagh toiled hard to stop slippery Griffiths from spoiling as Gallagher's jab and body shots took their toll late on.

Paul Hyland Jnr dropped Pepi Perov in the first round and constantly engaged with the Bulgarian en route to a 40-35 success.

Gerard Healy defeated Bulgaria's Yanko Marinov 40-36 and there were wins for Darren Cruise, Julio Cesar and Michael McKinson.

Dee's Domestic Destruction: Maughan Mowed Down Early – 26th November 2014

Belfast's Dee Walsh reinforced his status as one of Ireland's hottest prospects with an emphatic second-round blitz of Terry Maughan. Now 10-0 (4) Walsh's win at the Devenish Complex bagged him the vacant Irish light-middleweight title.

Maughan was the bigger man so 'Wealthy' Walsh (11st) set about slamming right hands into his torso. Maughan (10st 13lbs 2oz) tried to respond when able but midway through the second round (scheduled for 10) he started shipping a series of brutal head shots. Referee David Irving hovered with intent and dived in at 1-08 to save the Nottingham man from further punishment.

Dee is now keen on a Celtic or British title shot with an Irish title defence against mandatory contender Dennis Hogan also under consideration.

"Winning the Irish title means everything to me," said Walsh.

James Fryers had too much firepower for Hungary's Sandor Horvath (9st 7lbs 8oz). James hit the visitor hard and often enough to persuade referee Paul McCullagh to intervene at 2-57 of the second-round. Belfast's Fryers (9st 7lbs 2oz) , 6-0, took the initiative in this eight-rounder and scored his first knockout victory while collecting the vacant International Masters Bronze lightweight title for his efforts.

Ryan Burnett returned after a year of inactivity to stop Bulgaria's Valentin Marinov at 3-00 of round one. As soon as Belfast's Burnett (8st 4lbs), 5-0 (4), dropped Marinov (8st 9lbs 3oz) with a right uppercut this scheduled six-rounder looked ready to conclude. Marinov beat John Lowey's count but was caught again and clinically dispatched.

Paddy Gallagher (10st 10lbs) boxed impressively to a 40-36 decision over Bognor Regis' Liam Griffiths (11st 1lb 8oz). Belfast's Gallagher, 6-2 (4), showed improved boxing skills and coasted home on Paul McCullagh's card.

Belfast's Paul Hyland Jnr (9st 9lbs 7oz), 4-0, dropped Pepi Perov (9st 7lbs 4oz) in the first round and constantly engaged with the Bulgarian en route to a 40-35 success. Paul McCullagh officiated.

Belfast's Gerard Healy (11st 5lbs 3oz), 4-4, completed a 40-36 shutout of Bulgaria's Yanko Marinov (11st 7lbs 3oz) on John Lowey's scoring.

Roscommon's Darren Cruise (12st 0lbs 2oz), 5-3, outboxed Omagh's Dee Taggart (11st 11lbs 9oz) 40-36 for Paul McCullagh's reckoning.

Belfast-based Michael McKinson (10st 6lbs 8oz), now 3-0, defeated Bulgarian Teodor Stefanov (10st 6lbs 2oz) 40-36 on John Lowey's card.

Mr Lowey also awarded Portugal's Julio Cesar (12st 5lbs) a 39-37 debut victory over Brighton's Iain Jackson (12st 8lbs).

Back with a Bang: Burnett Bops Bulgarian in One – 27th November 2014

Ryan Burnett is back on the boxing beat following a resounding one-round stoppage of Valentin Marinov in the Devenish Complex. Ryan was pleased to be punching again after a frustrating one-year spell away from the ring.

"I knew after the first uppercut landed that I could get him again with it but I didn't want to just go straight ahead so I worked my way in. I threw it again and caught him perfect, right on the chin," said Burnett.

"I'm going to have Christmas with my family and then straight back in the gym. It's been emotional for me being out of the ring for a year. The past load of months I've been through a lot and I let it out with a big roar at the end there!"

Opponent Marinov looked confident before the opening bell as he stalked Burnett across the ring when the Belfast prospect made his entrance.

"Everyone fancies it until they get hit," Burnett dryly assessed.

Ryan boxes in London's York Hall on November 29 against Bulgaria's Stefan Slavchev. The 22-year-old is currently ranked at number six in the BoxRec rankings and a few timely wins against the right sort of opposition should see him boxing for a British title sooner rather than later. New trainer Adam Booth is certainly thinking along those lines.

"We are hoping to move fast and Adam believes I'm capable of it so I'll just do what he says. I've been with Adam for about three months now and it's been going brilliant. He's taught me a lot and it showed on the night. I'm fighting again in London on the 29th so I'm straight back in the gym."

Having handled David Haye's career for so many years Booth is perfectly placed to guide his young charge to glory. Things may have not have exactly gone to plan towards the end of his stint with Ricky Hatton but Ryan's career is now on the move once again.

"I didn't waste much time in there as I had a game plan and did exactly what Adam said, which came off perfect. After this next fight if all goes well then I'm looking at a big 2015," said Burnett.

Former British light-welterweight champion Curtis Woodhouse certainly believes Burnett is going to the top.

From @woodhousecurtis to @cohcfc @irishboxreview: *"Adam thinks he's mustard, if he says that I listen".*

Photograph: © Damian McCann/Kronk Gym

McCarthy Pleased with Pro Progress and Promises More to Come – 28th November 2014

Belfast cruiserweight Tommy McCarthy is enjoying the early stages of his professional career and insists that he left the amateur code with no regrets, but perhaps a couple of disappointments. Speaking on the day before his third fight (what turned out to be a first-round blitz of Dimitar Spaiyski) McCarthy briefly discussed his days in the unpaid code and laid out his hopes for the future.

"I'm still in the club with Patsy and Bernardo Checa has been working with me as well," enthused McCarthy who took on board the value of competing in the World Series of Boxing before committing to the pro game.

"It [the WSB] was a good experience for me with no vests and bouts over five rounds. I had two fights and lost both of them but the second one was a complete robbery! I was watching it back again the other night."

Tommy acquitted himself well with the rigours of the amateur game but despite his successes it was always likely he would eventually turn pro. After signing with savvy veteran Pat Magee the future is bright for the 24-year-old who now looks back on the amateur achievements that got away.

"The Olympics is obviously the big one as anyone from any sort of discipline wants to go to the Olympics," he admitted. "I was gutted when I didn't qualify that time. I gave it a good go and I would've had more regret if I hadn't even tried. It's more disappointment than regret really. I was more disappointed not to take a medal in the Europeans and Worlds last year because the two fights were so close. No regrets just a few disappointments."

Following his stint in the WSB McCarthy's head was turned by the allure of the paid circuit and decided to draw a line on his amateur career and aim for world titles without a head guard and vest.

"I thought about staying amateur and trying to right those wrongs but after you win the medals it doesn't mean anything the next year. You're world champion one day and the next day you're not and there are only so many medals you can win.

"The glory isn't there like if you win any kind of title as pro it stands forever. People know if you won a British title, or European or

Commonwealth and if you win a world title they paint you on the walls! I've always wanted to be a pro anyway from the start of boxing when I began at 11."

Veteran coach Patsy McAllister is handling Tommy's training affairs alongside his Oliver Plunkett BC understudy Jimmy McGrath and Panamanian master-strategist Bernardo Checa. Patsy is pleased with what he sees and reckons there is no reason why the talented power-puncher cannot be stepped up sooner rather than later.

"Well, progressing the way he's progressing we are hoping for a title shot inside the next 14 months. We have to up the opponents and go into six rounders straight away. It's no good knocking people over in one round. Tommy's got big experience, he's boxed world champions and all in the amateurs and just missed out on the Olympics," said McAllister.

Frampton Joins the Northern Ireland Sporting Greats – 29th November 2014

Carl Frampton has now joined an illustrious group of Northern Ireland sporting heroes. In the week following his world title win the 27-year-old was paraded out in Belfast City Centre to meet the fans after a civic reception.

"It means the world, honestly. It still hasn't sunk in to be honest. I'm sore everywhere and I'll go to bed tonight, have a sleep and then realise what a big deal it is. I'm very honoured," said Frampton who revealed that he and Kiko had exchanged some civil words after their war.

"I went back to his changing room and spoke to him. We shook hands and I've never respected a fighter more in my life. I said that I hope I never see you again! I apologise for the way I acted at the weigh-in. He shook my hand, we had a hug and I met his girlfriend and the rest of his team. They were all very respectful."

Frampton's status has been enhanced from boxer to role model but he insists that he does not intend to change the way he operate out of the ring.

"It's humbling to be a role model but I'm just being myself, I'm not doing anything differently," he said.

"That was one of the reasons he turned pro and now over the next 14 months or so, maybe earlier, we are looking for title shots. It depends on the opposition," said McAllister.

Ringside Pundits Assess Frampton's World Title Glory – 6ᵗʰ December 2014

There is no doubt that September's Titanic Showdown captured the public's imagination as Carl Frampton swept home to word title glory in front of a capacity crowd. Not only did the event draw a mammoth gathering of ardent fans but there were plenty of familiar faces planted around ringside lapping up the big fight atmosphere.

Former WBC light-heavyweight champion **John Conteh** was very impressed with what he witnessed: "It's absolutely fantastic, the best atmosphere I've ever experienced, even as a fighter. They've both improved so much and Frampton had a tough job on his hands tonight but he was in great condition. The world's his oyster now; it's all about the next level. I'm not sure who would win out of him and Quigg to tell you the truth. A lot depended on how he got on tonight. The fights will be a lot harder from now on. I love coming to Belfast."

One-time WBA super-bantamweight champion **Bernard Dunne** experienced a few special nights himself in Dublin during his heyday and he was lauding 'The Jackal's' display: "Carl was absolutely fantastic tonight and a worthy world champion on a fantastic evening. Kiko didn't just steamroll in, he respected his power. The crowd were a bit subdued during the fight. When Carl used his jab Kiko couldn't get out of the way of the shots. Carl's footwork and movement was phenomenal, he was one step ahead of Kiko for every moment of the fight. It was only when he stopped using the jab that Kiko could get close to him."

Limerick's former world title challenger and 2004 Olympian **Andy Lee** also weighed in: "He caught him with the same punch that he knocked him down and stopped him with eventually in the last fight. Up until that point in round five Kiko Martinez was having his best round and Carl showed tremendous courage, bravery and tenacity. I actually thought it was closer myself judging the fight and Kiko showed skill and condition, especially in the last round when Frampton went to finish him."

The BoxNation team, led by **Steve Bunce**, will now be hoping that Team Cyclone renew their agreement with the subscription station so that they can enjoy more evenings of this magnitude.

BoxNation summariser and former WBO super-featherweight boss

Barry Jones said: "The concentration was tremendous and the accuracy was spot-on. He made a 28-year-old world champion look like a pedestrian old man. The whole city will be enjoying themselves. It's been freezing cold but a great night."

Veteran commentator **John Rawling** added: "You have to go back to Ricky Hatton-Kostya Tszyu for a night with this type of passion. A fight with Santa Cruz is potentially huge. He has a big following in the United States and they will have been watching this from across the pond."

The Future's Bright for Irish Boxing Star Dee Walsh – 6th December 2014

Dee Walsh landed the Irish title in explosive style on Saturday, November 22 by removing fellow challenger Terry Maughan in the second round of a scheduled 10. Walsh took home the domestic crown at light-middleweight and this victory may only be the start for the talented Belfast starlet. Dee has certainly turned his career around after pushing through a spell of adversity away from the ring to finally land his first major belt.

"Before I came out I was pacing up and down thinking about the future," said Walsh. "I was beating my gloves together because I've never been so pumped up for a fight in my life. At the end of the first round I noticed he could take a few good shots but I knew that there were better shots to come for him and when I did really hit him it was going to be all over. I knew the end was in sight so I landed the big punches."

The uppercut that landed flush on Maughan and started a final flurry that resulted in David Irving's stoppage was not an accidental blow. 'Waldo' had been practising the same shot on former Irish champion Ciaran Healy in a pre-fight training camp.

"I was sparring Ciaran Healy a few weeks' ago and I caught him some similar uppercuts and he was saying to me to make sure and throw a few of those uppercuts on the night. So it was in my mind," he continued.

"Winning the Irish title means everything to me. I think about this time last year, not boxing and being depressed and stuff, then having Mark Dunlop come in for me. I'm just doing the best I can to make everybody proud. Next year I might go for other titles like the Celtic or British and get in to the Ulster Hall and keep building."

Unbeaten Kildare man Dennis Hogan may be next in line for Walsh as the Australian-based boxer, who boasts a 20-0-1 (7 KOs) record, has been mandated to fight for the title by the Boxing Union of Ireland.

"Yes that's no problem but we'll have a wee rest first," responded Walsh. "I hear he's highly ranked with the IBF and stuff so we'll see what happens."

The 24-year-old was also quick to praise the fervent Devenish crowd and his opposite number, Terry Maughan, who arrived alongside trainer Carl Greaves to have a go but was rapidly outgunned.

"The crowd were at an away match today so they created some atmosphere for me. To be honest I was looking at Terry coming into the ring and thinking that he's probably the tallest fighter I've ever fought. He took his top off and he looked meaty too so I tried to test him out early with a few right hands but I didn't catch him cleanly until the second round. I gave everybody a round this time which is better than getting rid of him in 20 seconds!"

There are many reasons behind Walsh's recent success, including the dedication and support of manager Mark Dunlop and his training team led in the St John Bosco gym by Gerard McCafferty. Another factor is down to Dee boxing regularly at his natural weight class rather than mixing with light-heavyweights as was the case before his ring hiatus.

"I only fought one light-middleweight in my first five fights and that was Gerard Healy who was tough. The next four have been at light-middleweight and you see what happens when I fight people at my weight," he added.

Dee Walsh is Going to the Top Says Expert Trainer Gerard McCafferty – 7th December 2014

Highly-touted Irish boxing talent Dee Walsh is ready to take the light-middleweight division by storm. After claiming the Irish crown in comprehensive fashion last month the 24-year-old puncher, now 10-0 (4 KOs), is relishing life both in and out of the ring. On the night, Walsh's title-winning gameplan was expertly constructed by head trainer Gerard McCafferty. Despite having little in the way of video footage to study their taller foe (Nottingham's Terry Maughan who was blown away in two rounds) Gerard remains confident that his boxer possesses the talent to work things out and adapt in any situation.

"We had no footage of him to see how he boxed so we weren't sure what to expect," said McCafferty. "Maughan said that an Irish title was like a world title to him and he wasn't coming here for a payday. I was speaking to [Maughan's trainer] Carl Greaves the other day and he said the same thing, that Terry was coming over to have a go and test Dee. He did not get a chance to test him because Dee was just too smart and too quick."

McCafferty views every fight as a learning experience for his young charge. Dee has been enjoying highly competitive sparring session with the likes of Gerard Healy which has helped both boxers to mature and progress. Walsh and Healy made their debuts together and now they're dedicated sparring partners, pushing each other inside the ring but enjoying a convivial relationship when the hard work is done for the day.

"Last week Dee was sparring Gerard as well as Tommy Tolan, Ciaran Healy and Joe Hillerby, one after the other and he could have done 20 rounds," continued Gerard McCafferty.

"Now that he's got this fight over him he will move on and Mark will pick out who he's going to fight next. We wanted 10-0 before Christmas and an Irish title is even better. He's still young and I can remember when he packed boxing in. I was on the receiving end [in 2012] when Tommy Tolan boxed him two-and-a-half years ago. He did such a good job on Tommy and I knew Dee was special. Tommy had been in against people who had fought for European titles and gone on to fight for world titles and for that kid there to do that in his third fight was unbelievable. We later had Dee up sparring Ciaran Healy for a fight in France and now we are both in his corner. It's funny the way things turn out."

With Dee walking around at over six feet tall and comfortably making the 11 stone weight limit Gerard is perplexed as to why his man was previously being routinely matched with light-heavyweights instead of campaigning at his natural limit. With hefty weight jumps no longer an issue Walsh trains every day and lives the life outside of the gym, passing his time as a family man when away from the limelight.

"For such a young lad he's showing great maturity. I saw him boxing Eamonn O'Kane in the final of the Ulster Seniors, I think he was 17 at the time, and I personally thought he beat O'Kane and I knew he was one to watch for the future. He is a great boxer but there's a dark side to him. When people ask me what I like to see in a boxer it's people who can box, yes, but you need a dig and a bit of venom."

Walsh clearly possesses that requisite "venom" and Gerard sees no reason why he cannot soon find himself in the company of more esteemed names at British title level.

"Listen, at light-middleweight Liam 'Beefy' Smith is the British champion and I remember being over with Gerard Healy when he fought 'Beefy' and his style would suit Dee. He's going to come forward and walk on to shots like that tonight. I'd like to see Dee getting a few rounds under his belt because he's going to be in some fights down the line where he won't get it so easy. We concentrated last week on a 10-round spar and after the first spar he was flying. It was about getting it into his head that he can do the distance and now he knows he can."

The St John Bosco head coach trusts Dee's future plans to expert manager and promoter Mark Dunlop of MHD Promotions who has carved out a niche for his band of Belfast boxers to ply their trade, on a regular basis, in the Devenish Complex every few months. If things go to plan Australian-based unbeaten talent Dennis Hogan could be next in line for a shot at Walsh's Irish title if Hogan can reconcile any concerns that the IBF may have with him accepting the bout.

"Hogan would be a great fight for Dee because Hogan will come to fight. There are a load of fights out there but we don't make the fights, that's Mark's job and we'll fight whoever he gets for us," added Gerard.

Ulster Elite Championships Finals Round-Up
– 13th December 2014

Kurt Walker won his bantamweight crown in impressive fashion at the Unite Ulster Elite Championships last night. The Canal club man swept home to a unanimous victory over Sean Higginson (St John Bosco) at the Dockers Club. Walker took a close opener although Higginson found a home for his right hand and persistently tried to force the issue. Walker took over in the second session, slamming home right hands of his own with increasing regularity as the bout progressed. Higginson was visibly tiring and shipped Walker's one-twos but his vocal supporters, along with trainer Gerard McCafferty, helped push the Bosco man over the line.

TJ Waite appeared unfortunate to concede the flyweight final to Canal's Jason McKay. There was plenty to shout about for McKay in the final round as he tucked up and landed hooks but Cairn Lodge product Waite appeared to have bossed the first two with his superior movement and well-timed shots. Setting McKay up with a feint and waiting for the Canal man to commit, Waite lashed home shots from both stances but the judges preferred McKay's endeavour more.

Michael Glendenning claimed a deserved unanimous decision over Sean Duffy at light-welterweight. Errigal's Glendenning used his jab to good effect, keeping Holy Trinity's Duffy at bay for extended periods. Glendenning wasn't afraid to bite down on his gumshield and mix it in the trenches when required either. Both men left the ring with battle scars from an excellent contest.

Caoimhin Hynes won the battle of the Holy Trinity at middleweight against club mate Taylor McGoldrick. The opening session was a slugfest as both men came out swinging with southpaw McGoldrick roughing up Caoimhin. Hynes added some refinement to his work in the second and settled down by anticipating McGoldrick's lunges and slipping his shots inside the gaps. McGoldrick became increasingly ragged and took a count in the third round.

St Paul's man Gerard Matthews outboxed Spartens' Connor Kerr at lightweight. Southpaw stylist Matthews landed his shots early but stayed inside for too long and soaked up a few swings from brave Kerr. He learned his lesson from the second onwards and remained one step ahead of a fatigued Kerr.

Two Castles' Ryan Donnelly earned a surprising split decision win at light-heavyweight over Padraig McCrory. Marauding southpaw Donnelly tried to turn it into an inside scrap but Holy Trinity's McCrory was able, for the most part, to land his spearing shots at distance. McCrory's work was crisper but the judges preferred Donnelly's come-forward aggression.

JD Meli defeated Connor Doherty in the welterweight final. Skilful Immaculata man Meli was always one step ahead of his Holy Trinity opponent. Meli used his jab and timed his punches to perfection.

Holy Trinity heavyweight Stephen McMonagle pressed Dockers boxer Thomas Copeland for the duration of their contest. Well-supported Copeland was strong and resilient but McMonagle won a split decision.

In the women's 64kg final Sarah Close (Holy Family) stopped Joanna Barclay (Holy Family) in the first round.

In the battle of the big Holy Trinity super-heavyweights Jason Barron claimed a unanimous decision over Damien Sullivan. Barron showed good movement and skills for his size. Michael Glendenning claimed the award for boxer of the tournament.

Andy Lee's Dream Come True by Winning World Title – 14ᵗʰ December 2014

From the desk of Kronk Press Officer Damian McCann: "Andy Lee from Limerick, Ireland wakes up this morning [written on Sunday] as the new WBO world middleweight champion following an impressive sixth round stoppage win over Matt Korobov last night in Las Vegas, USA. Lee started the fight by keeping matters at long range and was patience using his jab and picking his punches.

Both boxers utilized their respective technical boxing skills in the early going with not much to split them. In round six Lee stepped up and unleashed a ferocious right hook which stunned Korobov to his boots, sensing blood Lee moved in and unleashed a barrage of heavy punches forcing referee Kenny Bayless to stop the fight at 1:10 into the round.

It was an emotional victory for the Irishman; he was elated with happiness that he had won the prestigious prize of the world middleweight championship title and his name would be added to the boxing record books alongside champions such as Marvin Hagler, Sugar Ray Robinson and Carlos Monzon. The former Athens 2004 Olympian had now realized his boyhood dream, the fruits of his labour and dedication had finally paid off. He had stayed the course, battled with adversity and came out on top. After the fight Lee paid homage to the two most influential people in his boxing career, the late Emanuel Steward and Adam Booth. Lee signed with the legendary boxing guru, Emanuel Steward on December 15, 2005 and left the comfort zone of Ireland to live with Emanuel in Detroit and pursue a professional boxing career.

He served his apprenticeship and learnt his craft at the famous Kronk Gym in Detroit and obtained valuable experience in numerous training camps. Emanuel and Andy lived like father and son looking out for one another. Sadly Emanuel passed away after a short illness on October 25, 2012. Lee relocated to London and teamed up with another world class trainer and manager, Adam Booth. In the past two years Adam has made adjustment to Andy's game enhancing his boxing skills and ability both mentally and physically. Adam and Andy also have a strong friendship and working relationship.

Andy commented: "I would like to say thank you to my manager and trainer Adam Booth, who has done so much for me over the last couple of years, but it's also for the man who made me, Emanuel Steward."

Emanuel Steward will be smiling from Heaven proud of his protégé, saying I told you all my Irish Tommy Hearns would be world champion. He has done it. Premier US promoter, Lou DiBella was delighted that his fighter, Andy Lee won the championship belt with such an impressive stoppage. Lou has projected Lee's talent in recent years through boxing events on HBO television and advanced his career with wins against Craig McEwan, Brian Vera and John Jackson.

Andy will now celebrate and enjoy Christmas before contemplating his next fight. Ireland has another world champion and there will be a few pints of Guinness drank to toast Andy's victory in Limerick, Dublin and around the country for a few days to come.

Photograph: © Damian McCann/Kronk Gym

Frampton in Confident Mood Ahead of Maiden Defence Against Avalos – 19th December 2014

Carl Frampton does not suffer fools gladly. The 27-year-old has little time for the time-wasters and trash-talkers of the boxing community and quickly set about dissecting the credentials of IBF mandatory challenger Chris Avalos. Arriving in Belfast to promote the February 28 show entitled "The World is Not Enough" Avalos immediately began goading Frampton who responded with a scathing assessment of his opponent's record so far.

"The difference in this fight will be simple," said Frampton. "The two times he's stepped up he's boxed two half decent fighters, fringe world class, and both of them beat him. I'm the first world class fighter he's fought and that's going to be the difference. Chris, you're going to get knocked out."

Carl went on to stress that despite the mass public attention and huge boost in his profile away from the ring he remains as humble and hungry to succeed as ever. The Tigers Bay man has a world title in his possession and is in no mood to hand it over any time soon.

"Chris' manager says he has come up from the bottom but so have I," continued Carl. "He doesn't deserve this any more than me. I've been doing this my whole life. He may think this is going to be easy but I'm training for a tough fight."

Frampton is used to training over the festive period and will enjoy his Christmas despite the rigours of an intense training camp as he whips his body into supreme condition ready for the late February Odyssey Arena headliner. Even though Avalos appears tall for the 122lb weight class Carl pointed out that the loquacious visitor's high-heeled shoes represent just another psychological trick. The hometown hero also reckons that his opponent looks like he needs to stay off the sweet stuff over the next few weeks.

"I'm well used to training over Christmas and I'll be having a nice big dinner but I don't think this lad [Avalos] will be having a dinner because he looks a wee bit heavy and podgy at the minute so he'll be skipping the Christmas dinner. It's going to be like nothing he's ever experienced before but he does have a point when he says that a ring's a ring no matter where it is.

"But the atmosphere is noisier here than anywhere he's ever been and it's going to be a great night," said Frampton.

Chris Avalos: 'I'm Taking Frampton's Title By Knockout' – 19th December 2014

Carl Frampton will defend his 122lb strap against mandatory challenger Chris Avalos in the Odyssey Arena on February 28. A smiling Avalos swaggered into yesterday's Europa Hotel press conference with the air of a man fully confident that he is destined to take home the IBF super-bantamweight title. Champion Frampton, of course, has other ideas and the Belfast boxer appeared to get the better of the verbal spars between the pair at top table. Avalos admitted that he had never been to a press event of that magnitude before and thanked the hefty crowd of journalists and members of the public for their warm applause. The heavily-tattooed visitor -a stereotypical boxing product who has worked his way up from the bottom- then proceeded to discredit Frampton's abilities.

"I'm not going to lose, I'm here to win the title and it is not going to be by decision," the 25-year-old professed, pointing across Barry McGuigan directly at undefeated Frampton.

"I know that, he knows that and everyone might laugh like it's a joke but I'll prove it. It doesn't matter if the fight is here, out in Los Angeles where I live or wherever, he is going to lose, I promise you that. Fifth or sixth round it's over - it ain't going no longer."

Even though Avalos claims to have no respect for Frampton he has been diligent in his homework. The Californian routinely watches footage of his foe and believes that he has the tools needed to exploit the Belfast boxer's flaws.

"I've been studying Frampton for over a year now and I notice what he throws and what he gets hit with. He makes mistakes and I do as well but I've been in the gym correcting mine. I've noticed what catches him and how he moves; that's why I feel like I can beat him. I know it and he knows it. You ain't got no power, you're weak dude! I'm not Kiko, I'm a different fighter."

"I know, Kiko's better than you!" replied Frampton, much to the delight of his crowd.

Even Avalos grinned at that one, before explaining how the raucous Belfast atmosphere will not faze him on fight night. He is coming over for one purpose and that is to take possession of "his title".

"I'm going to be victorious, wherever the fight takes place. You paid to fight Martinez. I could've got Martinez out way earlier than you."

"Like you did with Jhonatan Romero?" Frampton spat back.

"Kiko Martinez absolutely destroyed Jhonatan Romero and you couldn't even beat him," continued 'The Jackal', who then took the visitor to task over his decision not to box Guillermo Rigondeaux despite holding a WBO number one ranking.

"Avalos didn't take the Rigondeaux fight because Rigo would've absolutely boxed the ears off him for 12 rounds. He's taken this fight thinking it's an easier fight. The difference is, Rigo would box the head off him but I'll knock him out."

Which prompted trainer Shane McGuigan to shout across the table: "Chris, you've picked the wrong Jackal."

Shane McGuigan Backs Frampton to Knock Out Avalos – 20th December 2014

Carl Frampton's trainer Shane McGuigan has a knack of picking results for his man. Shane often weighs in with his pre-fight predictions and this time is no different. He reckons mandatory challenger Chris Avalos will fail to hear the final bell on February 28 and Frampton will spark him in the middle rounds.

"I'm going to predict a knockout but it's the other way around," Shane opined, in response to Avalos' own five or six round demolition claim.

"I predict that Carl will knock you [to Avalos] spark out in six-eight rounds. Chris chose the wrong Jackal."

One aspect of Frampton's pre-fight preparations that will not be lacking is the physical side of the game. Frampton's strict dietary regime will not be interrupted by the Christmas period and if recent video evidence of his monkey bar challenge effort is anything to go by he is already in pretty fine fettle.

"We've started preparation and we are already in good shape, sparring 29 rounds this week," agreed Shane McGuigan. "More importantly he's getting better with each camp. [Frampton is] going to walk through Chris Avalos and achieve massive things. Scott Quigg, all the top super-bantamweights out there, he's going to unify the division and move up because he's got the right team behind him."

Irish Boxing Prospects Ready to 'Stand and Deliver' – 22nd December 2014

2015 promises to be an exciting year for Irish pugilists and fight fans with two world champions, Carl Frampton and Andy Lee, leading the way at super-bantamweight and middleweight respectively. Belfast is widely recognised as Irish boxing's fight capital and Mark Dunlop has found a niche venue for his fighters.

MHD Promotions' Saturday fight nights at the Devenish Complex are providing a regular platform for local prospects, from all over Ireland, to showcase their talents. With each passing show, Mark Dunlop's talented stable are building up a solid fan base are more importantly keeping themselves active.

Irish Champions Dee Walsh and James Tennyson are ready to seize their big opportunities in 2015 and hopefully progress on to Celtic and Commonwealth title fight.

Both Walsh, 10-0 (4 KOs), and Tennyson, 10-1 (8 KOs), are now back in full training camp for their ring returns on the stacked *'Stand and Deliver'* card in Belfast's Devenish Complex on Saturday, February 7, 2015.

The card also sees young North Belfast super-featherweight prospect Ciaran McVarnock, 2-0, make his long awaited home debut.

The fantastic line-up once again also features: James 'The Future' Fryers, Daniel 'Insane' McShane, Paul 'Hylo' Hyland, Gerard 'Boom Boom' Healy, Alan Donnellan, Darren Cruise, Gerard Whitehouse and Michael McKinson.

McGuigan Says America is Calling for Frampton
– 23rd December 2014

Barry McGuigan is expecting a huge 2015 for Carl Frampton and has laid down ambitious plans for his undefeated star. The suggestion has been for a while that Frampton is close to making his highly-anticipated American debut. The Belfast boxer's fan-friendly style would no doubt mesh well with the likes of Leo Santa Cruz or Abner Mares but so far WBC title holder Santa Cruz at least has been difficult to pin down for a unification. Barry reckons that it will only be a matter of time before Carl travels across the pond to enter the lucrative US market.

"America has been calling for some time and we will go out there when we're ready and the time is right. We know what we're doing and I've been down this road before," said McGuigan Snr who is cautious of looking past February 28 opponent Chris Avalos.

"We had two main objectives and the main one was to win the world title - preferably at home. We also wanted to fight here [in Belfast] on a regular basis, then conquer America and go to England as well. All of these things are planned for next year. Number one is February 28 and we'll sort this fellow [mandatory challenger Avalos] out here first."

One thing that has yet to be resolved is the television situation. McGuigan refused to be drawn on a couple of issues during the press conference and that was one of them. Belfast journalist David Kelly asked how new sponsor CWM (Cyclone have now been re-branded as CWM Cyclone Promotions) would take operations to a new level. The response of "watch this space" adds an element of intrigue.

"We will announce our broadcasting partner in January," added Barry.

That now appears unlikely to be boxing subscription station BoxNation who, despite televising Frampton's last three fights, are currently scheduled to show Tyson Fury and Chris Eubank Jnr in London on that same February date. If BoxNation were to remain involved then perhaps a split between the Frampton and Fury shows could be viable. Back in 2009 Frank Warren's Martin Rogan-Sam Sexton rematch in Belfast and Paul McCloskey's European title fight with Daniel Rasilla in Magherafelt (promoted by Brian Peters) were both screened live on the same night.

Alternative options could include a pay-per-view internet stream or the dark horse option in the background of Sky TV. Matchroom Boxing head honcho Eddie Hearn is involved in the fight on a tangential level but Avalos' manager Mike Criscio admitted that all of their dealings are with Top Rank and not with Hearn himself. It is possible that McGuigan could negotiate a standalone deal with the powerhouse network independent of Matchroom, similar to the broadcaster's interest in Amir Khan.

"Apparently Tyson Fury is fighting on the same night yeah," was Barry's non-committal stance on BoxNation.

If, as expected, Frampton finds himself back on Sky Sports that will conceivably help prize the doors open a little wider for a domestic blockbuster with Scott Quigg. However, by the time Quigg is fit and ready for such an encounter, 'The Jackal' could already be off conquering America.

'Hungry Avalos Came from the Bottom' Says Manager Criscio – 29th December 2014

Chris Avalos insists that the IBF super-bantamweight title should be his personal property. Speaking to the Californian on the telephone recently he described his displeasure at the Frampton-Martinez world title affair and described it as a "secret fight".

Once again, at the most recent Belfast press conference, organised to formally announce the February 28 show entitled "The World is Not Enough", Avalos accused Team Cyclone of paying for the Martinez rematch. The 25-year-old also claimed that the IBF were threatening to demote him in the rankings if he didn't agree to a fight with Japan's Yasutaka Ishimoto which took place earlier this year in China, resulting in an Avalos eighth-round knockout win.

"Chris has been waiting for this fight for a long time," agreed the American's manager Mike Criscio. "This will be a tough fight. Carl's a tough competitor and I'm not taking anything away from him but Chris' very hungry. He came from the bottom up, has a family to feed and he wants this bad."

Frampton was unimpressed by Criscio's assessment, arguing that he also has a young family to look after and has been handed nothing on a plate, having risen from a tough housing estate through the boxing ranks to the highest level. Frampton also cast aspersions on his opponent's record, especially his two defeats to supposedly lesser opposition.

"Yes, Chris does have two losses but against Chris Martin he had a 102 fever, the other guy was 12 pounds overweight and we should've never fought the fight," argued Mike Criscio. "I told Chris not to take the fight but he has Mexican pride and he took it. We went the distance, lost and never got the rematch. Against [former IBF title holder Jhonatan] Romero, as you all know, we beat Romero very comfortably. Gary Shaw has deep pockets and I think he paid off a couple of guys. The whole media frenzy after that was ridiculous. Chris won that fight."

With both combatants seated across the table from one another at the press conference Frampton visibly rolled his eyes at Criscio's reasoning. The tall, imposing manager cuts an authoritative figure who has spent his entire career trying to do his business with a level of integrity. Criscio's words were well considered and delivered concisely, offering a nice counterbalance to his client's brash predictions and perceived arrogant nature.

"Carl thinks he's going to come in here and knock Chris out but Chris has never been knocked out before by the way," continued Criscio. "If he thinks he is going to push Chris around then it's a rude awakening. This fight's going to be held in the middle of the ring, 100 punches each per round, nobody's going to back down but Chris will come out with a victory – I guarantee that."

Frampton Out to Make Avalos Pay for Lack of Respect – 2nd January 2015

Carl Frampton is intent on punishing IBF mandatory challenger Chris Avalos for a perceived lack of respect. Avalos arrived in Belfast intent on stoking up the tension with a bit of trash talk. Frampton was not amused by the American's antics but unsurprised by his crude attempts at engaging in psychological warfare.

"I expected it from him to be honest," shrugged Frampton. "He was just annoying me a wee bit, showing me zero respect as the champion. He said that he doesn't respect me as a fighter but he'll respect me when I hit him in the first round. I've got the motivation, I've got the belt."

Avalos' manager Mike Criscio claimed that his man was hungry for success after a tough career trying to reach this kind of level. Frampton listened intently to the hard-luck story but does not believe that Avalos deserves the title any more than himself.

"He's just the same as me as a young, hungry fighter. We don't need all that to sell tickets but it helps a wee bit. It's mind games but it doesn't bother me. I think he's a bit daft as well to be honest."

Any concerns about Carl's hands not being ready for fight night were quickly dismissed by the champion who has been limbering up on the monkey bar challenge at a complex in Twin Spires, Belfast.

"The hands are fine. I just waited and did no punching until I was told to and got the all clear. I've been sparring a bit and they're fine. Avalos' tall but he's wearing platform shoes; sticking the big heels on to look bigger."

Avalos may look bigger but the champion poked fun at his challenger for looking "a wee bit podgy". Frampton's supporters still crave big fight against the likes of Quigg, Santa Cruz and Rigondeaux but next in line is Californian Avalos in 'The Jackal's' late February Odyssey assignment. Carl has already predicted that the American's lack of respect will prove his downfall.

"The mistake this guy's making is he's saying he doesn't respect me. I am training hard for him. There are some big fights out there and as the champion they aren't going to be easy now. Some hard fights against hungry competitors," admitted Frampton.

National Elite Championships Report
– 23rd January 2015

The Irish National Elite Championships once again threw up its customary mix of thrills and spills in Dublin's National Stadium on Friday evening. Seasoned medal winners and promising breakthrough talents were busy battling it out for domestic bragging rights across 10 contests.

Leading the way in a 69kg battle of former Olympians was Adam Nolan who outsmarted John Joe Joyce by unanimous decision. Nolan's herky-jerky southpaw style gave the more conventional Joyce (St Michael's Athy) fits as the Bray ABC man constantly lashed home shots before taking a walk to admire his handiwork. True to type Adam started fast but showed no signs this time of fading down the stretch. Joyce tried to get his jab going but Nolan, trained by Katie Taylor's dad Peter, coasted home to a fourth Elite crown.

Dean Walsh edged Ray Moylette on a split decision at 64kg in a high-quality encounter. Walsh (St Joseph's/St Ibar's) retained the Elite light-welterweight accolade by using his jab, combinations and maintaining a consistent output. Classy Moylette (St Anne's), a 2008 World Junior gold medallist, bit down on his gumshield to release spiteful flurries but a rampant Walsh refused to be denied. Dean's night was complete when he later collected the Best Boxer Award.

Ireland's 2012 Olympic captain Darren O'Neill made the big jump up from middleweight to heavyweight to tackle Athlone behemoth Ken Okungbowa. Despite being dragged inside by Okungbowa's lunging attacks, O'Neill (Paulstown) was able to land his single shots with eye-catching accuracy to earn a split decision win at 91kg. Darren suffered nasty cuts across both eyes during the contest.

Defending 75kg champion Michael O'Reilly (Portlaoise) boxed within himself for the majority of his middleweight clash with Dundalk southpaw Stephen Broadhurst but still enjoyed a unanimous points win. O'Reilly's sharp jab and one-twos were enough to keep Broadhurst (Dealgan) at range and Michael cleaned up on the scorecards with wide totals.

Once super-heavyweight Dean Gardiner (Clonmel) figured out the range and got his broomstick jab working he was able to nullify the raw assaults of Meath slugger Constantin Popovicu (Johnstown). Buoyed on by a semi-final knockout of Belfast's Jason Barron, Popovicu swung in the left hook and tried to shorten the distance but Gardiner's superior skills told as he boxed to a unanimous decision at 91kg+.

Canal stylist Kurt Walker added the Irish 56kg title to the Ulster bantamweight crown he earned in December by beating the same opponent on a unanimous decision. Sean Higginson (St John Bosco) once again played his part but Lisburn's Walker was always landing the cleaner blows as Higginson repeatedly fell short.

Roy Sheahan (St Michael's Athy) befuddled and beat up Matthew Tinker (St Francis'), posting a wide unanimous points success at 81kg. This was Sheahan's first venture at the light-heavyweight limit and he looked comfortable against last year's finalist (Matthew lost to Joe Ward). Sheahan slipped in and out of range, bopping his southpaw foe often enough to cause bleeding from Tinker's nose and mouth.

Belfast's Sean McComb (Holy Trinity) did enough to snatch a split verdict over Dublin's George Bates (St Mary's) at 60kg. There was little to choose between southpaw McComb and upright Bates as they toiled and tangled throughout. McComb lost in last year's final to David Oliver Joyce and refused to be denied in his latest stab at Elite glory.

In the show opener Brendan Irvine (St Paul's) claimed a unanimous decision victory at 49kg over Hugh Myers (St Brigid's). The margins were tight for the majority of the contest as the combatants traded back and forth. Former finalist Myers diligently rolled forward but the judges preferred Irvine's crisp work off the back foot.

Myles Casey (St Francis') took a split decision over Evan Metcalfe (Crumlin) following a bad-tempered scrap at 52kg. Clean punches were few and far between with both men suffering cuts and rumbling on the canvas following lengthy grapples. There was certainly more endeavour than quality but Myles, brother of Willie 'Big Bang' Casey, ultimately prevailed.

Total Results

49kg Brendan Irvine (St Pauls) beat Hugh Myers (St Brigids) 3-0
56kg Kurt Walker (Canal) beat Sean Higginson (St John Bosco) 3-0
69kg Adam Nolan (Bray) beat JJ Joyce (St Michael's Athy) 3-0
75kg Michael O'Reilly (Portlaoise) beat Stephen Broadhurst (Dealgan) 3-0
91kg Darren O'Neill (Paulstown) beat Ken Okungbowa (Athlone) 2-1

64kg Dean Walsh (St Joseph's/St Ibars) beat R Moylette (St Annes) 2-1
52kg Myles Casey (St Francis) beat Evan Metcalfe (Crumlin) 2-1
60kg Sean McComb (Holy Trinity) beat George Bates (St Marys) 2-1
81kg Roy Sheahan (St Michael's Athy) beat Matthew Tinker (St Francis) 3-0
91kg Dean Gardiner (Clonmel) beat Constantin Popovicu (Johnstown) 3-0

Tennyson Ready to 'Stand and Deliver' in the Devenish – 4th February 2015

James Tennyson is preparing to live up to the 'Stand and Deliver' tagline on Saturday night when he headlines at the Devenish Complex. Tennyson boxes Simas Volosinas over six rounds in what is little more than a rust-shedding exercise with bigger tests waiting in the wings for 2015.

Featherweight Tennyson knows that another solid victory here will help him secure a space on more high profile shows as he climbs the rankings towards a shot at the (currently vacant) British featherweight title. There's increasing talk of the 21-year-old boxing his way into an eliminator within the next few bouts and show promoter Mark Dunlop believes his fighter is ready to push on.

Tennyson has rebounded well after a shock loss in 2013 and now boasts an impressive 10-1 record that includes an Irish title up at super-featherweight. 'The Baby-Faced Assassin' was last seen pounding tough veteran Ian Bailey over eight rounds in May but a mix of injuries and outside of the ring issues meant he did not fight for the remainder of 2014.

"That wasn't an easy time but it's over now and I can't wait to box again at the Devenish," said Tennyson. "The Bailey win was a good learning fight for me. I stayed calm, picked my shots and I was pleased with the performance."

Further down the card Tyrone McKenna takes part in his first professional outing on home soil. Welterweight McKenna started his paid career in America and amassed a 5-0 record before returning home to try his hand on the domestic circuit. The former Oliver Plunkett stylist faces Bulgaria's Teodor Stefanov over four rounds.

Co-headlining the bill is Paul Hyland Jnr. The improving lightweight enjoyed an active 2014, making his debut in May and boxing four times. He now steps up to six-round class against Yordan Vasilev.

Another boxer relishing his Belfast debut is featherweight Ciaran McVarnock who tackles Lithuanian Aivaras Balsys. McVarnock is based in Manchester and will have recent world bantamweight champion Paul Butler in his corner.

Darren Cruise, Alan Donnellan and Michael McKinson make up the remainder of the card.

Photograph: © Mark Dunlop

Tennyson's Ready for British Title After Volosinas Demolition – 8ᵗʰ February 2015

James Tennyson marked his ring return with a comprehensive second-round mauling of Simas Volosinas on Saturday night at the Devenish Complex. After battling through a frustrating nine-month ring absence the 21-year-old Irish champion is intent on hunting down a shot at the British featherweight title. Tennyson never allowed Lithuania's Volosinas to get a grip on the bout. 'The Baby Faced-Assassin' slammed home a variety of punches to frequently pin the visitor on the ropes and Volosinas barely managed to make it through the first round. Tennyson continued his assaults in the second and a weary glance across to his corner indicated Volosinas was looking for assistance under the increasing pressure.

Referee Paul McCullagh read the signals and called the bout off at 1-33 of the second session. James, now 11-1 (9), is expected to take up a place on the undercard of Carl Frampton's February 28 Odyssey world title defence.

"I'd definitely like a British title shot," enthused Tennyson. "I'm up there [in the rankings] at the minute so that's what I'm aiming for."

"He will destroy any featherweight in Britain, bar none," added manager Mark Dunlop who is busy chasing down an eliminator.

Paul Hyland Jnr comfortably moved up to six-round class to defeat lively Bulgarian Yordan Vasilev 60-54 on referee Hugh Russell Jnr's card. Hyland Jnr (9st 9lbs 3oz), 5-0, has an exciting style and used his superior skills to better Vasilev (9st 9lbs 1oz).

Tyrone McKenna enjoyed a 40-37 success over Bulgaria's Teodor Stefanov. Returning home from a spell in America where he had amassed an impressive five wins and sparred the likes of Matt Korobov. McKenna (10st 8lbs 6oz), 6-0 (2), is huge for a welterweight and toiled to make his advantages tell. John Lowey refereed.

Hugh Russell Jnr awarded Manchester-based super-featherweight Ciaran McVarnock a 60-54 victory over Lithuania's Aivaras Balsys. Originally from Belfast, McVarnock improved to 3-0 but was left frustrated by Balsys.

Galway's Alan Donnellan (12st 0lbs 3oz), 7-3 (2), had it all his own way against Omagh's Damian Taggart (12st 10lbs 8oz), scoring a 40-36 shutout on Paul McCullagh's reckoning.

Roscommon stylist Darren Cruise (12st 1lb 3oz), 6-3, notched a 40-36 formality over Brighton survivor Iain Jackson (12st 5lbs 8oz). Hugh Russell Jnr officiated.

Portsmouth's Michael McKinson (10st 5lbs 1oz), 4-0, opened the show with a 40-36 win over Lithuania's Aleksas Vaseris (10st 3lbs 9oz) on Mr Lowey's scorecard.

Photograph: © Mark Dunlop

Tennyson Has British Title in His Sights After Devenish Demolition – 17th February 2015

James Tennyson returned with a bang on Saturday, February 7 when the promising featherweight blitzed Simas Volosinas in two rounds. Bigger tests will certainly come for James but after an unfortunate nine-month hiatus the 21-year-old was just glad to be back in the ring and exciting his loyal following.

"I'm very happy with that because I've been training hard for nine weeks," he said. "The cornermen basically told me to go in and not to give him a minute to settle, just see how he copes. I've been out for nine months so it's good to get back in and get a good win and get back on track."

Tennyson is highly placed in the British rankings and wants to gets his paws on the Lonsdale belt or at least fight some sort of elimination bout before the year is out. The reigning Irish super-featherweight king was originally scheduled to box 15-0 Scottish boxer Michael Roberts in Belfast on March 28 but now it has been confirmed that Celtic title holder Kris Hughes has been tempted over to the Andersonstown Leisure Centre on the same date.

"I'd definitely like a British title shot. I'm up there [in the rankings] at the minute so that's what I'm aiming for. It was frustrating because I got a good win over Ian Bailey but then I was out of the ring and it's great to get back on track," said Tennyson.

Volosinas was no world-beater but he had reasonable form in the past. The Lithuanian troubled Declan Geraghty and went the six-round distance with Anthony Cacace in Liverpool last year.

"He put down Jon Slowey from Scotland so he's usually strong," added Tennyson.

"As soon as the uppercut landed and it damaged his nose he turned away so I stepped it up a wee bit. He didn't want to know from that point on."

Manager Mark Dunlop is keen to find a space for both James Tennyson and Paul Hyland Jnr on the big February 28 Odyssey undercard.

"Look at the support they both got and the wins, both were punch perfect," elaborated Dunlop. "Carl Frampton is the IBF champion of the world and he went away impressed with these kids tonight. The same with

Paul Butler."

Mark has been busy poking and prodding at the British Boxing Board of Control for a featherweight eliminator and was exploring other routes for the Poleglass puncher. The head of MHD Promotions revealed that there was talk of his man fighting for an IBF Intercontinental title.

Speaking immediately after Tennyson's impressive dismissal of Volosinas, Dunlop told Irish Boxing Review: "I'm trying to get James in an eliminator for the British title and I'm trying to get him ranked in the European as well. The British title's vacant, there are four boxers up there and nobody wants to fight this young man. I've asked to fight any of the top ten fighters for an eliminator and we don't care who it is, they're the ones who are going to care."

Mark's wishes appear to have come true as since that interview took place Tennyson has been pushed into a Celtic featherweight title shot by the Board in a bout that will also serve as the British title eliminator his Belfast team crave. The current Celtic champion is former Carl Frampton-victim Kris Hughes who will travel to Northern Ireland to box James on March 28. The winner of that Celtic clash will then fight for the British title which is set to be contested by Samir Mouneimne and Ryan Walsh whenever the various parties can agree a date and location. Mouneimne's previous crack ended badly when he was knocked out by current European champion Josh Warrington back in 2013. Dunlop is unconcerned about who faces his man and believes it is the opposition that needs to be worrying about Tennyson's abilities.

"James is the real deal. His defence is rock solid and this man [trainer Tony Dunlop] has dedicated himself for ten weeks building this kid up. Morning, noon and night the pair of them are out and they proved it tonight. If that fight hadn't been stopped by the referee then that kid was out of there.

"He will destroy any featherweight in Britain, bar none," buzzed Mark Dunlop.

A Win's a Win for Frustrated Ciaran McVarnock
– 19th February 2015

Purposefully striding into the ring amidst a cacophony of cheers and adulation Ciaran McVarnock was relishing his Belfast debut. After all, the 22-year-old had been eager to return home and display his skills to a burgeoning fan base after winning two bouts across the water. Following a bruising six-twos against Lithuanian survivor Aivaras Balsys, Ciaran moved his fledgling record to 3-0 by virtue of a 60-54 success on Hugh Russell Jnr's Scorecard. The youngster later revealed, however, that he was not happy with his overall performance.

"I loved the whole thing, the atmosphere and everything for my first fight back at home in front of an unbelievable crowd," said Ciaran.

"The tickets I sold was great and all, but I was nowhere near as good as I've been in sparring. I sparred better in the gym against Paul Butler than I did there tonight. I wasn't at my greatest but I'm happy to get the win when not performing at my best. He was frustrating me on the inside and holding."

What McVarnock insists he wanted was an all-out brawl but cagey Balsys was unwilling to comply.

"At times I wanted him to stand and have a war but he was holding on and I was trying to bend my knees and work and step to the side but no matter what I did he was holding on and I couldn't break free. This is going to be a big year for me and Frank Warren's going to keep me busy. To be honest I want more home fights and I proved I can sell the tickets in my first fight back home. I can't wait to do it again with these brilliant fans."

Selling out smaller hall venues is clearly a tick in the box for Ciaran as he strives for more opportunities. Could Frank Warren be tempted back over to Belfast for a show with his young fighter making an appearance?

"It all depends because I can sell near enough 200 tickets on a small hall show in just my third professional fight so imagine what I could do if I got on to the Frampton bill?" said McVarnock. "Loads of people were asking me today for tickets but I was under pressure and just couldn't do it so I told them to pay at the door. I've never come up against anyone with that sort of style before so if I do box that style again I'll know how to deal with it next time. I know I can box a million times better but I still won so I'm happy with that. I have to thanks Mark Dunlop for putting me on the show."

Now based in Manchester but keen to avail of any free spots on Irish cards, McVarnock is reaping the benefits of the top-class sparring partners he enjoys mixing with at Anthony Farnell's gym.

"My main sparring partner is Paul Butler who is fighting for his second world title and I have no doubt he will win it. I've been sparring the likes of Ross Burkinshaw, Commonwealth and English champion, and other unbeaten fighters," he added.

"I made the right move going over to Arnie's gym because he's an unbelievable trainer and if I was here I wouldn't get that kind of quality sparring. I stopped sparring Paul Butler in camp because he needs a southpaw so Arnie got me Burkinshaw which just shows how good Arnie is with me."

Butler Open to Conlan Scrap but Has IBF Business First – 20th February 2015

Paul Butler is relishing his March 6 clash with hard-hitting South African Zolani Tete in Liverpool. The talented super-flyweight is not content with winning a world title at bantamweight but he is now chasing history when he moves down in weight to battle Tete for the IBF crown one division south. Speaking in Belfast recently, when Paul was over watching gym mate Ciaran McVarnock make his Irish debut, the Chester boxer explained how well his preparations have been moving along.

"It's gone perfect and obviously we've had a long time to prepare for this. He pulled out [after the fight was originally scheduled] in October which was a bit of a disappointment but we've had from before Christmas to look forward to the March 6 bill. Now I can finally get my hands on him! I'm trained hard, sparring's gone well and hopefully everything goes to plan on March 6 when I take the world title off him."

Butler won the IBF bantamweight title in June 2014 by defeating Darlington's "Cinderella Man" Stuart Hall over 12 rounds. Hall had defied the odds previously by taking the title against Vusi Malinga and one defence later (a spurious Technical Decision win over Martin Ward) Stuey was busy boxing Butler. Despite a close, intense battle it was Butler who took the spoils and left the arena with the world crown on a night he fondly recalls.

"It was a great night and obviously the biggest win of my career so far," agreed the 26-year-old who plies his trade on BoxNation TV. "Every boy wants to go out and win the Lonsdale titles or the Commonwealth but I always dreamt of winning a world title and that night my dream came true. Obviously you set goals and I want to win a world title and I want to unify a division so dropping back down to my natural weight of super-flyweight means I can do it again now. I'll never forget the night I beat Stuey Hall, it was unbelievable."

Butler may not be a regular visitor across the water to Belfast but he is well aware of one unbeaten boxer flittering close to his radar of late. West Belfast stylist Jamie Conlan has been itching for a big opportunity for a number of years and it seemed possible that Conlan and Butler could meet for a WBO title showdown.

"I've seen quite a lot of Conlan. I boxed him as an amateur and beat him, but that's amateurs and this is a completely different sport so it means nothing. From what I've seen of him he's a good fighter but I believe it's all about levels in this sport and I believe I'm a couple of levels above Jamie at the moment.

"We were due to fight; it got put down as a WBO final eliminator which we accepted and they didn't so we got made mandatory for the WBO. I'm now mandatory and I think he has got a good ranking with the WBO. So if I win this IBF title and have a voluntary then I want to unify the division and hopefully me and Jamie can get it on."

For now it's Tete and the world title bout that occupies Butler's thinking, although he was impressed with what he saw of Mark Dunlop's Devenish show on February 7.

"I came over to support my gym mate Ciaran [McVarnock] who had a good win over six-two minute rounds. It's my first time in Belfast and there were some cracking little fights on tonight," he said.

Another Win for Paul Hyland Jnr Who Has Irish Title On His Radar – 21st February 2015

Paul Hyland Jnr got another solid six rounds under his belt at the Devenish Complex recently and now the Belfast boxer is closing in on an Irish title shot. Paul was thorough and controlled during his 60-54 domination of Yordan Vasilev and admitted his hands were aching post-fight due to the excessive hurt he had piled on poor Yordan.

"I enjoyed the six rounds, I felt fit and the same from start to finish," said Hyland Jnr. "My fitness is dead-on but he was a tough guy and my left hand's aching from the jabs. He took them all though so fair play. My jab set everything up and kept him at reach and he was trying to get me to rush in a bit with his taunting. I went in a couple of times and he took all I threw at him inside too. I just boxed and got the win comfortably.

"I was pushing him at the end and I couldn't miss him with the jab, I hit him that much with it. I'm happy with my performance."

Manager Mark Dunlop has proven that he can deliver for his fighters and help push them on to the next level. Paul is therefore leaving his destiny in the hands of MHD Promotions.

"Whatever Mark wants, I want too. I want to keep moving and stepping up because that's how you get places. I want to fight as much as I can, whatever Mark can get for me. He promised me four fights again so if I get on any other bills I'll take it. Soon enough I'll be stepping it up. Mark said hopefully this year I'll get an Irish title and whatever after that. If he gets me an Irish title then I'll be ready.

"If that Irish title opportunity arrives there is no doubt that Hyland will be ready and so will his fervent group of diehard fans that pack the Devenish on each and every fight night.

"Thanks to everyone who came and bought tickets, they give me amazing support. I'm really grateful for that. You have to be able to sell tickets," said Hyland Jnr.

Paul is already scheduled on BoxRec for his sixth fight. Abdon Cesar will be the opponent at the Andersonstown Leisure Centre on March 28 over eight rounds. An intriguing eight-round clash between undefeated duo James Fryers and Mark Morris is also down alongside a return for former light-middleweight Joe Hillerby boxing up at cruiserweight. James Tennyson headlines the enticing bill against Celtic champion Kris Hughes.

Tyrone McKenna Wins Belfast Debut After World-Class Stateside Sparring – 23rd February 2015

Tyrone McKenna is back boxing in Belfast and ready to take the domestic scene by storm. Following five successful bouts in America the promising welterweight has returned home to be closer to his family and found his way on to Mark Dunlop's February 7 Devenish card. After four rounds of honest toil, McKenna walked away with a 40-37 victory over Teodor Stefanov and the first step on the road to titles was taken in a competent manner.

"It was the first time I had that kind of support after being out in America so there was a kind of pressure," admitted McKenna. "I dealt with it well and I was probably the least nervous I've been for a fight because I had my coach of 15 years [Patsy McAllister] here with me. I felt comfortable in the ring and that guy was awkward, he kept on coming at me, lunging with big hooks and grabbing with headbutts. It wasn't as good of a performance that I wanted to give my own crowd but I got the win so I'm happy enough."

Tyrone showed a mix of untapped potential and a few rough edges that need to be smoothed out by veteran coach McAllister and his team of Jimmy McGrath and unbeaten cruiserweight Tommy McCarthy. Two things McKenna does have going for him are the massive height and reach advantages he will enjoy over the majority of welterweight foes.

"Most people see me and rush on in for the body, just trying to hit anything they can. I'm used to that style as everyone has done that against me. He [Stefanov] was a strong guy and he hit hard so I'm happy I got through the fight OK.

"It's my professional debut in Ireland and it's kind of a weird experience. No one really knows me over here as a professional even though I was getting a bit of a fanbase in America, slowly building it up. Now I've got to start afresh by getting my name out there again but over here this time."

Tyrone is still young but reckons there is little time to waste. The 24-year-old is targeting a cluster of victories and then a move into title class - starting with the BUI crown.

"I want to get to 10-0 as quickly as possible and then start to get titles under my belt. I'll hopefully get 10 wins and then go for an Irish title, then maybe a Commonwealth or Celtic title and then a British title hopefully," he said.

If ever there was an indication that setting up base in the US has its benefits then McKenna's sparring sessions with Matt Korobov provide exactly that. Quality Russian Korobov may have fallen short against Andy Lee in their recent world title affair but the former top-class amateur provided Tyrone with high-level stateside workouts.

"I'm a welterweight and he's a middleweight so I thought it would be quite different but I held my own against him. I felt that Andy was going to win because every spar I was having I hit Korobov with right hooks and that's Andy's best punch so I went straight home and bet on Andy to win! I learned a lot out there but I've got two kids so it's good to be home in Ireland."

'Quiet Man' Felipe Avalos Predicts KO for Son Chris Over Frampton – 26th February 2015

Midway through the final press conference at Belfast's Europa Hotel, world title challenger Chris Avalos was ready launch into another illogical assessment of champion Frampton's supposed struggles with Kiko Martinez. Even though the IBF super-bantamweight champion had knocked out the Spaniard in their first meeting and dominated him for long spells in the second, Avalos remained suitably impressed. Just as the Californian prepared himself for another tirade he got a touch on the shoulder and shake of the head from the smaller, unimposing figure seated to his left.

Father and trainer Felipe Avalos was not present at the first press conference back in December but he quietly made his presence felt here. Felipe was keen to monitor his offspring's behaviour this time around and maintain a tighter leash even if his wife struggled to keep herself in check as she spewed out verbal assaults at Frampton from behind a TV camera. Not that Felipe's unassuming demeanour should be mistaken for a lack of confidence. Far from it in fact as the veteran coach is predicting a sixth-round knockout victory for his son later this evening.

"I've seen some tapes of Carl and he's a good fighter but Chris will knock him out in six rounds," said Avalos Snr, holding up six fingers to force home his point.

"Frampton's a decent guy and I don't see this as an easy fight. This is it for us. We aren't concerned about what's next, we are taking one step at a time and this fight is our only concern."

Despite the lofty reputation of the Belfast big fight atmosphere (entirely justified might I add) Felipe does not see the fight being won and lost outside of the ring. The fans can shout and scream and the two combatants can trade verbal volleys at press tables but ultimately it's the exchange of leather from around 11pm and beyond that matters most.

"It's my first time in Belfast and it's nice, the people are very nice. We won't be bothered by the crowd, we are ready to fight and I don't think it will affect Chris at all. We don't need the referee or the judges. We have no concerns."

Avalos Snr is completely unperturbed by the choice of referee. The IBF have given the job to England's Howard Foster but Felipe sees Foster's only task being the count he will administer to Frampton after his son has dispatches him in the mid rounds.

"I don't know this referee but I think it's going to be fine and he'll be fair. We are not concerned about the referee or anything because Chris is going to knock him out anyway," he said.

'The World is Not Enough': Europa Hotel Final Press Conference – 26th February 2015

On Thursday, February 26, just two days before "The World is Not Enough" show in Belfast, the main combatants gathered for a press conference in the Europa Hotel. Here are the main points covered during the big-fight build-up.

Challenger Chris Avalos, never one to shy away from giving his opinions on matters, stepped up to the mic first:

"For your information, I'm going to win and take the belt home. I haven't come all the way out here to lose, that would be pretty stupid, it makes no sense. I'm going to do my talking in the ring. I'm still gonna whoop your ass anyway, it's going to happen. I've seen his fights with Martinez and he claims Martinez is the strongest fighter he's ever fought. He was running from that dude in both fights."

Belfast Telegraph journalist David Kelly suggested that Avalos appeared to be a little jittery and nervous at the prospect of a world title tilt:

"I'm not nervous at all. I've boxed away before, I've beaten undefeated guys. This doesn't worry me."

Champion Carl Frampton then waded in with his opinions. The Belfast boxer more than matched Avalos in the verbal sparring this time.

"He usually talks a little bit more than that so he must be tight at the weight and in a bad mood. I'm expecting a tough fight and I've prepared hard for it. He's lost twice before to guys who don't compare to me. It's another loss for him and he's used to it already so it'll be more of the same for him. I'm from the ghetto, I'm from T Bay. If he thinks I'm going to run away from him then let him believe that.

"I'm prepared to do whatever it takes to win this fight. I'll outfight and outbox him. I know he's a good fighter but I'm better. I do rate him higher than the likes Scott Quigg but this isn't about Quigg to be honest, he's a Sky TV hype job. Avalos is a better fighter than Quigg and this will be a tougher fight but I'm focused on Chris and no one else.

"We've got a gameplan and it just depends on his this guy comes out can deal with anything he puts in front of me. Did he actually watch the Kiko fights? I knocked him out the first fight and held centre ring in the second one. Raul Hirales was my first 12-rounder and I was pacing myself to see if I could do 12 rounds. I'm a different fighter now. I could've put it on him but I just outboxed him. Avalos is a good fighter but he's there to be hit and I'm the hardest punching super-bantamweight in the world."

Avalos' manager Mike Criscio had his turn next and tried to goad Carl into taking a £10,000 side bet in the outcome.

"I hate to tell you Carl but you're going to lose your title and it'll be a short stay for you. Would you like to bet some of your purse 'cause I'd love to take your money. I'm not here to popular I'm here to win a title."

Frampton's trainer Shane McGuigan is totally confident that his man will be too good on the night.

"It's been a great camp. Carl's trained exceptionally hard and I'm sure Chris has too but I believe Carl is going to knock him out. I'm really looking forward to the fight."

Conrad Cummings Ready to Show Off His Refined Skills – 26th February 2015

Middleweight puncher Conrad Cummings is flying after an intense training camp and cannot wait to excite the fans at the Odyssey Arena on Saturday night. Since hooking up with trainer Shane McGuigan and relocating to train in London, Conrad has been busy refining his skills. The unbeaten prospect now faces the first test of his fledgling career when he takes on fellow undefeated fighter Roberto Palenzuela in a six-round contest.

"Yes this fight is scheduled for six rounds and I could do six rounds standing on my head to be honest," said Cummings.

"I'm flying in training and I can't wait. I got a couple of niggles during camp but I suppose every boxer does. Shane's working on my style all the time. I'm a come-forward fighter who likes to put the pressure on and hurt you but I've been working on throwing more jabs, showing more movement and the subtler things. I'm not smothering my work as much and I really felt in my last fight that it was coming together and hopefully on fight night I can show everyone the improvements I've been making."

Conrad competed at a high level before turning pro and is hoping to move back up to box the best after cutting his teeth against lesser foes. His 5-0 ledger has been built on journeymen and the Coalisland man is now itching to step on the gas.

"As an amateur I was fighting at world level and also in the World Series of Boxing so I've had to drop back, so to speak, to fight these journeymen. They can be awkward and have losing records but this next guy's different, he's coming to win. He has it in his mind that he's going to beat me but I know what's going to happen on the night."

Despite his lofty ambitions and desire to hunt for belts, Cummings insists he's only focusing on one fight at a time. He has already spoken to Barry McGuigan about going for titles in his next few contests.

"Belts have definitely been mentioned and we're looking at the Celtic title in the not-too-distant future," admitted Conrad. "So we'll be pushing on and maybe even look at a WBO European title or something like that. All being well this will be my last six-rounder and we'll move to eight rounds."

Cummings has a sizeable number of supporters following him to Belfast and is hoping to pack out a corner of the Odyssey.

"I'll have around 400 fans coming up to support me which is very humbling. I'm a second year pro in my sixth bout, in a competitive fight and I'll enjoy it as much as I can. Don't blink!"

'Howard Foster is a Great Guy!' Says Avalos Manager Mike Criscio – 26th February 2015

Carl Frampton's first IBF title defence will be refereed by Howard Foster. The popular official may have a reputation for possessing an itchy trigger finger after some quickfire stoppages of late but world title challenger Chris Avalos' manager Mike Criscio is trying hard to embrace the appointment.

"I don't want to say anything negative or anything positive," said Criscio.

"We've got the right judges and with refs you get what you get. As long as Chris doesn't get hurt then I guess we'll be OK."

George Groves might offer evidence to the contrary. The super-middleweight was controversially wrestled away from the tornado-like assaults of Carl Froch last year when many thought he should've been allowed to continue. British referees in general have taken a bashing in recent months with Ian John-Lewis' "hover stoppage" and Phil Edwards' 10 count antics both coming under public scrutiny. Former heavyweight contender Terry O'Connor has also been on the receiving end. Boxing Asylum pundit Kurt Ward was quoted describing O'Connor as being, "Too fat to referee." The British Boxing Board of Control has not responded to Ward's accusations and the IBF have deemed Foster as fit to take charge of the big Belfast event.

"If Chris gets hurt then this guy might pull the trigger and that's what I'm worried about," continued Mike Criscio. "I don't think that will happen though because Chris has never been hurt. I don't want this guy to say, 'hey you talked shit about me before so I'm stopping the fight', because that's the way these refs are."

Rather than castigating the beleaguered Doncaster official, Criscio instead has a message for Howard.

"He's a great guy! And a good referee.....that's all I'm saying."

The Tactician: Chris Avalos' Brother Has Been Monitoring Frampton – 27th February 2015

Amidst all the hustle and bustle and outrageous hyperbole, Chris Avalos and his team have a plan. The world title challenger's words won't win him the IBF title later tonight but a cunningly-devised and well-executed strategy just might. Even if the visitor and his crew are understandably reluctant to divulge their best laid plans they do strongly claim to have identified key flaws in Frampton's game. One of the key figures behind Team Avalos' efforts is Chris' brother Shawn. More softly spoken and articulate than his brash sibling, Shawn arrives in Belfast with a keen eye for a good boxer and, as he puts it, the knowledge to prepare for the Odyssey headliner. He has been working behind the scenes on a big fight blueprint by engaging in some extremely diligent background work.

"There's nobody in the world rankings at 122 lb, in any governing bodies' ratings, that I don't know about because I have researched them all thoroughly," said Shawn Avalos.

"I've been watching Frampton for a very long time, way back to his early fights, because I believe that the devil is in the detail. We know we can get this win. Frampton has got strength but I wouldn't say he's the biggest puncher in the world. When Frampton fought Steve Molitor, Molitor had spent 18 months out of the ring and was basically contemplating retirement. He's also disappointed me by not going over to Manchester to challenge Scott Quigg."

After I challenged Shawn on the latter point -mostly on the basis that Quigg isn't a huge draw in Manchester and Frampton is a huge draw in Belfast so it made little sense for the Belfastman to travel- he conceded ground on that issue. Avalos revealed that he has scrutinised every fight 'The Jackal' has taken part in since the vacant Commonwealth title drubbing of Australia's Mark Quon back in 2011.

"I've seen quite a few of Frampton's fights, including the one against Raul Hirales, right back to Mark Quon. Of course I've seen him fight different styles and when they're taller he runs and when opponents are shorter he engages. You can see the difference in the quality of opponents and against Kiko in the first fight he landed a lucky punch. It was lucky because Frampton was fading and I had him up by two rounds but he was definitely fading. By the second fight he knew that he had to stay back and keep Martinez at a distance because he didn't have confidence in his power to get the knockout again."

The Avalos clan seem to have some beef with Frampton's two wins over Martinez and I'm not sure I concur with any of their points. Both wins over Kiko, particularly the breakout win in the first fight, were hugely reputable victories that sit solidly on Carl's record. Frampton has 13 knockouts on that slate but Shawn Avalos thinks he has been pushed into world class too early.

"Frampton says he is a big puncher but he only has 12 knockouts. On his record of course it says 13 but I dismiss the one against Hugo Cazares because Cazares looked away, made a rookie mistake and got counted out. Frampton's good, I mean he's alright, but it's all too much too soon. They should've held him back for about 18 months from a world title. In the first fight with Kiko it was a dogfight because Martinez knew how to handle him. Jeremy Parodi had a good record but only five knockouts, so he basically has pillow fists.

"The things my brother [Chris] says aren't always that eloquent because he wants to get to the point. Speaking out here in press conferences isn't going to do anything in the ring. The question is, can Frampton keep Chris off him? Everybody tells us that the atmosphere here is so great that it defeats people and eats you alive. But we've been in this situation a couple of times before. Chris fought Jose Nieves who was supposed to be the next big guy out of Puerto Rico and Yenifel Vicente who was the next big thing out of the Dominican Republic. He beat Rolly Lunas and Drian Francisco, both big punchers who gave good boxers the fights of their lives and Chris got rid of both those guys."

Boxing in Frampton's hometown makes things even tougher for Chris Avalos and Shawn reckons that having the fight in Northern Ireland means his brother has to win by knockout as he cannot win a fair decision. That's debatable but he does have a point when he says Chris is a versatile operator with better skills and resolve than some (not the champion, it's fair to say) are giving him credit for.

"Frampton says he's ready for everything, well we're going to test that. Chris is a strong puncher, he's a young guy and you can dismiss the two losses. We will find out if Frampton is indeed a strong puncher and if he has a good chin.

"Frampton's walking into the ring on Saturday with a guy who doesn't care about what he brings to the table," concluded Shawn.

Cacace and Cummings Ready for Spanish Tests – 27th February 2015

Anthony Cacace has described his fight against Spain's Santiago Bustos as the first test of his career. Tired of feasting on journeymen with lopsided records, Cacace believes Bustos will bring an element of danger.

"Every other fighter I've fought so far I've had no problems at all with and lesser opponents can demotivate you," admitted Cacace.

"I'm just going to do it at my own pace but I'm sure I'll need to dig deep in this one. I would love a stoppage and at my best there's no reason why I can't stop him. I know he's a tough man who doesn't usually get knocked out but I might be the one to do it."

Anthony says he will thrive on the big fight nerves and remains fully focused on his opponent. Bustos is shorter and brings pressure but Cacace is well prepared for that style.

"That's what I've been sparring for the past eight weeks so I'll be completely ready for that," he revealed. "I think if someone's coming to have a go then that makes it easier for me because I can pick him off with hard, single shots. I just hope he walks on to one."

Conrad Cummings, meanwhile, could have his hands full with Roberto Palenzuela. The Spaniard is unbeaten and coming off the back of an upset away win. Conrad is determined not to become his next scalp.

"This guy's coming to win and he believes he's going to beat me but he's going home with his first loss," said Cummings.

"I like to come forward and let the hands go. I'll be doing the same against Palenzuela and I'm sure the fans will get some excitement on the night."

The likes of Billy Joe Saunders and Chris Eubank Jnr are edging towards world level and Cummings reckons he is not far behind.

"I feel like I'm on all their heels, including the bigger names. I'm sparring the best in the UK and the world and giving them lots to think about."

Another Cyclone signing, Portsmouth's Josh Pritchard, makes his professional debut in a four-rounder.

McCullough and Gallagher Relishing Their Limelight Spots – 27th February 2015

Belfast duo Marc McCullough and Paddy Gallagher are shaping up nicely for their bouts on tonight's Odyssey undercard. McCullough will box an eight-rounder with Malkhaz Tatrishvili. The Georgian visitor has a 9-8 record and fought last weekend in Sheffield.

"He's a Georgian guy and that's all I know, I haven't seen anything of him," admitted McCullough.

There is plenty of incentive for Marc to get past Tatrishvili with Blain McGuigan hinting at a potentially huge opportunity sitting in the pipeline. The 25-year-old is just focusing on getting this job done first.

"I just want to keep active, get a few rounds under my belt and then start pushing up in the rankings of the governing bodies," said McCullough.

Veteran trainer John Breen has confidence in both of his boxers and does not foresee Marc's hand injury causing any problems.

"Marc's looking very good and working hard for the fight. He's been using his right hand in the gym, no problem," said Breen.

John is also pleased with the progress of Paddy Gallagher who he believes is using his head more in the ring and bringing in to play his underused ringcraft.

"I want Paddy to box more and it's been very hard to get sparring for him. He's had 40 rounds of reasonable sparring. Paddy's getting on alright and doing what he has to do," explained Breen.

Gallagher faces Miguel Aguilar over four rounds and is expected to drop down and campaign at light-welterweight after this contest.

"This is the biggest show in town and every boxer in Ireland would love to get on it," said Gallagher. "I've sold my tickets and I want to impress and hopefully get on the other shows. I've seen bits and pieces of Aguilar. He's lost to good people but his record doesn't reflect how well he fights."

Aguilar scored an upset win recently and Paddy reckons the Nicaraguan will arrive in Belfast full of confidence but thinks he will have enough to prevail.

"John reckons I'm improving and getting faster and smarter so hopefully I'll put in a good performance," he said.

'Apache' Cacace Ready to Bust-Up Bustos
– 27th February 2015

Belfast super-featherweight Anthony Cacace has completed an intense training camp and is ready to excite the Odyssey crowd this Saturday. 'The Apache' views his eight-round bout with Spain's Santiago Bustos as the perfect opportunity to showcase his talents.

"Everything's been going perfectly to be honest. I've had great sparring and I'm just looking forward to getting it done now," said Cacace.

"I'm boxing Bustos and things are going to plan. He beat Ben Jones in his last fight and Jones was pretty highly ranked with BoxRec so I know Bustos is a tough wee man who's been in with good opposition. I'm ready for what he has to bring."

After turning pro with Emerald Promotions Anthony went on to spend eight months training in America. Unfortunately things didn't exactly go to plan for the 26-year-old and he eventually decided to head home and relocate to train with Shane McGuigan.

"I prefer to be training away from home because it allows me to put in the hard work and focus on my boxing which is the most important thing. My experience of Philadelphia wasn't too good but now I'm settled in well and enjoying life. I sparred with some professionals out in the US which should benefit my career but I'm glad to be home and travelling back and forth to London is a lot better. Shane's a brilliant trainer who suits me down to the ground."

Cacace will have to be wary of Bustos as the Mallorcan is used to arriving in prospects' backyards and causing an upset. Santiago knocked out 12-0 Matty Tew in his hometown of Southampton back in 2013 and the 32-year-old has never been stopped since turning pro in 2011.

"I've got a good opponent and I'm fighting on ITV4 in the Odyssey Arena so I think this is going to be my biggest fight to date," added Cacace. "It's going to be a great night with lots of support. I've had a mixture of sparring partners and they've all been half decent. I went in with two of the Mexicans that came over to spar Carl and a French guy as well."

Coach Shane McGuigan has gone on record saying that his man has the ability to handle the likes of Gary Sykes and Liam Walsh who are currently mixing at British title level. Cacace already has an Irish title in his trophy cabinet and is hungry to start a domestic haul.

"I'm looking at Celtic, Commonwealth or British, any title that comes my way. I want to box for them all and I believe I've got the tools to mix it with some of the top guys," agreed Cacace.

Marc McCullough Has WBO Fight On the Horizon After Tune-Up – 27ᵗʰ February 2015

Marc McCullough is refusing to let a hand injury derail his big plans for 2015. The reigning WBO European champion was unable to accept a chief supporting role on February 28 due to metacarpal problems but the 25-year-old was not ready to take a rest either. Marc has accepted an eight-round contest on "The World is Not Enough" undercard as he continues chasing the big boys of the featherweight division.

"I need to fight as often as I can because I don't want to get ring rust. I'm feeling fine and in good shape," said McCullough.

"This time it was a shorter camp for a change, due to the hand injury. I've only started punching again in the last two or three weeks and that's too much of a risk to try and get back quickly so I've just taken an eight-round fight to keep me active. I'm still back and forward from hospital getting a bit of work on the hand but they've told me I'm alright to go ahead and fight even though it's still getting checked out. With a wee bit of luck I'll be in big fights soon."

Promoter Barry McGuigan offered Marc a chance to sit this show out and recuperate but after the Shankill Road man got the all-clear from a specialist he was raring to go.

"I want to fight every chance I get. I've done a bit of sparring with Paul Hyland and James Tennyson and a couple of the amateurs they brought in for me. It's a good mixture because the amateurs are high paced and intense. I've been sparring the pros for four or five rounds and then bringing the amateurs in for the last couple."

McCullough is excited about the prospect of fighting on terrestrial television and believes that his most recent wins, like the stoppage of former world champion Dmitry Kirillov last September, have helped nudge him to a new level.

"Ever since the Willie Casey fight I've had a wee bit of confidence and a buzz. I sparred Paul Appleby before the Kirillov fight in what was a really good camp. I just want to move on up while the confidence is high and I'm on a good run."

After suffering spells out of the ring early in his career Marc has compiled an impressive 11-1 slate with seven knockouts. He is already soaking up the fight week atmosphere and ready to enjoy his supporting role at the Odyssey.

"The build-up to Frampton fights is always crazy. Even more so being against Avalos who has done a bit of talking himself so it will be a good atmosphere. I'm really looking forward to it," said McCullough.

Gallagher Has Changed His Ways and Preparing to Box Clever – 27th February 2015

Paddy Gallagher is eager to display the improvements he has made to his game when he tackles Miguel Aguilar on Saturday. Despite making his name as a crowd-pleasing brawler, Gallagher has settled down on his skills since hooking up with new trainer John Breen.

"I'm boxing a bit smarter now. I'm using my head and working the jab a lot more," said Gallagher.

"John says that I'm a better boxer than a fighter. Sometimes I get in a fight as it's hard to get out of old habits but he's changed things and made it natural for me to box. So far, so good."

Paddy was disappointed with his performance in the Prizefighter tournament last April and felt he did not give a true account of his abilities. Gallagher now views his Odyssey undercard slot as a way to alter fans' perceptions of what he can offer.

"Getting on the TV would be good exposure and people can see what I can do, in a good way. I got a few compliments after boxing on the last Devenish show with people saying that I boxed better and I can still be aggressive and go in for the kill but also box clever. That's the way boxing should be.

"Everything's going so well. I've had some hard sparring sessions and tough training and I'm ready to go. I've sparred a few boys in the gym, like Declan Dalton an amateur who tries MMA and makes you work because he's a bit heavier and very strong. I've been put through my paces and John said the last spar on Friday was my best yet."

Paddy is looking to push his record beyond 6-2 and contest titles at some point in 2015. The 25-year-old former Commonwealth Games gold medallist trusts his future to trainer and manager John Breen.

"John's a good manager so it's up to him what comes next. I'll throw a few ideas at him and we'll just progress as much as we can. An Irish title at the end of the year would be good. If I can get the win here then hopefully I'll step up and be ready for whatever comes next."

Opponent Aguilar, a Spanish-based Nicaraguan, generally knows how to go the distance but has been stopped by the better names on his record.

"It's only four rounds but the stoppage could come, you never know. As long as I can put in a good performance and beat him then I'll be flying. He's fought Cardle and Jenkins and other unbeaten guys and his wins are into double numbers.

"I think he's going to go for it and on paper he's a good fighter," added Gallagher.

Carl Frampton-Chris Avalos Big Fight Scorecard
– 29th February 2015

Round 1:
Avalos swaggers out confidently but Frampton begins to find his range as the round progresses. Avalos' left eye slightly swells. Avalos takes centre ring with his jab but Frampton times the right hand well. Avalos' left eye starting to swell.
Frampton 10-9 Avalos

Round 2:
Neither man takes a backward step as the challenger lunges in with wide shots. Carl's left-right combinations land with chilling accuracy. Avalos aiming for the body and both men engage in the trenches. Frampton takes advantage when Avalos walks away citing an apparent shoulder problem.
Frampton 10-9 Avalos

Round 3:
Frampton's work is calculated and composed while Avalos reaches with desperate right hands. Carl's left hook is hitting the target. Frampton's work is calculated and composed. Avalos, meanwhile, is reaching with desperate right hands. Carl's left hook is finding its way home.
Frampton 10-9 Avalos

Round 4:
The champion's jab is landing cleanly and for the first time during his visit Avalos seems to be losing belief. 'The Jackal's' footwork and timing is sublime. Avalos lands a right uppercut but little else. The American challenger is caught in a daze.
Frampton 10-9 Avalos

Round 5:
Frampton hurts Avalos with a left hook. The American tries to fight back but consistently heavy punches force the referee's intervention. Avalos is being beaten around the ring. The champion is toying with him. Referee Howard Foster has to stop the challenger as he takes a barrage of unanswered punches. Frampton is superb.
Fight stopped by referee Howard Foster at 1:33 of round five.

Wins for Local Talent On Big Odyssey Undercard – 29ᵗʰ February 2015

Anthony Cacace led the way on Saturday's Odyssey undercard with a wide points win over Santiago Bustos. Cacace shrugged off a hand injury, suffered in the second round, to take the spoils by an 80-71 margin on Hugh Russell Jnr's reckoning. Anthony started brightly, using his sizeable height and reach advantages to blunt the crude assaults of Spaniard Bustos.

"He beat a highly-ranked fighter in his last fight and I outpointed him easily enough so I have much more to give," said Cacace.

Conrad Cummings defeated Roberto Palenzuela 60-54 on Paul McCullagh's scorecard. Someone's 0 had to go in this battle of unbeaten boxers and it was Spain's Palenzuela that went home with a first loss. Cummings moves to 6-0 and was pleased with his night's work against a tough opponent.

"He caught me with a couple of shots in there but that's boxing. I feel like I'm learning all the time and when I throw at range I land more," said Cummings.

Marc McCullough is expecting a big title opportunity later this year and the 25-year-old ticked along with a routine first-round stoppage. His bout with Malkhaz Tatrishvili never looked like lasting the scheduled eight rounds once Marc landed the right hand. Tatrishvili shipped one and turned his back, prompting a flurry from McCullough and swift intervention from referee Hugh Russell Jnr at 1-09.

"Everytime I hit this guy his legs wobbled. They're talking about me fighting again in April or May so I needed something tonight," admitted McCullough.

Paddy Gallagher posted the most impressive win of his career while outpointing Nicaraguan Miguel Aguilar 40-35. Referee Paul McCullagh deducted a point from Aguilar in the third round for holding. Disciplined Gallagher boxed to instructions and was well worth his win.

London heavyweight Dillian Whyte knocked out Beka Lobjanidze in the fourth round of a 10-rounder. Referee Phil Edwards counted the Georgian out at 1-10 after a knockdown.

Denton Vassell's career hangs by a thread after he was widely beaten by Ukraine veteran Viktor Plotnykov. Vassell hit the deck in rounds 10 and 12 en route to a unanimous points loss.

Portsmouth's Josh Pritchard won his debut on points.

Dominant Frampton Ready for the Big Fights After Avalos Destruction – 29th February 2015

Carl Frampton comprehensively dispatched world title challenger Chris Avalos in the fifth-round of their IBF showdown on Saturday, February 28. The 28-year-old Belfast puncher set his stall out from the off, catching cocky Avalos with a variety of classy blows. Avalos landed a few shots of his own but appeared to lack the power to trouble Frampton. Landing a thumping right hand, followed by some meaty left hooks, Carl refused to let up and consistently peppered the American visitor with a multitude of shots. English referee Howard Foster jumped in following a sustained barrage and ended the contest early. Despite having to take oxygen to aid his recovery Avalos was asking for a rematch after the dust had settled. It's safe to say there is little possibility of that happening.

After boxing recently on the BoxNation TV platform Frampton fought on ITV and enjoyed a solid terrestrial television audience with a huge number tuning in from Northern Ireland. Frampton will now target a summer showdown with Scott Quigg who holds the WBA 'Regular' title at 122lb. The division's main ruler, Cuba's Guillermo Rigondeaux, must also be considered, although WBC king Leo Santa Cruz is probably not on the radar given that he has been earning huge purses for fighting substandard opposition lately and would require a monster offer to unify his strap. Former Rigondeaux victim Nonito Donaire has also been mentioned.

If Quigg and Frampton do enter negotiations then it is believed that Quigg's promoter Eddie Hearn would push for the fight to be on Sky TV, possibly as a Pay-Per-View attraction. Venue-wise, Barry McGuigan is expecting to travel to England and arrange a fight in London or potentially Manchester rather than staying in Belfast.

Undercard Round-Up

Anthony Cacace vs. Santiago Bustos

Belfast super-featherweight Anthony Cacace recorded a comprehensive 80-71 victory over Santiago Bustos on 'The World is Not Enough' undercard. Making the most of his supporting role and prime slot on terrestrial television, Cacace described his fight as the first real test of his career. Spain's Bustos always remained competitive.

Cacace flittered between southpaw and orthodox, using his silkier skills and ring smarts to time Bustos, lure him in and slam home spiteful counters. A flurry in the third round saw Bustos taste the canvas and receive a count from referee Hugh Russell Jnr. The well-travelled Mallorcan is no stranger to being the "opponent" and he never stopped throwing throughout the eight-rounder.

26-year-old 'Apache' Cacace improved his record to 11-0 and is now looking to gatecrash the mix at British and Commonwealth title level. Anthony reckons that hooking up with trainer Shane McGuigan will help push him all the way.

"I've only started working with Shane McGuigan and this is just the beginning" admitted Cacace. "I hurt my right hand in the second round and I could've got rid of him a wee bit earlier but I'm happy enough. He beat a highly-ranked fighter in his last fight and I outpointed him easily enough so I have much more to give.

"My right hand was sore. I hit him in the second round and felt it go. I changed my stance up and as it happens the left is as good as the right. I'm definitely ready to step-up."

Marc McCullough vs. Malkhaz Tatrishvili

Marc McCullough made short work of Georgian opponent Malkhaz Tatrishvili, knocking the visitor out at 1-09 of round one. Shorter Tatrishvili looked tentative early on and understandably so as McCullough raked home heavy shots from the start. Marc landed a stinging right hand that shocked Tatrishvili who turned his back and staggered to the safety of a neutral corner. McCullough was quick to follow him and landed enough unanswered shots to persuade referee Hugh Russell Jnr's intervention in this scheduled eight-rounder.

McCullough and his team have big plans for a contest later in the year that will see him step up in levels. Marc was pleased to have tested his right hand which was hurt in the build-up but posed no problems here.

"I wanted to test the hand and it held up lovely," said McCullough. "I barely got a sweat on me there but it gives me a bit of confidence knowing I can throw and land the shots. Every time I hit this guy his legs wobbled.

"They're talking about fighting again in April or May so I needed something tonight. It'll possibly be an Intercontinental title or something and I'd also like to move up the rankings of the other governing bodies."

Conrad Cummings vs. Roberto Palenzuela

Conrad Cummings enjoyed a 60-54 success over Spain's previously unbeaten Roberto Palenzuela. The stocky middleweight motored forward throughout the contest and took a landslide decision on Paul McCullagh's scorecard.

Cummings forced some of his work at times, pushing Palenzuela against the ropes and throwing plenty of punches. The Spanish fighter was content to lie against the ropes and throw sporadic counters and even though he did occasionally land there was little power to trouble Cummings. The 23-year-old is looking to fight for a Celtic title later in the year.

Speaking after the bout the Coalisland man explained how he has been working on boxing more in the gym and felt he showed those improvements in his performance.

"I feel like I'm learning all the time and when I throw at range I land more and the plan was to show my progression and I felt I did that," said Cummings.

"He caught me with a couple shots in there but that's boxing. He was certainly durable enough and a solid opponent - that's what it's all about."

Dillian Whyte vs. Beka Lobjanidze

Brixton heavyweight prospect Dillian Whyte knocked out Georgia's Beka Lobjanidze in emphatic fashion. Whyte started crisply, poking out a solid jab and landed some heavy blows in the fourth session causing Lobjanidze sunk to his knees. Beka had shipped a body shot and the grimace on his face indicated that he was not ready to continue. The Eastern European was counted out by ref Phil Edwards at 1-10 of the round and the win sees Dillian push his record to 14-0. Whyte is now lining up a British title eliminator against undefeated Scottish heavy Gary Cornish. This one was scheduled for 10 rounds.

"That guy was just running all night and I'm not happy at all about that even though I got the win," scathed Whyte. "I don't even know what I finished him with. He had a go for three rounds and then gave up, after all the talking he did before the fight too.

"I don't know if Gary Cornish will even fight me but it he does then I'm ready for a better fight. I'll fight all the British heavyweights out there."

Paddy Gallagher vs. Miguel Aguilar

Paddy Gallagher is hunting down an Irish title shot after outpointing Miguel Aguilar 40-35. Paddy had his hands full with lively Aguilar, a Nicaraguan based in Spain, but managed to pull through on Paul McCullagh's scorecard. The crowd were sensing that their man was in a real scrap midway through the second round and tried to rally to his cause. The 25-year-old Belfast scrapper responded, boxing well to instructions, he only engaged when Aguilar was sufficiently softened up and backed into corners. 'Pat Man' sensed his man was wilting in the third and Mr McCullagh deducted a point from Aguilar for persistent holding.

"I boxed a lot more in there and I'm pleased but he was tough," said Gallagher. "I've made changes and training with John Breen has brought my boxing skills out." There's plenty more to come from me."

Denton Vassell vs. Viktor Plotnykov

Viktor Plotnykov is the new IBF Intercontinental welterweight champion after posting a unanimous decision victory over Denton Vassell.

Plodding Plotnykov was not easily deterred and worked hard for the duration of the contest. The Ukrainian's heavier hands were too much for a tired and listless Vassell to endure. Denton did his best to get into a rhythm but his 37-year-old opponent was surprisingly fresh.

Former Commonwealth champion Vassell was dropped in the 10th round and began to suffer soon after. The Manchester boxer was visibly hurting and repeatedly stung by Plotnykov who put him down again in the 12th and final round. Referee Phil Edwards was watching closely in the final session but Vassell narrowly lasted the course.

The scores of 118-108 (twice) and 115-111 all favoured Plotnykov. Vassell's record falls to 21-3 and the 30-year-old will have a tough time rebuilding his career after suffering a third stoppage loss. Opening the card was Portsmouth's Josh Pritchard who won on points over four rounds.

View from Press Row: How the Boxing Media Called Frampton vs. Avalos – 1st March 2015

"The debate over who is the number one fighter in the super-bantamweight division is surely drawing to a close. Carl Frampton's brutal fifth round stoppage of Chris Avalos leaves little room for further argument. A year ago WBA/WBO champion Guillermo Rigondeaux would probably have had the edge over Frampton. Not now. WBC champion Leo Santa Cruz and Frampton would have been a 50-50. Not now. That leaves bitter rival Scott Quigg who frankly seems likely to face a similar fate to Avalos when - as seems highly probably- they meet in an open air sports stadium his June.

"Those ignorant of the Noble Art and Californian Avalos may think his challenge did not match the hyperbole but that would be to underestimate two special a talent Frampton truly is -and will become- as Saturday night was evidently the start of the Tigers Bay man's peak years."

David Kelly, Belfast Telegraph

"This was what brought ITV back to boxing, an absolute barnburner in Belfast that saw Carl Frampton retain his IBF super bantamweight title with a fifth round stoppage. The challenger, Chris Avalos, had gone toe to toe for four rounds of incredible hostility before giving way in the fifth beneath a barrage of sledgehammer blows.

"The referee stepped in with the American almost out on his feet. The doctor was across the ropes in an instant to establish the condition of a man who had walked into a storm. Promoter Barry McGuigan claimed his man was a top five box-office star before the bout. On this evidence both know how to put on a show."

Kevin Garside, Independent

Barry McGuigan: 'Quigg Needs to Realise That Carl is the Best in the World' – 5th March 2015

The dust had barely settled on Carl Frampton's fifth-round blitz of Chris Avalos before enthusiasm for his next fight began gathering speed. Talk of a September blockbuster with Scott Quigg in Manchester is churning around on the rumour mill but nothing is yet concrete. Cyclone Promotions' CEO Barry McGuigan, a former world champion himself of course, says that he has his own preferences but many factors still need to be agreed on.

"We genuinely don't know what is next," said McGuigan. "We know Quigg turned up tonight, so he's obviously interested in the fight and we are genuinely interested in a fight with him. We're willing to compromise. Quigg has to remember that this kid [Frampton] has the most valid title and is the best super-bantamweight in the world and is the one who fills arenas. He put 16,000 in for his world title fight and 9,000 tonight and could have filled it twice over. He [Quigg] has got the regular title and he has to understand that."

Guillermo Rigondeaux's manager Gary Hyde may have a thing or two to say about this proposed situation. Hyde is looking to put a roadblock in the way of any Frampton-Quigg fight and force Quigg to put his WBA trinket on the line against Gary's Cuban stylist. Bury man Quigg, to his credit, travelled over to Belfast on his own to put his hat into the ring.

Given that details have emerged over his Sky deal not being on as solid foundations as first thought, perhaps a pathway could be created for Scott to move over and compete on ITV. His promoter Eddie Hearn feels the fight is PPV worthy and wants the domestic blockbuster to take place on Sky TV where both fighters can enjoy a healthy payday.

"Eddie thinks of the numbers all the time, but let's do a Chris Eubank and Nigel Benn thing with this one - this fight could make superstars out of these kids. I understand Quigg is not on a deal with Sky, so the deal can be done," enthused McGuigan.

"Eddie Hearn keeps pushing the pay-per-view thing, but this fight is a much better fight on terrestrial television. I think the fight would be a 30,000-seater, so of course it would be outdoors. You could do the old MEN in Manchester, that's 20,000 indoors, the O2 in London is 19 or

20,000, and there is always the likes of Queen's Park Rangers' ground. Our sponsors sponsor Chelsea, so there's always Stamford Bridge. There are many possibilities and we really want the fight."

Once the number crunchers had done their calculations of the ITV/UTV audience on Saturday evening, figures of around 2 million were revealed. Barry views interest both in Ireland and across the water as an indicator of a possible terrestrial television dust-up between two unbeaten titlists.

"Let's think about the possibility of it being free-to-air, and millions and millions of people being able to see it. It would be a great fight - until Carl hits him! No, that's cheeky, but it will be a great fight and it has the potential to be huge, absolutely huge. Boxing has a future on terrestrial TV, and if we mix it with what these guys do a 24/7, we can do diary stuff and bios in conjunction with the actual event.

"Nobody can tell you that event tonight wasn't a spectacular event and worth watching," added Barry.

Frampton: 'Now is the Time to Make Quigg Fight Happen' – 6th March 2015

Carl Frampton has made his desires known that there will never be a better time for the Scott Quigg fight to happen. Carl says that he is happy for the fight to take place at any location and believes he would bring the bigger crowd no matter where they trade leather.

"It doesn't matter where it is, I'm happy, and I'm sure the fans would love an away trip," said Frampton. "I bring a lot of people from England to watch my fights. If Belfast is the stumbling block, we can have it at a neutral venue, London, I suppose. If that's what it takes to do it, well, there are plenty of places where we could do it outdoors.

"Now is the perfect time to do it. It should happen now. From the start of my career I always said I wanted to win a British title but it never happened and obviously I'm well past that level now, but this fight has been brewing and brewing. Luckily I haven't been beaten and he's had a couple of draws; it's time for it to happen now."

Frampton explained that his hand was okay apart from a touch of swelling (hazard of the trade you'd imagine) and the left hand, that he damaged in the Kiko win, was fine - nothing that a bit of ice wouldn't sort out. While hand problems are one of the things Frampton has to deal with inside the ring there are burdens on his shoulders outside of the ring too. The pressure of being a national icon from one side of the politics divide, married to a girl from the other could bring complications. The Tiger's Bay hero makes his work in his own way.

"I'm just being normal. I just happen to be married to a girl from a different religion but that's all, really," he responded. "It's nice and it's humbling that people look at it that way, but I'm just trying to treat people right, the way I like to be treated. I'm not doing anything different," said Frampton.

Barry McGuigan agreed with the sentiment of his fighter: "It's a thing we like to put in the past. We deliberately don't do anything. We deliberately tell our fighters not to wear colours that would alienate people. We really put a lot of effort into doing things right. Carl is a lovely, lovely kid, and the thing of him coming from a Protestant and Loyalist area and marrying a girl from a Catholic and Nationalist area – that's gone! They love each other and they married each other and that's the way it should be. He's such a great role model, such a great example. We live threescore and ten if we're lucky, so just get on with life and get on with each other."

Shane McGuigan Puts Quigg and Donaire On the Frampton Hit List – 7th March 2015

Shane McGuigan reckons that Carl Frampton can dispatch any of the title holders at the 122 lb weight class. In fact, Frampton's trainer, who has adapted seamlessly to training at world level, has been saying this for a while and now will be the perfect time to prove it.

"I said to Dad about a year ago that Carl could beat them all; Dad said, 'well, yeah - in time'," revealed Shane.

"I believed that then and I believe it now even more so. Carl was always good at going back but now he can fight aggressively, but do it in style. What he did to Chris Avalos was ruthless – that's the level you have to bring out of a fighter and he brought it out tonight. He keeps raising the game, raising the bar. He's a world-class fighter; he's always been world class but he's going to be one of the very best."

McGuigan Jnr believes that Scott Quigg is the obvious next opponent but he still remains hopeful of tempting Leo Santa Cruz out his Al Haymon bubble for a unification bout. Another fighter Shane fancies is Nonito Donaire who is now campaigning back down at super-bantamweight. After these fighters have been dealt with then a massive encounter with Guillermo Rigondeaux would be on the agenda. After speculating on the next opponent Shane broke down 'The Jackal's' blitz of Chris Avalos and revealed just at what point he thought the fight was won.

"I thought the final factor was when Carl hit him in the second round. He went to break and Carl jumped on him and hit him hard. About 20 seconds before that Carl thumped him as well with a right hand, and after that Avalos slowed right down. He was a sitting duck, Carl started pushing him back and he can't fight on the back foot. The difference is Chris Avalos is a fringe world class fighter and a mandatory challenger with two governing bodies, but Carl Frampton is a level above that.

"Not being disrespectful to Avalos, he wilted and turned away and that's why Howard Foster intervened," added Shane McGuigan.

Carl Frampton concurred: "Avalos seemed very slow to me and I knew everything that was coming. I was hitting him with my right all the time; Shane was telling me to throw the left hook after it, and I was throwing the left hook on its own as well."

Best Super-Bantamweights On a Mega-Fight Collision Course – 7th March 2015

Guillermo Rigondeaux and Carl Frampton are by general consensus the two best super-bantamweights in the world and a buzz is slowly building around a potential unification bout. Rigondeaux's manager Gary Hyde has made it clear that he wants either Frampton or Scott Quigg now that a potential Leo Santa Cruz fight has been scuppered by the WBC champion's loyalty to Al Haymon's career plan. Frampton's team are averting their gaze towards Quigg but the Rigondeaux fight must surely be on the radar at some point.

"Here's the thing about Rigondeaux - it doesn't make sense," countered Barry. "Everybody is screaming about Guillermo Rigondeaux but look what happened him in his last fight. He fought a Japanese guy [Hisashi Amagasa] - a big stringy kid who couldn't really punch - and he was dropped twice, but when Frampton hits them he knocks them out.

"Rigondeaux is not an exciting fight at the minute and it's not something that attracts us. Quigg does, Santa Cruz does, so we want the unification fights. Quigg was here tonight. Nonito Donaire has come down as well. We want those unification fights and there are many options out there. The other options make more sense, Quigg and Santa Cruz and then, further down the line, we can do business with Rigondeaux. The other two make much more sense for now."

Barry then went on to assess Frampton's destruction of mandatory challenger Chris Avalos.

"I suppose the perfect scenario would have been for it to go another couple of rounds, but it indicates Carl Frampton's power. I've always did that he's the hardest punching super-bantamweight in the world. There isn't a harder puncher in the division in the world," opined McGuigan.

Post-Fight Reaction: Barry McGuigan Responds to Media Questions – 8th March 2015

Carl Frampton, Barry McGuigan and Shane McGuigan took to the top table at the post-fight press conference to discuss Carl's fifth-round knockout of Chris Avalos in the Odyssey Arena on February 28. Cyclone Promotions' main man Barry McGuigan discussed some of the talking points generated during the evening, both in and out of the ring.

How is Carl maturing as a fighter and growing into this Odyssey atmosphere?

It is a remarkable venue and Carl is a remarkable fighter. I really believe that Frampton is an exceptional fighter and that he can go on to be one of the best Irish fighters there has ever been. Tonight he fought a kid who was number one in the world with the IBF, number one in the world with the WBO, and in the top five in the world with all the other governing bodies, and Carl just dismantled him and took him apart. And, as always, the atmosphere was just fantastic and just gets better and better. Can anyone here remember a more raucous atmosphere?

Where will Carl box next and what's the TV situation?

We feel like we want to go and box in England now and box in America as well, but we want to get the timing right. We really believe that there is a future to be had with ITV. Look at what's happening across the water? What's Al Haymon doing? And NBC? They realise the value of boxing being on free-to-air television and we should too. If we're all less greedy, this could be a major event in the summer on ITV.

Where does WBA 'Regular' champion Scott Quigg fit into all of this?

I don't want to be rude to him - he, obviously can draw a fair number of people in his hometown - but Carl Frampton is THE attraction and I really can't wait to see what the result for ITV was tonight. He really is an amazing talent and an amazing draw. The arena tonight was just incredible; I honestly don't think it has ever been like that before. We haven't got the feedback yet, but we'll sit down with ITV over the next week.

Dillian Whyte Talks Joshua Rivalry and Klitschko Training Camps – 13th March 2015

Unbeaten heavyweight Dillian Whyte is desperate for a fight with UK golden boy Anthony Joshua. The 26-year-old Brixton man beat Joshua as an amateur and reckons that he can repeat the trick in the pro game if the pair ever meet. Dillian is galled by some of Joshua's recent comments and admitted that he doesn't like the 2012 Olympic gold medallist.

"I want to fight him now, just to knock him out," raged Whyte. "It's not about a pay day or anything, it's personal now. If they offered me to fight him for the British title tomorrow then I'd fight for free - that's how much I want him. He says that there's no beef but he doesn't like me and I don't like him, it's as simple as that. I would like to get in the ring with him and settle it as professionals.

"I fought Anthony Joshua as an amateur and we were both raw. I beat him, he took it personally and got angry. He started calling me names, calling me a cheat and this and that. That pissed me off and I responded. Now he has stirred up a hornets nest and these hornets are ready to bite."

Speaking ahead of his recent bout on the Frampton-Avalos undercard Dillian revealed that even though it was his first time fighting in Belfast he had been over to train back in 2010. Cork manager Gary Hyde was managing Vladimir Chanturia at the time and called the Londoner over to help him out, resulting in two weeks of sparring. Fast forward to February 2015 and Whyte was back in Belfast to dispatch another Georgian, hapless Beka Lobjanidze, in four one-sided rounds. Whyte views 2015 as a year for stepping up in class as he closes in on Scotland's Gary Cornish in a British title eliminator.

"This year for me is about stepping up. I've been around a while now and I was off for two years but I'm back fighting and I want to keep busy and climb the ranks. I don't want to keep fighting journeymen and knocking them over. I want to test myself and see what I need to work on and go the rounds. I want to be active and get ring timing, experience and ring fitness. I've been training but I want to get experience by fighting. The more a lawyer stays in the courtroom, the better he gets at his job and I'm 26, I've got time and this is my educational stage, which I'm taking full advantage of."

Even though Whyte's time inside the ring has been limited, mainly due to a hotly-contested drugs ban that saw him sidelined for a whopping two years, he has been making up for lost time in high-quality training camps. Dillian has compiled an impressive sparring CV, helping some of the sport's top heavyweights to prepare.

"I never had a long amateur career so that's how I've learned. I've sparred David Price, David Haye, Tyson Fury, Hughie Fury, both Klitschko brothers and that's how I've learned my skills. Sparring needs to be current to be beneficial but you always learn from it and if I sparred Wladimir today and I was fighting next week then it would be very beneficial. I took something from each fighter and I'm impressed with one thing from each of them. With Wladimir it's his discipline and desire, with David Haye his timing and reflexes, Tyson Fury has heart and desire and David Price can punch. I look at what they can do, how they run, how they warm-up, how they train and all that stuff because I'm still relatively new to boxing so watch the guys at the top of the game.

"Vitali's awkward, he can punch and he's a tough man who can trade with smaller fighters in the pocket. He's a nice guy with no ego and he'll have a hard spar with you and at the finish say 'well done, I appreciate that' and encourage you. He used to tell me to keep going, stay discipline and dedicated and then I can make it. He said I had a lot of talent but it's still raw and with more experience I can go all the way. For him to say that to me at the time, I was 3-0 then, gave me a lot of inspiration. I used to watch this man on TV as a kid, fighting Lennox Lewis and Herbie Hide so for me that was a great boost."

Of all his sparring experiences Whyte holds the Klitschkos in high regard for their rigid training schedules and ultimate professionalism.

"The Klitschkos are very professional. They have a programme and they stick to it regardless. Everything is on time, diligent and runs smoothly. Wladimir comes to the gym, does his shadow boxing and stretching and the spars. In the morning he gets everyone at the gym and he trains and wants everybody else to train. Watching the Klitschkos has given me something to aspire to. I want to run my camps similar to their camps."

Now sporting a 14-0 slate with 11 opponents falling early, Dillian is hunting down arch rival Joshua but content with a British title shot while he waits for his nemesis to accept a rematch in the paid ranks.

"We [Whyte and eliminator rival Gary Cornish] have until March 11 for purse bids and then the end of June for the fight to happen. I hope he takes the fight. It will be a good fight because he's a tall, strong guy and we can put on an excellent show."

Tennyson Ready to Cruise Past Hughes in Title Tilt – 28th March 2015

James Tennyson has described tonight's fight with Kris Hughes as the biggest challenge of his career so far. Headlining Mark Dunlop's show at the Andersonstown Leisure Centre James will move one step closer to a British title shot if he can dispatch 'Badger' Hughes.

"This is undoubtedly the biggest fight so far for me," admitted Tennyson. "There's a British title fight at the end of it and a Celtic title on the line so the outcome is huge."

Hughes was beaten by Carl Frampton back in 2012 and arrives in Belfast with a 17-5 record. Tennyson sees the Scottish visitor as a more difficult proposition than 2013 Irish title victim Mickey Coveney.

"Coveney is my biggest opponent to date but I'd say that Hughes is going to be a tougher test for sure. I don't know too much about him but he's a southpaw and definitely a step up because he's above me in the rankings. He's had more fights and got that bit more experience but my training team have devised a fight plan on how to deal with him."

Tennyson is only 21 but maturing nicely and a move up to super-featherweight is likely at some point in the future. That is why manager Mark Dunlop feels the time is right to hunt domestic glory in the nine stone weight class. James' Kronk training team of Tony Dunlop and Daniel Boyle have been busy monitoring potential British title rivals.

"I just focus on my own game and let my trainers watch and learn about the other fighters," said Tennyson. "I'm focused on Hughes and training's gone very well. I've done a bit of sparring with Paul Hyland and plenty of rounds with James Fryers.

"I always get great support and the fans will be rewarded with a great win on the night," he added.

On the undercard unbeaten Belfast pairing James Fryers and Mark Morris clash in a lightweight eight-rounder. Reigning Irish light-middleweight champion Dee Walsh boxes Peter Orlik while Paul Hyland Jnr tackles Imre Nagy. Tyrone McKenna, Joe Hillerby and Daniel McShane all feature.

Tennyson Able to Cruise Past Hughes After Andytown Brawl – 29th March 2015

James Tennyson added the Celtic featherweight title to his collection with a seventh-round disqualification win over Kris Hughes. Headlining at the Andersonstown Leisure Centre in front of a raucous crowd the Belfast boxer had too much physical strength for spindly southpaw Hughes who resorted to clinching and grappling to make it through.

Tired of the Bellshill man's spoiling tactics, referee Ian John-Lewis deducted two points in round six after issuing formal warnings from the fourth round. The second point was for a deliberate headbutt that opened a cut across Tennyson's right eye. The 21-year-old local man stayed calm and continued to try and get his boxing going. After a third point was taken, Hughes attempted one wrestle too many and was rightly ejected at 2-31. The fight doubled as a British title eliminator.

"I'm here to fight so if it's the British title next then I'm ready," said Tennyson. "Getting my second title is a huge confidence boost. I hurt him at a point but he kept on holding all the time.

"I think the referee made the correct decision because James Tennyson was just too strong for me," admitted Hughes.

Dee Walsh wasted little time removing any threat opponent Peter Orlik may have possessed. The 25-year-old dispatched his hapless Hungarian foe in the first of a six-rounder. Walsh was never required to call upon the fine array of skills that have made him one of Ireland's hottest prospects. 'Waldo' dropped the left hook and right uppercut on a stumbling Orlik, prompting referee John Lowey to terminate the bout at 1-29. Belfast's Dee moves to 11-0 and is next out in the Devenish Complex on June 6 with his sights set on a Celtic shot or Irish title defence as he manoeuvres towards a British title.

James Fryers won the battle of Belfast when Mark Morris failed to come out for the sixth session of their eight-rounder. Fryers is a neat boxer who is finding his power as the level of opposition increases. Well-conditioned Morris, now 2-1 (1), started strongly but was dropped in the second round and started showing signs of desperation from the third onwards. Fryers, 7-0 (2), picked his shots to perfection as referee David Irving hovered on several occasions. James collected the BUI Celtic Nations crown for his troubles.

Paul Hyland Jnr put a heavy beating on Hungary's Imre Nagy right up until the fifth round when Nagy literally crumbled to the canvas at 2-39. This was well-supported Hyland's first step into eight round class but Nagy did start well. Referee John Lowey deemed an opening-round Hyland touchdown as a slip and Belfastman Paul battered Nagy for as long as the bout remained. Hyland Jnr increased his record to 6-0 (1) and is chasing an Irish title shot.

In an all-southpaw six-rounder Belfast's Tyrone McKenna halted Istvan Kiss at 1-30 of the third round. McKenna's jab and left hand were sharp and accurate and the Hungarian visitor took a count in the third. Moments later McKenna, now 7-0 (3), encouraged John Lowey to call a halt.

Daniel 'Insane' McShane suffered his first pro defeat after dislocating his right shoulder against Zoltan Horvath in the second round. This six-round scrap was a rough and untidy affair and Paul McCullagh struggled to keep the pair in check. Hungary's Horvath was cut across the nose but celebrated his win, at 2-49, in style. Belfast's McShane falls to 9-1 (3).

Belfast's Joe Hillerby enjoyed a 40-36 victory over Omagh's Dee Taggart on Paul McCullagh's scorecard. Neither man arrived in peak shape but Hillerby moves to 10-2 (2).

James Tennyson (8st 13lbs 15oz), 12-1 (9), w dq 7, Kris Hughes (8st 13lbs 6oz), 17-6 (2); Paul Hyland Jnr (9st 8lbs 6oz), 6-0 (1), w rsf 5, Imre Nagy (9st 9lbs 5oz), 11-6 (4); James Fryers (9st 7lbs 5oz), 7-0 (2), w rtd 5, Mark Morris (9st 7lbs 3oz), 2-1 (1); Dee Walsh (11st 3lbs 3oz), 11-0 (5), w rsf 1, Peter Orlik (10st 11lbs 6oz), 8-7-1 (2); Daniel McShane (9st 10lbs 9oz), 9-1 (3), l rsf 2, Zoltan Horvath (9st 9lbs 5oz), 2-32 (2); Tyrone McKenna (10st 7lbs 4oz), 7-0 (3), w rsf 3, Istvan Kiss (10st 11lbs 2oz), 17-17 (9); Joe Hillerby (13st 12lbs 9oz), 10-2 (2), w pts 4 Dee Taggart (13st 12lbs 5oz), 5-9 (1).

Tennyson Gets Past Hughes and Has British Title in His Sights – 30th March 2015

James Tennyson took one step closer to a British title shot after snatching Kris Hughes' Celtic featherweight crown on March 28. James may not have taken the title in emphatic style but it was his physical strength on the inside that made the local hero simply too hot to handle for Hughes. The Scottish former champion was disqualified by referee Ian John-Lewis in round seven for persistent holding.

"I hurt him at a point but he just kept on holding all the time," said Tennyson. "He was very honest about that. He told me and he told the referee as well that I was too strong for him and that was all he could do. Every time I tried to get a shot off he was just clinging on to me so I couldn't really get the shots off. The ones I did land were hurting him and that showed. He was burying in the head as well."

James ended up with a cut eye following a sixth-round headbutt from Hughes but never seemed close to losing his cool. The Poleglass boxer showed a temperament belying his 21 years, by refusing to be dragged down to Hughes' level, in front of a fervent crowd at the Andersonstown Leisure Centre.

"I tried to keep as composed as I could and just box. He was open to the right hand which I expected. I expected more of a fight from him than what I got to be honest," added James.

The self-styled 'Baby-Faced Assassin' will now cast his gaze towards potential Lonsdale belt opponents. Samir Mouneimne and Ryan Walsh are set to box for the vacant title with Tennyson leading the pack to fight the winner. Which one would *he* like to fight next?

"That's down to my team and Mark [Dunlop, promoter]. I'm here to fight so if it's the British title next then I'm ready.

"That's a huge confidence boost for me getting my second title and it was a British title eliminator as well which I'm working towards next," concluded Tennyson.

Walsh Hungry for Celtic Crack After Dispatching Orlik in One – 1st April 2015

Dee Walsh limbered up for a possible title fight on June 6 with a one-round blowout of Hungary's Peter Orlik last Saturday. Dee could now defend the Irish title he won against Terry Maughan last year or even step across to box at Celtic title level.

"I want the Celtic title next and that's what Mark [Dunlop, promoter] has planned for me anyway. Hopefully that'll get me en route for a British title," said Walsh.

Even though referee John Lowey's intervention may have been deemed a little premature, there was no danger of Orlik lasting the distance let alone winning the fight. Dee says that despite what it seemed like outside of the ring, inside the ropes he was hurting his Hungarian foe with every shot.

"Everybody says that about my stoppages but I can feel it right up my arm. Everytime I hit him he didn't want to know. He wobbled so I stepped back and then hit him again and that was when John Lowey stepped in. I hit him with a right hand straight away and everytime he came in he had the head down because he didn't want to get on top of it. He had a bit of a cut on his eye too and that was down to the uppercut."

Perhaps a solid, competitive opponent capable of going a few rounds would benefit Walsh's progression as he chases down domestic rivals? Not a bit of it. Dee knows he can do distances after some solid sparring sessions at the St. John Bosco gym.

"I'm not so worried about the rounds because I get my rounds in the gym sparring with Joe [Hillerby] and Frankie [Carrothers]. I could've done 10 rounds in there tonight," he said.

"This is the hardest hitting light-middleweight right now in the world," added trainer Gerard McCafferty. "No doubt about it. There's no light-middleweight that will stand with this man. We'll fight for a Celtic title or defend the Irish title on June 6."

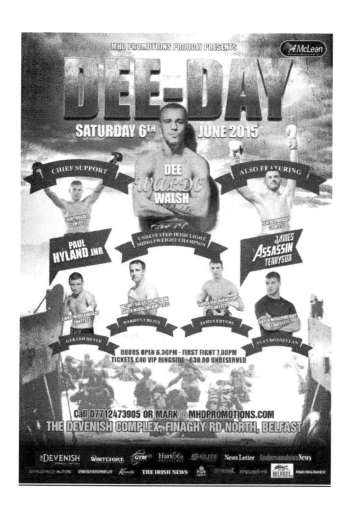

O'Kane Relishing Big Fight in Lavey
– 10th April 2015

Eamonn O'Kane is relishing his big fight with Lewis Taylor on May 2 in Lavey. The Dungiven middleweight was busy outlining his plans at a press conference yesterday and believes he is closing in on a world title fight.

"I'm really looking forward to putting on a good show and seeing what Lewis Taylor is made of," said O'Kane.

"I know he's orthodox, unbeaten and he throws a lot of punches. That'll suit because nobody likes to throw more punches than me. It should definitely be an all-action fight."

Hassan N'Dam is expected to box David Lemieux for the vacant IBF belt soon and Eamonn believes he can take on the winner. N'Dam is managed by Cork's Gary Hyde who has expressed an interest in tackling the former Prizefighter champion.

"If N'Dam wins then a fight between us could certainly be made," reckoned O'Kane. "That's the fight I would like so I hope he does it. If I get the win first on May 2 then I'll be pushed up the rankings after that and into position. I'm only focused on Lewis Taylor at the moment though."

Eamonn was trained by Immaculata veteran Gerry 'Nugget' Nugent when he turned pro before briefly switching to Bernardo Checa. He is now based in England under the tutelage of George Groves' coach Paddy Fitzpatrick.

"I've made a lot of improvements with Paddy and I want to move on after this fight. I'm boxing now instead of street fighting. It's being explained to me all the time about what I need to do and why we are doing certain things in training and I'm boxing to a system with a gameplan. I'm working on making sure everything is technically correct."

The 33-year-old has been travelling across England enjoying valuable sparring sessions against a variety of opponents, including plenty of rounds with Groves himself.

"I've been in with cruiserweights, light-heavies and even welterweights. They all have different styles and I've got a wide range of spars. I had a good knockout in Swindon in my last fight and it'll get even better on May 2. There won't be a better night for boxing with Mayweather-Pacquiao afterwards. Hopefully people will watch my fight and then stay up to watch Mayweather.

"I'm hoping for a great atmosphere and I'm sure the fans will get behind all the home boxers to push us over the line," said O'Kane.

O'Kane Can See a World Title Shot On the Horizon – 2nd May 2015

Eamonn O'Kane believes a shot at World glory is within reach and victory over Lewis Taylor tonight could seal the deal. O'Kane's IBF inter-continental title is on the line when the pair clash at the Lavey Centre with a 2,000-strong crowd expected.

"I hope we have a rough and ready crowd and an unbelievable atmosphere to help get me over the line," said O'Kane.

"The support will give me that extra one or two per cent needed. Hassan N'Dam and David Lemieux are fighting for the IBF belt. They are ranked one and five and I'm at seven so we are in touching distance of a World title. I intend to do a great job and if I get the win I am right in the mix."

Sheffield's Taylor, 16-0-1 as a pro, insists he's putting his undefeated ledger on the line for a reason and is expecting to have too much for his Dungiven opponent. The 25-year-old has been begging manager Dennis Hobson for a step-up in level.

"Eamonn's a good kid but I'm confident and I've been training hard," said Taylor. "I'm ready to show what I can do. I am not coming over here to lose my unbeaten record and I've wanted this fight because this is my time now."

This is 33-year-old O'Kane's 16th contest but the Commonwealth gold medallist has packed in Prizefighter and Irish title wins since turning over in 2011. After starting out as an aggressive slugger, O'Kane has refined his style of late and reckons he can box more in this bout.

"I have to pick my moments and use that aggression, strength and power at the right time. I have to box smart and show what I have been working on," he added.

Trainer Paddy Fitzpatrick, who also handles George Groves, has been behind the stylistic transformation. He believes a win for his man could lead to fights with the likes of Chris Eubank Jnr.

"Eamonn is ranked at number seven with the IBF and if Lewis wins then he breaks the top 10. There are some massive fights for the winner," said Fitzpatrick.

Unbeaten Belfast super-featherweight James Fryers is on the undercard alongside Luke Watkins, Alan Donnellan, Garvey Kelly, John O'Donnell and Junior Saeed.

Sutcliffe Leads the Way in Dublin with Points Win – 2nd May 2015

Philip Sutcliffe Jnr enjoyed his biggest win to date last night at the Red Cow Hotel in Dublin. Sutcliffe outpointed Yoann Portailler by a score of 79-72 but was made to work hard for his victory by a solid and well-chosen opponent who refused to be dispatched like so many of the puncher's previous foes.

Portailler was ranked number 15 at lightweight in the recent EBU rankings. In his last contest he lost a 12-round decision to Belgian Jean Pierre Bauwens for the EU title so the 28-year-old clearly had title experience and was able to negotiate a championship distance. Yoann was no stranger to hitting the road either and winning away from home, having knocked out Brett William Smith (15-1 at the time) in his native Queensland, Australia in 2013.

Portailler began strongly, bobbing and weaving behind a high guard, the Frenchman pumped the jab and tried to give Sutcliffe angles. The 25-year-old Dubliner sized up what his opponent had to offer early on and set about him as the round progressed, unleashing the usual plethora of slashing right hands and left hooks mixed in with some tasty body blows. Portailler was clipped at the end of the first and staggered across the ring, opting to take a knee as Phil buzzed around looking for the finisher.

The plucky visitor managed to see out the opener and started having a go back in the second round. This trend continued through the third and fourth as even though Yoann was not bossing the fight he was giving Sutcliffe something to think about with some decent overhand rights. Portailler took the fifth on my card as Sutcliffe's corner team screamed for their man to box behind the jab, work the body and let the shots flow more naturally as Phil rushed in for the kill too often.

By the sixth round Sutcliffe was beginning to time his man again and found a second wind. After putting his foot on the gas in the seventh 'Sucko' decided it was futile trying to remove the man from Blanzy and boxed in circles, in and out, throughout the eighth to take home a deserved, wide points win on Emile Tiedt's scorecard. For the record, Mr Tiedt refereed all six contests on the card.

Father and trainer Phil Sutcliffe Senior commended the toughness and bravery shown by Portailler who was the perfect opponent for young Phil at this stage of his career. Manager Pat Magee is now looking for another step-up in levels. Despite a few grimaces post-fight as Bernardo Checa removed his gloves (which were the Japanese "Winning" brand as the team search for a softer option to preserve Philip's brittle digits) it appears that there was no obvious hand damage.

"He was a tough guy and I expected a couple of rounds off him but he went the distance which is something I needed," said Sutcliffe Jnr, now 8-0 (6 KOs).

"The hands are OK. There's a bit more padding in the Winning gloves and hopefully we'll be using them from now on. Hopefully Pat can push me on again and we can get bigger fights. I would like another eight-rounder but I'll leave it to Pat to see where we go next."

Belfast boxer Alfredo Meli made short work of Valentin Stoychev. The talented southpaw came out aggressively and whacked Stoychev with snippy portside leads and flurries of shots. The hapless Bulgarian soaked up a right hook to the body but seconds later stumbled into the ropes and looked at Emile Tiedt for help. The Dublin referee doled out a count and tried to coax Valentin back out for more punishment but the away man declined by wobbling around on unsteady legs. The scheduled eight-rounder was terminated at 2:10 of the first session.

Meli will no doubt get tougher tests than this one and he will need them as he closes in on title class. The Belfastman has skills and an Irish title fight with the likes of Luke Keeler or Anthony Fitzgerald would certainly whet the appetite.

Lightweight puncher Ciaran Bates defeated Pepi Perov 40-36. Bulgarian southpaw Perov always comes to have a go and provide some entertainment and this visit was no exception has he winged away gamely at Bates even copping the Dubliner with a few meaty hooks. Ciaran stayed calm and focused, however, and used his spearing jab and greater economy to subdue Perov who smiled as the rounds wore on and continued to take his lumps.

Bates was forced to travel a longer distance than usual but will be all the better for the experience.

There were wins for three local boxers earlier in the evening. Craig O'Brien opened the show with a 40-36 victory over Bulgaria's Asen Vasilev. Light-middleweight O'Brien made his size and reach advantages work for the most part and peppered his opponent's body with well-timed flurries. Podgy Vasilev, a well-travelled veteran, used his ring smarts to tie and smother and both men tired slightly as the bout wore on.

Despite this only being his second pro fight there are definitely signs that O'Brien has some skills to work with.

Gorey heavyweight Niall Kennedy enjoyed a 40-36 points success over Ugandan survivor Moses Matovu. Kennedy introduced a crisp, sharp jab from the start and landed enough variety to keep Matovu on his toes. The Belfast-based visitor displayed all of the feints and moves from his usual bag of tricks to keep referee Emile Tiedt at bay – not that Kennedy ever looked like stopping or really troubling his man. Trainer Paschal Collins implored his charge to keep throwing his range-finder and to ignore the antics of Moses.

Kennedy has ability and a bit of pop to go with it. Don't we just love a good heavyweight to get excited about?

All-action welterweight Gerard Whitehouse went to war with Bulgarian brawler Teodor Stefanov and prevailed 40-36 on Emile Tiedt's scorecard. Gerard threw plenty of leather to please his excitable following while Stefanov spoiled as much as he could to get through.

Midway through the show the Boxing Union of Ireland (BUI) presented their awards from 2014. Andy Lee was awarded Boxer of the Year, Gary 'Spike' O'Sullivan collected the Knockout of the Year for his first-round dismissal of Anthony Fitzgerald in the 3 Arena last November. Jono Carroll was announced as Prospect of the Year and shared the Fight of the Year accolade for his barnburner with Declan Geraghty.

O'Kane Moves Closer to World Glory with Gritty Win in Derry – 2nd May 2015

Written by Odhrán Crumley

Eamonn O'Kane came through a gruelling twelve round battle to retain his IBF intercontinental middleweight title, which doubled as a world title eliminator to keep his world title plans on track, with a points victory over previously undefeated Lewis Taylor in Lavey Community Centre.

After the fight O'Kane admitted, "I have to be better if I want to win a world title".

The Dungiven native had to battle hard to earn a majority decision with the three judges -Canada's Harry Davis, Poland's Gregorz Molenda and England's Dave Parris- scoring the contest 116-112,115-113 and 114-114 respectively. O'Kane picked up a hellish cut above his right eye as the result of a head clash in round five. This saw O'Kane fighting behind his jab and growing into the fight in the second half, winning the two final rounds to claim victory in front of an almost capacity home crowd. Eamonn's win handed Taylor his first defeat and kept his world title dreams alive by moving him into third position in the IBF middleweight rankings.

O'Kane said: "I want the big fights and an All-Ireland world title clash between me and Andy Lee would capture the imagination".

On the undercard Galway's former Commonwealth welterweight Champion John O'Donnell returned to the ring after almost two years out to claim an 80-73 points victory over Hungarian Laszlo Fazekas advancing his record to 29-2. O'Kane's stablemate at Fitzpatrick's Gym, Garvey Kelly got back to winning ways with a fifth-round TKO victory over Hungarian Gabor Feher knocking him down twice in the process. There was also points wins for Belfast man James Fryers who moved to 7-0, classy English man Junior Saeed (4-0) and Galway's Alan Donnellan (7-3).

You can follow Odhrán on Twitter @odhranc14 or contact by email at ocrumley@live.co.uk

Carl Frampton Joins Up with US Powerhouse Al Haymon – 11ᵗʰ June 2015

Undefeated IBF super-bantamweight champion Carl Frampton has signed a deal to work with American mystery man Al Haymon. Haymon, an influential boxing advisor who is rarely seen in public, currently works with a number of leading boxers including Floyd Mayweather, Amir Khan, Adonis Stevenson, Adrien Broner, Robert Guerrero and many others.

Haymon will work as an advisor to Carl Frampton, who will continue to be managed by IBHOF member Barry McGuigan and promoted by Cyclone Promotions. Carl's team have spent their time recently negotiating with Matchroom supremo Eddie Hearn about a possible July blockbuster with his man Scot Quigg but talks broke down with both sides blaming one another for the lack of progress.

Speaking on the agreement, Frampton said: "I am very happy to have signed with Al Haymon. Al Haymon has a formidable reputation in boxing and has been the catalyst to securing the biggest fights in recent years. This is an exciting stage of my career after winning my world title, and my team and I know that this relationship with Al Haymon will help take my career to the next level. I am looking forward to it."

Frampton's manager Barry McGuigan said: "We are delighted to add Al Haymon to the team. Al Haymon is the best at what he does, there is no question about this. Al works with many world class fighters in the super bantamweight and featherweight divisions, so there will be plenty of attractive fights for Carl in the coming years. Carl is moving towards the peak of his career and we believe this is the perfect time to strike up this partnership."

Hopefully the partnership with Haymon can bear fruit and Frampton will get paid well and achieve meaningful matchups against 122lb rivals like Leo Santa Cruz (who is also on Haymon's books) and Guillermo Rigondeaux. Unfortunately as mentioned it seems a fight with Scott Quigg is further away than ever and it is hoped that Carl will not get fed a succession of substandard opponents as Haymon has done with so many of his fighters since coming to prominence.

Frampton to Defend His World Title in the USA Live on CBS – 13ᵗʰ June 2015

Carl Frampton will make the second defence of his IBF world title against Alejandro Gonzalez Jr on July 18 at the Don Haskins Center in El Paso, Texas. This fight will be the main event on a CBS broadcast as part of the Premier Boxing Champions (PBC) series that will go out live coast-to-coast in the USA.

Cyclone Promotions are in discussions with a UK broadcaster to televise the second defence of Frampton's IBF title live on July 18. Undefeated Frampton, 20-0 (14 KOs), is already an established star in the UK and Ireland and has recently signed an advisory agreement with Al Haymon. The Gonzalez Jr fight will be Frampton's first bout in the USA and will take place as the headliner of a CBS terrestrial television show.

Alejandro Gonzalez Jr, a 22-year old Tijuana native with a 25-1- 2 (15 KOs) record, follows in the footsteps of his father Alejandro Gonzalez Sr when he challenges for the world title in Texas. Gonzalez Sr dethroned WBC featherweight champion Kevin Kelley in San Antonio, Texas in 1995 to become champion. Gonzalez Jr, ranked 13 by the IBF and 54 in the world by BoxRec, will have the majority of the support in El Paso for his first world title challenge.

Belfast's Frampton, meanwhile, won this version of the world title in Belfast in September 2014 in front of 16,000 ecstatic home fans. His first defence against the eccentric American Chris Avalos attracted a terrestrial television audience of over two million viewers (on ITV) across the UK and Ireland.

IBF king Frampton said: "I am delighted to be defending my title in the USA on July 18ᵗʰ live on CBS against Alejandro Gonzalez Jr. I want to become a star in the USA and this is my first step on that journey. Now that my team is working with Al Haymon I am set to defend my title in front of millions of US fight fans on CBS. Alejandro Gonzalez Jr. is a dangerous Mexican challenger but he has never fought anyone like me and on the 18ᵗʰ of July he is in for a big, big shock. I feel I am the best super-bantamweight in the world and I am excited to box in front of a huge television audience in the USA."

Frampton's manager Barry McGuigan said: "This is fantastic news for Carl Frampton. He is defending his title live on CBS in the USA and I believe Carl's all-action style will captivate the US fight fans. Frampton has all the ingredients needed to become a major star in the USA; he is an exceptional fighter with a brilliant personality who has a fanatical fan base in the UK. Alejandro Gonzalez Jr. is a hungry and dangerous young Mexican boxer who will be travelling to El Paso, Texas to rip that belt from Frampton. This is going to be a cracking fight."

Texas' undefeated Jermall Charlo challenges IBF World light-middleweight champion Cornelius 'K-9' Bundrage on the undercard of Frampton vs. Gonzalez Jr.

'New Beginning' for Conlan Who Gets Mexican Test in Dublin – 4th July 2015

Belfast boxer Jamie Conlan is ready to open a new chapter in his career when he headlines Frank Warren's 'New Beginning' show in Dublin tonight. A successful defence of the WBO Inter-Continental super-flyweight title against Mexico's Junior Granados will push Conlan closer to a world title shot.

"These are the type of fights that I've always wanted, to help me break into world level," said Conlan. "Beating Granados will show how far I am along and if I'm ready to take a step up or if I need a few more fights like this."

After leaving long-time trainer John Breen to hook up with Danny Vaughan at the MGM Marbella gym, Jamie has been engaged in a rigid Spanish training camp to prepare him for this big opportunity which will be televised on BoxNation.

"I've had a great camp and been pushed to the limits, doing things I've never done before," added Conlan.

"I was out in Spain for nine weeks flat-out and boxing was the first and only thing you thought about all day. It's got me mentally as well as physically prepared and I now know what a proper camp feels like. This is the training that I want, to be away from everyone and just focused on the fight and getting my head down."

At 28, Conlan is now approaching his peak and despite suffering some injury woes and promotional setbacks he has amassed a perfect 13-0 record. Granados turned pro at 17 and is now 13-2-1. The Mexican is a solid opponent but some suspect losses on his record suggest that Jamie will be a class above.

"I expect a really tough fight but I also expect myself to have the boxing brain to outsmart and outfight him," asserted Conlan.

"He likes to come forward and throw a good left hook to body and head from what I've seen. He's got good head movement and his defence isn't bad either. The main things I have over him are height and weight because he's naturally a flyweight moving up to super-fly. He has won a WBC Hispano title though so he must be doing something right in the ring."

If Conlan manages to get past this latest test his team have set out a blueprint to help guide their man to success with more fights planned before the year's end. Jamie, however, isn't looking at anything beyond getting his work done at the National Stadium this evening.

"My team have given me a guide from now until Christmas and I have to follow it, starting with a good job against Granados," he concluded.

On the undercard Ryan Burnett boxes Csaba Kovacs over eight rounds at bantamweight.

Barnburner: Conlan Rallies Back from the Brink to Tame Ferocious Granados – 4ᵗʰ July 2015

Undefeated super-flyweight Jamie Conlan was forced to call upon all of his reserves to grind out a points win over Junior Granados at Dublin's National Stadium. Even though the judges' scorecards of 96-92 (Dave Parris) and 95-93 twice (Jose Ignacio Martinez and Giustino Di Giovanni) were unanimous in the Belfast man's favour, they hardly begin to tell the story of a victory that nudged itself further into Fight of the Year territory as the bout progressed.

Conlan started strongly, looking to impose his clear size advantages over Granados who had spent the majority of his career campaigning at flyweight. The Mexican visitor made up for any height and reach discrepancies by timing his assaults with impressive fluency, mostly set up behind a sharp left jab.

After negotiating the early sessions fairly comfortably Jamie shipped a solid right hand late in the fourth and was suddenly on unsteady legs. Granados bulled forward to seize his opportunity but Conlan dug deep and even landed a tasty left hook to stave off the danger.

Conlan endured a disastrous seventh round but somehow made it through. Trying to box more than brawl was the strategy but Jamie found himself moving backwards too often and a Granados right hook scythed into his torso and sent the crowd favourite to the floor. He took advantage of every second before tentatively rising and opting for more. Yucitan man Granados, 22, duly dished out further punishment, leaping in with constant right hands and hooks, many finding the target.

Veteran referee Mickey Vann hovered in closely as Conlan tried his best to block and slip Granados' relentless onslaught. Trainer Danny Vaughan led the call from ringside for his man to throw back some leather. The fighter who ironically adopted a ring moniker of 'The Mexican' was being pummelled by the real thing as Junior landed a pair of slashing uppercuts to send Conlan back to the canvas and seemingly on the brink of a stoppage defeat.

The 28-year-old simply refused to lose his unbeaten record, summoning the courage and guts to not only stay competitive but regain control in the final rounds. Buoyed on by fervent support, Conlan made it to the final bell and retained his WBO Inter-Continental super-flyweight title.

Rather than being pleased with the fan-friendly war he had just served up for an appreciative Dublin crowd and BoxNation viewers, Jamie was disappointed that he allowed the fight to reach such a critical stage.

"I made a lot of mistakes and I could have done a lot better. It's a big learning fight, not a coming of age one," said Conlan who commended the immense atmosphere that helped drag him over the line.

"I felt like crying in the ring because they were giving me an extra boost when I came back to the corner and it sent shivers down my back. Afterwards Granados said 'you're a true Mexican' and to me that's a compliment because I had to dig deep."

While Conlan is leaving his next move to the MGM team, post-fight chatter suggests that a fight with Paul Butler could still be on the cards.

Tommy Langford needed just four rounds of a scheduled 10 to bludgeon Mexico's Julio Cesar Avalos and take home the WBO Inter-Continental middleweight title.

It was apparent early on that Avalos had little more to offer than stoic resistance and by the third round it was becoming a one-sided affair as Tommy repeatedly landed an impressive variety of shots. Referee Steve Gray jumped in at 2-41 with Birmingham's Langford punishing Avalos on the ropes.

Belfast bantamweight Ryan Burnett forced Hungarian opponent Csaba Kovacs to retire at 1-32 of the second round (of an eight-threes) citing a damaged left shoulder. Referee Emile Tiedt accepted his withdrawal as Burnett moves on to a possible British title shot.

Stephen Ormond shook off any negative effects from his disqualification defeat to Terry Flanagan in February with a second-round blitz of Poland's Jacek Wylezol. 'The Rock' found a home for his left hook to the body and the visitor started to crumble. David Irving read the signs and called the eight-rounder off at 1-47.

Anthony Fitzgerald enjoyed a confidence-building 77-75 points win over Telford's Kieron Gray at middleweight. Dubliner Fitzgerald was docked a point by David Irving in round eight for punching behind the head.

Dublin lightweight Declan Geraghty stopped Dinars Skripkins in round three of a six. David Irving waved it off at 2-54 after the Latvian visited the canvas for a third time.

Birmingham lightweight Michael Rooney opened the show with a second-round stoppage of the Czech Republic's Richard Walter. Emile Tiedt intervened at 2-42 of this scheduled four-rounder.

Dublin heavyweight Sean Turner made Latvia's Janis Ginters retire at the end of the first session (slated for four). Mickey Vann officiated.

THE VERDICT: Conlan may not yet be ready for the highest stage but this main event and accompanying atmosphere was reminiscent of the recent Bernard Dunne era.

FULL RESULTS : Jamie Conlan (114lbs 7oz), 14-0 (8), w pts 10 Junior Granados (113lbs 7oz), 13-3-1 (8); Tommy Langford (159lbs 8oz), 13-0 (4), w ko 4 Julio Cesar Avalos (160lbs 4oz), 15-5 (7); Ryan Burnett (120lbs), 10-0 (8), w rtd 2 Csaba Kovacs (124lbs), 7-6 (4); Anthony Fitzgerald (159lbs 8oz), 18-7 (4), w pts 8 Kieron Gray (163lbs 9oz), 8-41 (1); Stephen Ormond (141lbs 7oz), 18-2 (9), w rsf 2 Jacek Wylezol (139lbs 4oz), 12-10 (7); Declan Geraghty (133lbs), 8-1 (2) w ko 3 Dinars Skripkins (132lbs 9oz), 2-3; Sean Turner (271lbs), 5-0 (4) w rtd 1 Janis Ginters (244lbs), 5-10-1 (5); Michael Rooney (138lbs), 8-0 (1) w ko 2 Richard Walter (135lbs), 1-3 (1).

Gonzalez Jr Out to Spoil the Frampton Party
– 14ᵗʰ July 2015

IBF super-bantamweight world champion Carl Frampton will be using his July 18 American debut as an opportunity to formally announce himself to US fight fans and push on to bigger fights with fellow belt holders. However, Frampton's opponent this Saturday, Alejandro Gonzalez Jr, insists that he is not a man to be overlooked. The 22-year-old Mexican is coming to the Don Haskins Center in El Paso, Texas determined to spoil the party.

"I have a big chance, a great opportunity and I am going to take advantage of it," asserted Gonzalez Jr.

"It's Frampton's first time coming to the United States and he wants to be a superstar. But in order to become a superstar he must first get by me. I know that he's a great fighter with a lot of experience and a hard-hitting punch, but nothing that I can't handle. I'm not going to be afraid of anyone and even though this will be the biggest fight of my career, I won't be nervous."

Alejandro arrives in Texas boasting an impressive 25-1-2 record. Both draws came early on in his career and he has 15 knockouts. The Tijuana man's single defeat came in 2014 to fellow Mexican Juan Alberto Rosas and this will be only his second fight outside of Mexico. He insists that the loss was a learning experience and focusing on it too hard would be a mistake.

"Ever since my lone loss to Rosas last year, I've gained a lot of experience," said Gonzalez Jr. "Frampton's looking at me as the fighter who lost to Rosas, but I'm a different fighter now. I'm ready for this test."

Having signed with promotional powerhouse Al Haymon and boxing on free-to-air television both sides of the water, Frampton is eyeing money-spinning bouts with the likes of Guillermo Rigondeaux and Leo Santa Cruz. Gonzalez Jr, meanwhile, comes from solid boxing stock. His father, of the same name, enjoyed a fruitful 55-fight career that included a WBC featherweight title win over Kevin Kelley in 1995. Junior has taken that inspiration into pre-fight preparations.

"For this fight we worked differently in training camp than all my other camps. I've worked on my defence, my attack and counter punches. Everything has been done differently," he said.

"La Cobrita" is a tall, rangy boxer with respectable punching power and a hunger to gatecrash the party at 122lbs by bagging himself a world title. He believes that the crowd will be against the travelling champion with plenty of Mexicans packing the venue to offer support.

"From what I've seen of Frampton he is a very aggressive fighter. I don't have just one plan - whatever Frampton brings we'll handle it," he added.

World Title Night: "The Showdown At Thomond Park" – 14th July 2015

From Boxing Booth Press Officer David McHugh

Adam Booth and Frank Warren proudly present "The Showdown at Thomond Park" for the WBO Middleweight Championship of the World.

On Saturday the 19th of September, reigning WBO Middleweight Champion and Limerick native, Andy Lee, will defend his World title against undefeated Billy Joe Saunders. This unique outdoor global boxing event will take place at Thomond Park the home of Munster Rugby, live and exclusive on Box Nation in the UK and Ireland.

Booth Boxing and Queensberry Promotions are delighted to welcome all members of the media, dignitaries and special guests to Thomond Park for the announcement of this special sporting event.

An event of this magnitude in Limerick is unique. It offers sports fans, event fans and boxing fans a wonderful opportunity to witness a major global sporting contest on their doorstep and to get behind and support one of the most likeable and successful Irish sporting heroes.

"Hosting this event is a huge boost for the stadium and region, and we are very much looking forward to a first for Thomond Park with the staging of this WBO Middleweight Championship. Off the back of winning his title we were fortunate to have Andy Lee presented at half-time during the Munster v Leinster game last December and the reception he received that day was fantastic. I'm sure the supporters will be out in force again to cheer their local hero on as he defends his world title on home soil in September." ~ John Cantwell –Thomond Park Stadium Director.

"This is a dream come true for me. After becoming World Champion, my first wish was to defend my title in Limerick. It's important for me to repay the city and country who have supported me throughout my career. I want to thank everyone involved in organizing this event, it will be a very special night" ~ Andy Lee – WBO Middleweight World Champion

"I'm delighted to be headlining this fantastic event against Andy Lee with his WBO World Middleweight Championship on the line. Thomond Park is an amazing outdoor stadium steeped in sporting history and now it's going to play host to arguably the biggest boxing event staged in Ireland in recent years. The fight between me and Lee has been simmering for the last few years and now it's red hot. I can't wait for it and it's going to be a fight that will be talked about for many years to come." ~ Billy Joe Saunders – Mandatory challenger

Photograph: © David McHugh/Boxing Booth

Five Boxing Experts Break Down Frampton's Future Prospects – 16th July 2015

Carl Frampton will get a chance to display his skills to the world boxing audience once again on Saturday night when he faces Alejandro Gonzalez Jr in Texas. Five local boxing luminaries have been running the rule over Frampton's exciting American debut, potential super-bantamweight rivals and his overall ability.

Former WBA super-middleweight champion Brian Magee is looking forward to some big fights in the future for the Tigers Bay boxer.

"He has a fantastic style with plenty of action and likes to fight," said Magee.

"I think there's no doubt he can go all the way and top the division. It's about getting the fights to show that and I can't see there being a problem. He's got the ability and the mentality to go all the way to the top and stay there for a while. Frampton's young enough to be at his peak for three or four years.

"Everything they've done so far has been fantastic for him and they've brought him along nicely, getting the right opponents at the right times. Now he's ready to take on anybody and he has the fitness to match all of them."

Belfast's John Breen has trained many champions over the years and reckons 'The Jackal' is now capable of dominating his weight class.

"Carl's improved so much over this last year that he looks something special now," said Breen.

"I think Frampton beats Rigondeaux now - in fact I think he beats the whole lot of them [fellow belt holders]. He's a different class to Gonzalez Jr. I think he'll win in four or five rounds because this guy's not in the same league. The Americans love bangers and punchers so if he goes out and does what he's been doing here then he'll definitely do OK. If Carl keeps on winning then it's good for boxing in Ireland as well."

Monkstown man Neil Sinclair once fought for the world welterweight title and boxed in America in 2006.

"Carl's flying now and should be approaching his peak. Look at his performance at the Titanic where he boxed beautifully and then again in the first defence," said 'Sinky'.

"The noise of the crowd here in Belfast is brilliant and I'm sure he'll have some support with him in Texas but it'll be a different experience. He's exciting and not a brawler as such but he's a great boxer who can punch and will throw the big shots. Carl just seems to be getting better and better with each fight. There's no doubt the wee lad will rise to the occasion and revel in it all."

Belfast promoter Mark Dunlop believes there are some big fights on the horizon for Carl, both at home and in America.

"He can go on to superfights because it's a great division to be in at the moment," said Dunlop.

"I think he's phenomenal and they're doing a great job with him in terms of picking opponents and so on. It all depends on how he performs on the night but if everything goes to plan then Frampton will come through and if Scott Quigg does the same [in Manchester] then they can make that superfight. The Gonzalez Jr bout will be tougher than people think because his father was a world champion so I'm sure he's been in the gym all of his life."

Holy Trinity coach Harry Hawkins guided Dubliner Bernard Dunne to the WBA super-bantamweight title in 2009.

"The bigger plan is there and I'm sure Carl will be around for a long time," said Hawkins.

"Boxing in America is great but it will take three or four fights at least to get some kind of superstar status over there. It takes a lot to break into the American market but remember that Carl's already a superstar on this side of the pond. I still think Carl's a better fighter than Quigg."

Frampton-Gonzalez Jr: Round-By-Round Report from Texas – 18th July 2015

Carl Frampton successfully retained his IBF super-bantamweight world title with a unanimous decision win over Alejandro Gonzalez Jr but was made to work for his Texas win.

Frampton surprisingly found himself on the canvas twice in the opening round as his Mexican opponent raced out of the blocks. He responded to take control for the rest of the fight and claim a unanimous victory in a solid but unspectacular American debut.

Round 1
The action doesn't take long to heat up in Texas as Gonzalez Jr lands a looping left hook round the guard and Frampton touches down for a flash knockdown. Frampton down again later in the round in a disastrous opener for the Belfast man.
Frampton 7-10 Gonzalez Jr

Round 2
Gonzalez Jr lands a low blow but the dangerous right hand is also finding its target. Carl gets his rhythm back with some good combinations and body shots. Frampton throwing a few wild shots reminiscent of the Robbie Turley fight earlier in his career.
Frampton 10-9 Gonzalez Jr

Round 3
Gonzalez Jr deducted a point for persistent low blows after landing his third offensive shot below the waistline. 'The Jackal' has found his jab and looks calmer and more in control after a ferocious opening to the bout.
Frampton 10-8 Gonzalez Jr

Round 4
Carl lands a left hand late in the round that ruffles Gonzalez Jr. The taller Mexican is not holding the Tigers Bay man off as easily as in the first few rounds as Frampton narrows the distance quickly to get his shots off inside.
Frampton 10-9 Gonzalez Jr

Round 5

Gonzalez Jr is still dangerous and timing his shots well, especially the double left hook. The Mexican's body assault is also a concern but Frampton takes back control of centre ring with his better boxing brain.

Frampton 10-9 Gonzalez Jr

Round 6

Frampton starting to settle down now and picking his shots. Gonzalez Jr has a sneaky uppercut in his arsenal but Carl is bringing Alejandro forward before slashing him with classy hooks.

Frampton 10-9 Gonzalez Jr

Round 7

The world title challenger is giving a lot more than some observers expected and makes the champion work hard on his US debut. Reigning WBC king and potential future Frampton opponent Leo Santa Cruz is watching with interest at ringside.

Frampton 10-9 Gonzalez Jr

Round 8

The referee gets involved again as Frampton is warned mid-round for a low blow of his own. Gonzalez Jr lands some whipping shots and grows again in confidence. The early adversity appears to be drifting away as Frampton lands consecutive right hands.

Frampton 10-9 Gonzalez Jr

Round 9

Decent round for Gonzalez Jr who gets off with some good punches and shows that he is not about to go down without a fight. The challenger makes a solid argument for taking the round.

Frampton 9-10 Gonzalez Jr

Round 10

Carl naturally slowing down as the torrid pace begins to ease. Gonzalez Jr has never done the 12 round distance before but looks relatively strong. Carl just does enough to win the round.

Frampton 10-9 Gonzalez Jr

Round 11

Gonzalez Jr loses another point for low blows and the scorecards are starting to move Frampton further away towards victory. The Tijuana man surely needs to land a big blow to save this.

Frampton 10-8 Gonzalez Jr

Round 12

Carl wants to leave the American audience with a tasty closing session and he lands a big right hand. Gonzalez Jr duly sucks it up and continues to motor forward. 'The Jackal' squeezes home after a nerve-racking but exciting war.

Frampton 10-9 Gonzalez Jr

My scorecard: Frampton 116-108 Gonzalez Jr

Judges' scorecards:

Frampton 115-109 Gonzalez Jr
Frampton 116-108 Gonzalez Jr
Frampton 116-108 Gonzalez Jr

Post-fight comments

Carl Frampton: "I was in shock, I came out slow. I need to give Gonzalez Jr so much credit, he doesn't look like a big puncher but man he can punch. It was exciting but it wasn't the performance I wanted. I don't want to make excuses but I took too much weight off in the last few days. Big decision whether to stay at this weight or go to featherweight - I don't know.

"It was just a shock, they were flash knockdowns, it's never happened before. The canvas was very soft and I couldn't use my toes, my best attribute and he took a good punch. They were flash knockdowns and I recovered well. I showed a big set of balls and I showed excitement. Things like that happen. It wasn't my best performance of my career but I came back and won.

"I had some problems making the weight. I don't want to tell you exactly what I had to take off over the last few days but it was a lot of weight. It means we will have to seriously consider moving to featherweight. I wanted to win and I got the win, I wanted to give excitement and I gave excitement."

Barry McGuigan: "He struggled a bit at the weight and we might have to move up to featherweight. The ring canvas was very soft and I said to him don't get caught early on as you're in a haze for three or four rounds and that's exactly what happened. He showed tremendous courage to come back. It wasn't a brilliant performance but he showed he can come back."

Sensational Scott Quigg Blasts Kiko in Two and Targets Frampton – 19th July 2015

Scott Quigg made a huge statement by knocking out Kiko Martinez in two rounds at the Manchester Arena last night. Quigg's performance was always likely to be compared with rival Carl Frampton who twice beat Martinez, firstly by knockout for the European title and last September for the world title in Belfast's Titanic Quarter. Scott was too powerful in his attack and the diminutive Spaniard was unable to cope with the power in the Bury man's punches.

This was certainly the sternest test of Quigg's career and he started cautiously, pushing the jab as Martinez rushed forward looking to unload. Having such a destructive reputation, including many knockout wins on the road, Kiko was eager to get inside and land his big shots. Scott was backing up too much and conceding ground to his challenger.

Any nerves were swiftly eradicated in the second session of this WBA title affair as Quigg raced out of the blocks. Kiko was suddenly badly hurt in round two after a right uppercut landed flush and dropped him for a count from referee Terry O'Connor. This only started the damage and Martinez was quickly down again and out from Quigg's hard punches.

The bout was stopped at 1-04 of the round, sending the Manchester crowd into raptures for their man who has now made a potential fight with rival Frampton even more enticing. Quigg moves his professional record to 31-0-2 with 23 knockouts.

"I knew he was going to come out and gain a bit of confidence so I set him up on the shots we've been working on through the camp," said Quigg. "I wasn't reckless, I kept my cool. Hopefully I've changed a few opinions tonight and thanks to everyone in the arena tonight."

"We worked on the uppercut in camp and we tested his power in the first round and kept him reaching before he walked on to a big uppercut," added trainer Joe Gallagher.

Promoter Eddie Hearn is still interested in the Carl Frampton fight but sees other big bouts for his man: "We've got plenty of options and a Nonito Donaire fight is close. Scott's a quality fighter and we will see that when he fights quality opposition.

"He's a world champion and his stock will keep on rising. That was sensational tonight and no super-bantamweight can stand up to Quigg's power so he deserves respect," said Hearn.

Domestic Results: Professional Shows in Ireland

2014

February 15 - National Stadium, Dublin (Promoter: Gary Hyde, Nowhere to Hyde Promotions)
Middleweight: Hassan N'Dam N'Jikam WTKO4 Ricardo Marcelo Ramallo
Middleweight: Mark Heffron WPTS8 Mateo Damian Veron
Middleweight: Luke Keeler WTKO2 Edgars Sniedze
Cruiserweight: Youri Kayembre Kalenga WKO3 Cesar David Crenz
Super-middleweight: Darren Cruise NC2 Robert Long
Cruiserweight: David Maguire debut WPTS4 Moses Matovu
Welterweight: Sonny Upton WPTS4 Kevin McCauley

March 21 - Holiday Inn, Belfast (Promoter: Jane Wilton, Belfast Promotions)
Light-welterweight: Matthew Wilton WPTS6 Lewis O'Mara
Featherweight: Paul Quinn WPTS4 Joe Beeden
Middleweight: Alfredo Meli WPTS6 Festim Lama
Lightweight: Mark Morris WTKO1 Ryan Corrigan
Light-welterweight: Anthony Upton WTKO4 Alec Bazza
Light-middleweight: Casey Blair WPTS4 Billy Campbell

April 4 - Odyssey Arena, Belfast (Promoter: Barry McGuigan, Cyclone Promotions)
Super-bantamweight: Carl Frampton WKO2 Hugo Fidel Cazares
Middleweight: Conrad Cummings WTKO3 Zahari Mutafchiev
Lightweight: Stephen Ormond WTKO5 Karim El Ouazghari
Super-flyweight: Jamie Conlan WTKO7 Benjamin Smoes
Featherweight: Marco McCullough WTKO3 Elemir Rafael
Middleweight: Eamonn O'Kane WKO1 Alvaro Gaona

May 10 - Devenish Complex, Belfast (Promoter Mark H Dunlop)
Featherweight: James Tennyson WPTS8 Ian Bailey
Light-middleweight: Dee Walsh WTKO1 Krisztian Duka
Super-featherweight: Derek Potter WPTS4 Ben Mulligan

Flyweight: Luke Wilton WPTS6 Stefan Slavchev
Lightweight: Paul Hyland Jnr WPTS4 Zoltan Horvath
Middleweight: Alfredo Meli WPTS4 Samet Hyuseinov
Lightweight: James Fryers WPTS4 Alec Bazza
Featherweight: Martin Lindsay WTKO3 Krzysztof Rogowski

June 6 - Holiday Inn, Ormeau Avenue (Promoter: Jane Wilton, Belfast Promotions)
Middleweight: Luke Keeler WTKO4 Festim Lama
Lightweight: Ciaran Bates WTKO1 Mihaly Szalontai
Light-middleweight: Willie Thompson WPTS4 Liam Griffiths
Light-welterweight: Eamonn Magee Jnr WTKO2 Zoltan Horvath
Lightweight: Paul Hyland Jnr WPTS4 Joe Beeden
Middleweight: Alfredo Meli WPTS6 Dan Blackwell
Heavyweight: Kenneth Odeke WPTS4 Moses Matovu

June 14 - Holiday Inn, Ormeau Avenue (Promoter: Jane Wilton, Belfast Promotions)
Middleweight: Anthony Fitzgerald WPTS6 Dan Blackwell
Light-middleweight: Dee Walsh WTKO1 Jozsef Kormany
Light-middleweight: Casey Blair WPTS4 Liam Griffiths
Lightweight: Declan Geraghty WTKO1Renato Toth
Heavyweight: Sean Turner WTKO1 Zoltan Elekes
Light-welterweight: Kofi Yates WPTS4 Alec Bazza
Middleweight: Alfredo Meli WPTS4 Damian Taggart

June 20 - Waterfront Hall (Promoter: Barry McGuigan, Cyclone Promotions)
Featherweight: Marco McCullough WPTS10 Martin Parlagi
Super-flyweight: Jamie Conlan WTKO3 Gabor Molnar
Middleweight: Conrad Cummings WTKO2 Lajos Munkacsi
Featherweight: Willie Casey WPTS6 Krzysztof Rogowski
Cruiserweight: Conall Carmichael WPTS4 Moses Matovu
Lightweight: Isaac Dogbo WPTS4 Andy Harris

September 6 - Titanic Quarter (Promoter: Barry McGuigan, Cyclone Promotions & Sergio Gabriel Martinez, Maravillabox)

Super-bantamweight: Kiko Martinez WPTS12 Carl Frampton
Super-flyweight: Jamie Conlan WPTS10 Jose Estrella
Featherweight: Marco McCullough WRTD8 Dmitry Kirillov
Middleweight: Conrad Cummings WPTS6 Robert Talarek
Middleweight: Eamonn O'Kane DTD4 Virgilijus Stapulionis
Super-featherweight: Anthony Cacace WTKO2 Dawid Knade
Light-welterweight: Matthew Wilton WPTS 4 Adam Cieslak
Featherweight: Willie Casey WTKO6 George Gachechiladze

September 12 - Red Cow Moran Hotel (Promoter: Jane Wilton, Belfast Promotions)
Middleweight: Luke Keeler WPTS6 Laszlo Kovacs
Cruiserweight: Ian Tims WPTS4 Tamas Danko
Heavyweight: Sean Turner WKO4 Istvan Ruzsinszky
Lightweight: Ciaran Bates WTKO1 Miklos Szilagyi
Light-welterweight: Philip Sutcliffe Jnr WPTS4 Martin McCord
Lightweight: Declan Geraghty WPTS4 Ignac Kassai

October 4 - Devenish Complex (Promoter: Mark H Dunlop)
Light-middleweight: Dee Walsh WPTS4 Adam Grabiec
Super-featherweight: Daniel McShane WPTS4 Qasim Hussain
Lightweight: Paul Hyland Jnr WPTS4 Andy Harris
Light-middleweight : Alan Donnellan WPTS4 Iain Jackson
Light-middleweight: Gerard Healy WPTS4 Liam Griffiths
Super-middleweight: Darren Cruise WPTS4 Harry Matthews
Super-featherweight: James Fryers WPTS4 Lewis O'Mara
Welterweight: Michael McKinson WPTS4 Jan Salamacha
Cruiserweight: Tommy McCarthy WTKO1 Dimitar Spaiyski

November 1 - Downpatrick Cricket Club (Promoter: Jane Wilton, Belfast Promotions)
Featherweight: Paul Quinn WTKO6 Dawid Knade
Middleweight: Alfredo Meli WPTS4 Iain Jackson
Heavyweight: Sean Turner WPTS4 Moses Matovu
Lightweight: Ciaran Bates WTKO2 Lewis O'Mara
Welterweight: Michael McKinson WPTS4 Pawel Seliga
Welterweight: Gerard Whitehouse WTKO1 Jakub Czaprowicz

Light-middleweight: Casey Blair WPTS4 Liam Griffiths
Light-middleweight: Damian Taggart LPTS4 Dee Walsh

November 15 - 3Arena (Promoter: Eddie Hearn, Matchroom Boxing)
Middleweight: Jorge Sebastian Heiland WKO10 Matthew Macklin
Super-flyweight: Khalid Yafai WPTS12 Everth Briceno
Middleweight: Gary O'Sullivan WTKO1 Anthony Fitzgerald
Middleweight: Luke Keeler WTKO1 Gary Boulden
Featherweight: Patrick Hyland WPTS8 Oszkar Fiko
Lightweight: Declan Geraghty LDQ4 Jono Carroll
Welterweight: Sam Eggington WTKO1 Sebastien Allais
Light-welterweight: John Joe Nevin WTKO1 Jack Heath
Cruiserweight: Tommy McCarthy WTKO2 Martin Horak
Light-welterweight: Kofi Yates WTKO2 Oisin Fagan
Cruiserweight: David Maguire WTKO2 Paul Morris
Lightweight: Anthony Crolla WPTS6 Gyorgy Mizsei Jr
Cruiserweight: Ian Tims LRTD1 Paul Drago

November 22 - Devenish Complex (Promoter: Mark H Dunlop)
Light-middleweight: Dee Walsh WTKO2 Terry Maughan
Lightweight: Paul Hyland Jnr WPTS4 Pepi Perov
Light-middleweight: Gerard Healy WPTS4 Yanko Marinov
Welterweight: Michael McKinson WPTS4 Teodor Stefanov
Super-middleweight: Darren Cruise WPTS4 Damian Taggart
Super-featherweight: James Fryers WTKO2 Sandor Horvath
Welterweight: Julio Cesar WPTS4 Iain Jackson
Bantamweight: Ryan Burnett WTKO1 Valentin Marinov
Welterweight: Paddy Gallagher WPTS4 Liam Griffiths

2015

February 7 - Devenish Complex (Promoter: Mark H Dunlop)
Super-featherweight: James Tennyson WTKO2 Simas Volosinas
Lightweight: Paul Hyland Jnr WPTS6 Yordan Vasilev
Light-middleweight: Alan Donnellan WPTS4 Damian Taggart
Super-middleweight: Darren Cruise WPTS4 Iain Jackson
Welterweight: Michael McKinson WPTS4 Aleksas Vaseris

Featherweight: Ciaran McVarnock WPTS6 Aivaras Balsys
Welterweight: Tyrone McKenna WPTS4 Teodor Stefanov

February 20 - Red Cow Moran Hotel (Promoter: Pat Magee and Tony Davitt, P & T Promotions)
Heavyweight: Sean Turner W KO1 Peter Erdos
Light-welterweight: Philip Sutcliffe Jnr W KO1 Terry Needham
Cruiserweight: Tommy McCarthy W KO6 Jakub Wojcik
Cruiserweight: Steve Collins Jr W KO2 Viktor Szalai
Lightweight: Stephen Carroll WPTS4 Ladislav Nemeth
Welterweight: Gerard Whitehouse WPTS4 Karoly Lakatos
Light-middleweight: Craig O'Brien W PTS4 Jakub Czaprowicz

February 28 - Odyssey Arena (Promoter: Barry McGuigan, Cyclone Promotions)
Welterweight: Denton Vassell LPTS12 Viktor Plotnykov
Super-bantamweight: Carl Frampton WTKO5 Chris Avalos
Welterweight : Paddy Gallagher W PTS4 Miguel Aguilar
Super-featherweight : Anthony Cacace W PTS8 Santiago Bustos
Middleweight: Conrad Cummings WPTS6 Roberto Palenzuela
Featherweight: Marco McCullough WTKO1 Malkhaz Tatrishvili
Heavyweight: Dillian Whyte WKO4 Beqa Lobjanidze
Featherweight: Josh Pritchard WPTS4 Aron Szilagyi

March 14 - Devenish Complex (Promoter: Peter Turley)
Light-welterweight: Eamonn Magee Jnr WTKO1 Dinars Skripkins
Middleweight: Tommy Tolan WTKO3 Phillip Townley
Light-heavyweight: Matthew Fitzsimmons WRTD2 Aleksandrs Birkenbergs

March 28 - Andersonstown Leisure Centre (Promoter: Mark H Dunlop)
Cruiserweight: Joe Hillerby WPTS4 Damian Taggart
Featherweight: Kris Hughes LDQ7 James Tennyson
Light-middleweight: Dee Walsh WTKO1 Peter Orlik
Lightweight: Paul Hyland Jnr WTKO5 Imre Nagy
Lightweight: James Fryers WRTD5 Mark Morris
Super-featherweight: Daniel McShane LTKO2 Zoltan Horvath

Welterweight: Tyrone McKenna WTKO3 Istvan Kiss
May 1 - Red Cow Moran Hotel (Promoter: Jane Wilton, Belfast Promotions
& Tony Davitt)
Lightweight: Ciaran Bates W PTS4 Pepi Perov
Welterweight: Gerard Whitehouse WPTS4 Teodor Stefanov
Light-welterweight: Philip Sutcliffe Jnr WPTS8 Yoann Portailler
Middleweight: Alfredo Meli WTKO1 Valentin Stoychev
Light-middleweight: Craig O'Brien W PTS4 Asen Vasilev
Heavyweight: Niall Kennedy W PTS4 Moses Matovu

May 2 - Lavey Centre (Promoter: Mickey Helliet and Laurence O'Kane)
Middleweight: Eamonn O'Kane WPTS12 Lewis Taylor
Lightweight: James Fryers W PTS4 Zoltan Horvath
Welterweight: Garvey Kelly WTKO5 Gabor Feher
Super-featherweight: Junior Saeed WPTS4 Miklos Hevesi
Super-middleweight: Alan Donnellan W PTS 4 Jozsef Racz
Light-middleweight: John O'Donnell WPTS8 Laszlo Fazekas

June 6 - Devenish Complex (Promoter: Mark H Dunlop)
Featherweight: James Tennyson WTKO 3 Krzysztof Rogowski
Light-middleweight: Dee Walsh WPTS 8 Patryk Litkiewicz
Lightweight: James Fryers WTKO1 Sergejs Logins
Lightweight : Paul Hyland Jnr WTKO4 Ivans Levickis
Light-middleweight: Gerard Healy WPTS4 Piotr Tomaszek
Welterweight: Tyrone McKenna WPTS4 Sylwester Walczak
Lightweight: Joe Fitzpatrick WTKO1 Ignac Kassai

July 4 - National Stadium (Promoter: Frank Warren, Queensberry Promotions & Matthew Macklin, MGM Promotions)
Super-flyweight: Jamie Conlan WPTS10 Junior Granados
Bantamweight: Ryan Burnett WKO2 Csaba Kovacs
Middleweight: Anthony Fitzgerald WPTS8 Kieron Gray
Lightweight: Declan Geraghty WTKO3 Dinars Skripkins
Middleweight: Tommy Langford WKO4 Julio Cesar Avalos
Super-featherweight: Stephen Ormond WKO2 Jacek Wylezol
Lightweight: Michael Rooney WKO2 Richard Walter

Heavyweight: Sean Turner WRTD1 Janis Ginters

August 1 - Devenish Complex (Promoter: Charlie Tolan, Fianna Promotions)
Middleweight: Tommy Tolan vs. TBA
Light-heavyweight: Joe Hillerby vs. John Waldron
Light-heavyweight: Padraig McCrory vs. Jody Meikle
Lightweight: Mark Morris vs. Barry McGuigan
Light-middleweight: Conor Doherty vs. Matt Scriven
Light-welterweight: Darren Mangan vs. TBA

August 1 – Falls Park Marquee (Promoter: Pat Magee)
Cruiserweight: Tommy McCarthy vs. Courtney Fry
Lightweight: Joe Fitzpatrick vs. TBA

October 17 - Europa Hotel (Promoter: Mark H Dunlop)
Lightweight: Paul Hyland Jnr vs. TBA
Light-middleweight: Dee Walsh vs. TBA
Featherweight: James Tennyson vs. TBA
Super-featherweight: James Fryers vs. TBA
Lightweight: Joe Fitzpatrick vs. TBA

September 19 - Thomond Park Stadium (Promoter: Frank Warren, Queensberry Promotions)
Middleweight: Andy Lee vs. Billy Joe Saunders

World Results 2014

July 26: Billy Joe Saunders WKO8 Emanuel Blandamura (vacant European middleweight) - Liam Smith WTKO6 Jason Welborn (British light-middleweight) - Chris Eubank Jr WRSF1 Ivan Jukic (super-middleweight) - Tom Stalker WPTS6 Ben Wager (light-welterweight) - Gennady Golovkin WKO3 Daniel Geale (WBA middleweight title).

August 1: Leonard Bundu WPTS12 Frankie Gavin (*European and Commonwealth welterweight titles*).

August 2: Sergey Kovalev WTKO2 Blake Caparello (*WBO light-heavyweight title*).

August 30: Marco Huck WPTS12 Mirko Larghetti (*WBO cruiserweight title*).

September 6: Carl Frampton WPTS12 Kiko Martinez (*IBF super-bantamweight title*) - Juan Francisco Estrada WTKO11 Giovani Segura (*WBO and WBA flyweight titles*).

September 13: Floyd Mayweather WPTS12 Marcos Maidana (*WBC and WBA welterweight titles*) - Leo Santa Cruz WKO2 Manuel Roman (*WBC super-bantamweight title*) - Mickey Bey WPTS12 Miguel Vazquez (*IBF lightweight title*) - Scott Quigg WTKO3 Stephane Jamoye (*WBA super-bantamweight title*) - Anthony Joshua WTKO3 Konstantin Airich (*heavyweight*).

September 19: Omar Narvaez WPTS12 Felipe Orucuta (*WBO super-flyweight title*).

September 20: George Groves WPTS12 Christopher Rebrasse (*WBC super-middleweight eliminator and for Rebrasse's European title*) - Luke Campbell WTKO7 Krzysztof Szot (*lightweight*) - Kal Yafai WKO2 Herald Molina (*bantamweight*) - Kid Galahad WPTS12 Adeilson Dos Santos (*super-bantamweight*) - Javier Mendoza WPTS12 Ramon Garcia Hirales (*vacant IBF light-flyweight title*).

September 26: Juan Carlos Payano WPTS12 Anselmo Moreno (*WBA 'super' bantamweight title*).

September 27: Arthur Abraham wpts12 Paul Smith (*WBO super-middleweight title*) -Grigory Drozd WPTS12 Krzysztof Wlodarczyk (*WBC cruiserweight title*) - Denis Lebedev WKO2 Pawel Kolodziej (*WBA cruiserweight title*).

October 4: Rances Barthelemy WPTS12 Fernando Saucedo (*IBF super-featherweight title*) - Jhonny Gonzalez WKO11 Jorge Arce (*WBC featherweight title*) - Josh Warrington WTKO4 Davide Dieli (*vacant European featherweight title*) - Ricky Burns WPTS8 Alexandre Lepelley (*light-welterweight*) - Dave Ryan WPTS12 Tyrone Nurse by unanimous decision (*vacant Commonwealth light-welterweight title*).

October 8: Jermain Taylor WPTS12 Sam Soliman (*IBF middleweight title*).

October 11: Lee Selby WRSF9 Joel Brunker (*IBF featherweight title eliminator*) - Anthony Joshua WKO2 Denis Bakhtov - Cornelius Bundrage WPTS12 Carlos Molina (*IBF light-middleweight title*).

October 18: Gennady Golovkin WKO2 Marco Antonio Rubio (*WBA middleweight title*) - Nicholas Walters WTKO6 Nonito Donaire (*WBA featherweight title*).

October 25: Randy Caballero WPTS12 Stuart Hall (*vacant IBF bantamweight title*) - Martin Murray TD7 Domenico Spada (*WBC Silver middleweight title*) - Hekkie Budler WPTS12 Xiong Zhao Zhong (*WBA strawweight title*) - Luke Campbell WTKO5 Daniel Brizuela (*lightweight*) - Chris Eubank Jr WKO2 Omar Siala (*middleweight*) - Paul Butler WPTS10 Ismael Garnica (*super-flyweight*) - Kevin Satchell WPTS12 Valery Yanchy (*European flyweight title*).

November 1: Tomoki Kameda WPTS12 Alejandro Hernandez (*WBO bantamweight title*).

November 6: Wanheng Menayothin WPTS12 Osvaldo Novoa (*WBC strawweight title*).

November 8: Sergey Kovalev WPTS12 Bernard Hopkins (*WBA, IBF and WBO light-heavyweight*).

November 15: Wladimir Klitschko WTKO5 Kubrat Pulev (*IBF heavyweight title*) - Donnie Nietes WTKO8 Carlos Velarde (*WBO light-flyweight title*) - Jorge Sebastien Heiland WKO10 Matthew Macklin (*WBC 'international' middleweight title*) - Kal Yafai WPTS12 Everth Briceno (*IBF inter-continental super-flyweight title*).

November 22: Manny Pacquiao WPTS12 Chris Algieri (*WBO welterweight title*) - Vasyl Lomachenko WPTS12 Chonlatarn Piriyapinyo (*WBO featherweight title*) - Jessie Vargas WPTS12 Antonio DeMarco (*WBA 'regular' light-welterweight title*) - Takashi Miura WTKO6 Edgar Puerta (*WBC super-featherweight title*) - Roman Gonzalez WTKO6 Rocky Fuentes (*WBC flyweight title*) - Tony Bellew WPTS12 Nathan Cleverly (*cruiserweight eliminator title*) - Scott Quigg WPTS12 Hidenori Otake (*WBA super-bantamweight title*) - Jamie McDonnell WTKO10 Javier Chacon (*WBA bantamweight title*) - Anthony Joshua WKO1 Michael Sprott (*final eliminator for British heavyweight title*) - Callum Smith WPTS12 Nikola Sjekloca (*final eliminator for WBC super-middleweight*) - James DeGale WTKO3 Marco Antonio Periban (*super-middleweight*) - George Groves WTKO7 Denis Douglin (*super-middleweight*).

November 29: Tyson Fury WRTD10 Dereck Chisora (*British heavyweight title*) - Billy Joe Saunders WPTS12 Chris Eubank Jr (*European middleweight title*) - Terence Crawford WPTS12 Raymundo Beltran (*WBO lightweight title*) - Evgeny Gradovich DPTS12 Jayson Velez (*IBF featherweight title*).

December 6: Juergen Braehmer WTKO1 Pawel Glazewski (*WBA 'regular' light-heavyweight*).

December 13: Amir Khan WPTS12 Devon Alexander (*WBC Silver welterweight title*), Andy Lee WTKO6 Matt Korobov (*vacant WBO middleweight title*).

December 19: Adonis Stevenson WKO5 Dmitry Sukhotsky (*WBC light-heavyweight title*).

December 31: Takashi Uchiyama WTKO9 Israel Perez (*WBA super-featherweight title*) - Kohei Kono DPTS12 Norberto Jimenez (*WBA super-flyweight title*) - Alberto Rossel WPTS12 Ryoichi Taguchi (*WBA light-flyweight title*).

World Results 2015

February 28: Carl Frampton WTKO5 Chris Avalos (*IBF super-bantamweight title*) - Tyson Fury WKO8 Christian Hammer (*heavyweight*) - Chris Eubank Jr WTKO12 Dmitry Chudinov (*WBA 'interim' middleweight*) - Liam Walsh WRSF5 Joe Murray (*British and Commonwealth super-featherweight titles*).

March 6: Zolani Tete WTKO8 Paul Butler (*IBF super-flyweight title*) - Derry Mathews WTKO5 Gyorgy Mizsei Jr. (*lightweight*) - Jazza Dickens WPTS12 Josh Wale (*vacant British super-bantamweight title*).

March 7: Tommy Coyle WRSF5 Martin Gethin - Luke Campbell WTKO3 Lewis Morales (*lightweight*) - Bradley Saunders WTKO5 Stephane Benito (*welterweight*) - Keith Thurman WPTS12 Robert Guerrero by unanimous decision (*WBA welterweight title*) - Amnat Ruenroeng WPTS12 Zou Shiming (*IBF flyweight title*).

March 14: Sergey Kovalev WTKO8 Jean Pascal (*WBA, IBF and WBO light-heavyweight titles*).

March 21: Juergen Braehmer WTKO10 Robin Krasniqi (*WBA 'regular' light-heavyweight title*).

March 27: Ovill McKenzie WPTS12 Matty Askin (*British and Commonwealth cruiserweight title*).

March 28: Kell Brook WKO4 Jo Jo Dan (*IBF world welterweight title*).

April 4: Anthony Joshua WRSF3 Jason Gavern (*heavyweight*) - Anthony Nelson WTKO6 Jamie Wilson (*vacant Commonwealth super-flyweight title*) - Adonis Stevenson WPTS12 Sakio Bika (*WBC light-heavyweight title*) - Carlos Cuadras WPTS12 Luis Concepcion (*WBC super-flyweight title*).

April 10: Denis Lebedev WPTS12 Youri Kalenga (*WBA cruiserweight title*).

April 11: Josh Warrington WPTS12 Dennis Tubieron (*WBC featherweight* *eliminator title*) - Martin J Ward WRTD5 Maxi Hughes (*WBC international super featherweight title*) - Andy Lee DPTS12 Peter Quillin (*WBO middleweight title*) - Rocky Martinez WPTS12 Orlando Salido (*WBO super-featherweight title*).

April 16: Shinsuke Yamanaka WKO7 Diego Santillan (*WBC bantamweight title*).

April 18: Terence Crawford WTKO6 Thomas Dulorme (*vacant WBO light-welterweight title*) - Derry Matthews WPTS12 Tony Luis (*interim WBA lightweight title*).

April 22: Kazuto Ioka WPTS12 Juan Carlos Reveco (*WBA 'regular' light-flyweight title*).

April 24: Badou Jack WPTS12 Anthony Dirrell (*WBC super-middleweight title*) - Daniel Jacobs WTKO12 Caleb Truax (*WBA 'regular' middleweight title*).

April 25: Wladimir Klitschko WPTS12 Bryant Jennings by unanimous decision (*WBA, IBF and WBO heavyweight titles*).

May 1: Raymundo Beltran WTKO2 Takahiro Ao (*vacant WBO lightweight title*) - Takashi Miura WTKO3 Billy Dib (*WBC super-featherweight title*).

May 2: Floyd Mayweather Jr WPTS12 Manny Pacquiao (*WBC, WBA and WBO welterweight titles*) - Vasyl Lomachenko WKO9 Gamalier Rodriguez (*WBO featherweight title*).

May 9: Bradley Skeete WTKO6 Brunet Zamora - Frank Buglioni DPTS10 Lee Markham - Mitchell Smith WTKO5 Cristian Palma (*vacant WBO Inter-continental featherweight title*) - Anthony Joshua WTKO2 Rafael Zumbano Love (*heavyweight*) - Kal Yafai WTKO1 Isaac Quaye (*super-flyweight*) - Callum Smith WTKO1 Olegs Fedotovs (*super-middleweight*) -Matt Macklin WTKO2 Sandor Micsko (*middleweight title*) - Sam Eggington WTKO7 Joseph Lamptey (*vacant Commonwealth welterweight title*) - Saul Alvarez WTKO3 James Kirkland (*light-middleweight title*) - Jamie McDonnell WPTS12 Tomoki Kameda (*WBA 'regular' bantamweight title*) - Omar Figueroa Jr WPTS12 Ricky Burns (*light-welterweight*).

May 16: Gennady Golovkin WTKO6 Willie Monroe Jr (*WBA middleweight title*) - Roman Gonzalez WTKO2 Edgar Sosa (*WBC flyweight title*).

May 22: Grigory Drozd WTKO9 Lukasz Janik (*WBC cruiserweight title*).

May 23: James DeGale WPTS12 Andre Dirrell (*vacant IBF super-middleweight title*).

May 29: Amir Khan WPTS12 Chris Algieri (*non-title welterweight fight*).

May 30: Kell Brook WTKO6 Frankie Gavin (*IBF welterweight title*) - Jorge Linares WTKO10 Kevin Mitchell (*WBC lightweight title*) - Lee Selby WTD8 Evgeny Gradovich (*IBF featherweight title*) - Anthony Joshua WKO2 Kevin Johnson (*heavyweight*) - Nick Blackwell WTKO7 John Ryder (*vacant British middleweight title*) - Scotty Cardle WPTS12 Craig Evans (*vacant British lightweight title*) - Dave Ryan WTKO9 John Wayne Hibbert (*Commonwealth light-welterweight title*) - Nathan Cleverly WKO1 Tomas Man (*light-heavyweight title*) - Javier Mendoza WTD6 Milan Melindo (*IBF light-flyweight title*).

June 6: Miguel Cotto WTKO4 Daniel Geale (*WBC middleweight title*) - Jesus Cuellar WKO8 Vic Darchinyan (*WBA featherweight title*).

June 12: Erislandy Lara WPTS12 Delvin Rodriguez (*WBA light-middleweight title*).

June 13: Deontay Wilder WTKO9 Eric Molina (*WBC heavyweight title*) - Jose Pedraza WPTS12 Andrey Klimov (*vacant IBF super-featherweight title*) - Lee Haskins WTKO6 Ryosuke Iwasa (*IBF bantamweight title*) - Nicholas Walters WPTS12 Miguel Marriaga (*WBA featherweight title*).

June 20: Andre Ward WRTD9 Paul Smith (*non-title, catchweight 172lbs*) - Shawn Porter WPTS12 Adrien Broner (*non-title welterweight*) - David Lemieux WPTS12 Hassan N'Dam (*vacant IBF middleweight title*).

June 26: Tony Bellew WTKO10 Ivica Bacurin (*cruiserweight*) - Callum Smith WPTS12 Christopher Rebrasse (*super-middleweight*) - Rocky Fielding WKO2 Brian Vera (*super-middleweight*).

June 27: Timothy Bradley WPTS12 Jessie Vargas (*vacant WBO welterweight title*) - Amnat Ruenroeng WPTS12 Johnriel Casimero (*IBF flyweight title*).

July 4: Pedro Guevara WPTS12 Ganigan Lopez (*WBC light-flyweight title*).

July 11: Terry Flanagan WTKO2 Jose Zepeda (*vacant WBO lightweight title*) - Liam Walsh WKO6 Isaias Santos Sampaio (*vacant WBO Inter-Continental lightweight title*) - Keith Thurman WRTD8 Luis Collazo (*WBA 'regular' welterweight title*) - Donnie Nietes WPTS12 Francisco Rodriguez (*WBO light-flyweight title*).

Professional Boxers' Records

As always I would like to extend my thanks to legendary journalist Gerry Callan of the Irish Daily Star for providing a list of boxers' records and professional show statistics. Gerry regularly updates Boxrec.com and painstakingly compiles his records each week before sending them on to the Review for inclusion ~ SW.

CIARAN BATES

Light-welterweight - Born: Dublin: 5 November, 1985 - Irish light-welterweight runner-up 2007 (John Joe Joyce)
2014
June 5 Mihaly Szalontai, Belfast RSF 1
Sep 12 Miklos Szilagyi, Dublin RSF 1
Nov 1 Lewis O'Mara, Downpatrick RSF 2
2015
May 1 Pepi Perov, Dublin PTS 4
June 13 Danail Stanoev, London RSF 3
FIGHTS: 5 WON: 5 DREW: 0 LOST: 0

TONY BATES

Light-welterweight - Born: Dublin, 28 February, 1988 - Based in Sydney
2011
July 29 Jason Mac Gura, Homebush PTS 4
Aug 28 Matt Bune, Hurstville RSF 3
Oct 15 Troy Glover, Campsie RSF 2
2012
Mar 2 Jake Moulden, Mansfield PTS 4
Apr 6 Matthew Seden, Campsie RSF 3
July 13 Manopnoi Singmanasak, Campsie RSF 3
2013
Feb 23 Kurt Finlayson, Caloundra T-DRAW 1
June 13 Sapapetch Sor Sakaorat, Campsie RSF 2
Aug 30 EakKhunphol Mor Krungthepthonburi, Hurstville KO 3
2014
Mar 15 Eakkreenkrai Mor Krungthepthonburi, Kensington RSF 3

Dec 6 Gun Tinular, Hurstville RSF 1
2015
Inactive to date
FIGHTS: 11 WON: 10 DREW: 1 LOST: 0

ALEC BAZZA
Super-featherweight - Born: Belfast, 4 August, 1988
2013
Dec 7 Craig Hardy, London DREW 4
2014
Mar 8 Michael Devine, London L-PTS 4
Mar 21 Anthony Upton, Belfast L-RSF 4
May 10 James Fryers, Belfast L-PTS 4
June 14 Kofi Yates, Belfast L-PTS 4
Sep 6 George Thompson, Paisley L-PTS 4
Oct 25 Michael Joynson, Liverpool L-RSF 1
2015
June 13 Joe McCrory, London L-PTS 4
FIGHTS: 8 WON: 0 DREW: 1 LOST: 7

CASEY BLAIR
Light-middleweight - Born: Bangor, 18 November, 1979
2014
Mar 21 Billy Campbell, Belfast PTS 4
June 14 Liam Griffiths, Belfast PTS 4
Nov 1 Liam Griffiths, Downpatrick PTS 4
2015
Inactive to date
FIGHTS: 3 WON: 3 DREW: 0 LOST: 0

RYAN BURNETT
*Bantamweight - Born: Belfast, 21 May, 1992 - Agalarov Youth Memorial tournament
light-flyweight bronze medallist, Baku, 2009; Irish Under-21 light-flyweight champion,
2009; World Youth Championships light-flyweight silver medallist, Baku, 2010; Youth
Olympic Games light-flyweight gold medallist, Singapore, 2010.*
2013
May 24 Laszlo Nemesapati Jnr, Liverpool KO 1

June 28 Elemir Rafael, Belfast RSF 2
Oct 19 Reynaldo Cajina, Belfast RSF 2
Nov 16 Sergio Perez, Vratsa, Bulgaria PTS 6
2014
Nov 22 Valentin Marinov, Belfast RSF 1
Nov 29 Stefan Slavchev, London RSF 4
2015
Feb 27 Isaac Owusu, Sheffield RSF 2
Mar 27 Faycal Messaoudene, London PTS 6
Apr 11 Stephon McIntyre, New York KO 1
July 4 Csaba Kovacs, Dublin RSF 2
FIGHTS: 10 WON: 10 DREW: 0 LOST: 0

DEAN BYRNE
Welterweight - Born: Dublin, 11 September, 1984 - Based in Sydney until late 2007, then Los Angeles, now London
2006
Feb 18 Ronie Oyan, South Windsor RSF 2
May 12 Robert Oyan, Sydney PTS 6
Aug 4 Robert Oyan, Sydney PTS 6
Oct 21 Arnel Porras, Sydney T-PTS 5
(For vacant New South Wales light-welterweight title)
2007
Mar 9 Chris McCullen, Brisbane PTS 10
(Australian light-welterweight title challenge)
May 27 Brad Crookey, Sydney PTS 10
(Australian light-welterweight title defence)
2008
May 23 Michaelangelo Lynks, Montebello, California RSF 1
Aug 2 Daniel Gonzalez, Tacoma, Washington PTS 6
Sep 19 Geoffrey Spruiell, Woodland Hills, California KO 2
Dec 20 Francisco Rios Gil, Los Angeles RSF 4
2009
May 1 Jose Reynoso, Las Vegas PTS 8
2010
May 14 Justo Sanchez, Santa Ynez RSF 5
Aug 7 Konstantins Sakara, Dublin RSF 4

Dec 10 Sergejs Volodins, Dublin PTS 6
2011
Oct 21 Michael Frontin, London PTS 8
Oct 28 Frank Haroche Horta, Manchester L-RTD 8
2012
Apr 28 Terry Holmes, London L-PTS 6
Sep 15 Kevin McCauley, London PTS 4
Dec 8 Carson Jones, London DREW 8
2013
July 5 Danny Little, London PTS 6
2014
Feb 1 Roman Belaev, Monte Carlo L-PTS 12
(For vacant WBA Continental welterweight title)
Apr 5 Mark Douglas, London L-PTS 3
(Quarter-final of Prizefighter tournament)
2015
May 16 William Warburton, London DREW 4
June 27 David Avanesyan, Blackpool L-RSF 6
FIGHTS: 24 WON: 17 DREW: 2 LOST: 5

ANTHONY CACACE

Lightweight - Born: Belfast, 2 February, 1989 - Four Nations Junior Championships lightweight gold medallist, Liverpool, 2006; Dan Pozniak Junior Cup gold medallist, Vilnius, 2007; Irish Under-19 lightweight champion 2007 (Jamie Kavanagh); Ulster lightweight champion 2008 (Stephen Donnelly); Irish lightweight runner-up 2008 (Ross Hickey); Arfura Games lightweight bronze medallist, Darwin, 2009; Ulster lightweight champion 2009 (Eamon Finnegan)
2012
Feb 25 Ben Wager, Belfast RSF 1
Apr 7 Kristian Laight, Newark, Nottingham PTS 4
July 21 Mickey Coveney, Belfast RSF 6
Sep 7 Aivaras Balsys, London PTS 8
Nov 3 Mickey Coveney, Dublin KO 1
(For vacant Irish super-featherweight title)
Dec 8 Youssef Al Hamidi, Edinburgh PTS 4
2013
Mar 9 Zsolt Nagy, Dundalk PTS 6

Oct 12 Osnel Charles, Philadelphia PTS 4
2014
Sep 6 Dawid Knade, Belfast RSF 2
Dec 6 Simas Volosinas, Liverpool PTS 6
2015
Feb 22 Santiago Bustos, Belfast PTS 8
June 14 Karoly Lakatos, Budapest RSF 3
FIGHTS: 12 WON: 12 DREW: 0 LOST: 0

CONALL CARMICHAEL
Cruiserweight - Born: Belfast, 1 April, 1979 - Irish middleweight champion 1999 (Ian Tims); Irish middleweight runner-up 2001 (Kenny Egan); Irish light-heavyweight runner-up 2003 (Kenny Egan)
2012
Apr 14 Moses Matovu, Belfast PTS 4
Apr 27 Paul Morris, Belfast PTS 4
Dec 1 Darren Corbett, Belfast RSF 1
2013
Apr 27 Courtney Owen, Belfast RTD 4
May 18 Hari Miles, London L-PTS 3
(Quarter-final of Prizefighter tournament)
2014
June 20 Moses Matovu, Belfast PTS 4
FIGHTS: 6 WON: 5 DREW: 0 LOST: 1

JONATHAN 'Jono' CARROLL
Lightweight - Born: Dublin, 12 April, 1992
2012
Dec 16 Matthew Seden, Perth PTS 4
2013
Dec 7 Pornchai Sithpajuk, Madeley KO 2
2014
Nov 15 Declan Geraghty, Dublin DSQ 4
Dec 6 Stephen Foster, London PTS 3
(Quarter-final of Prizefighter tournament)
Dec 6 Gary Buckland, London PTS 3
(Semi-final of Prizefighter tournament)

Dec 6 Michael Devine, London PTS 3
(Final of Prizefighter tournament)
2015
Apr 11 Carlos Perez, Leeds PTS 6
FIGHTS: 7 WON: 7 DREW: 0 LOST: 0

STEPHEN CARROLL
Lightweight - Born: Dublin, 18 May, 1992
2015
Feb 20 Ladislav Nemeth, Dublin PTS 4
FIGHTS: 1 WON: 1 DREW: 0 LOST: 0

WILLIE CASEY
Super-bantamweight - Born: Limerick, 20 December, 1981
2008
Oct 26 Carlos De Jesus, Killarney RSF 2
2009
Oct 24 Stoyan Serbezov, Dublin PTS 6
Nov 14 Michael O'Gara, Limerick RSF 6
2010
Feb 13 Fernando Guevara, Dublin RSF 1
Apr 8 Tyson Cave, Toronto RSF 8
May 29 Mark Moran, London RSF 3
(Quarter-final of Prizefighter tournament)
May 29 Josh Wale, London PTS 3
(Semi-final of Prizefighter tournament)
May 29 Paul McElhinney, London PTS 3
(Final of Prizefighter tournament)
June 26 Faycal Messaoudene, Cork RSF 5
Aug 7 Emiliano Salvani, Dublin PTS 8
Nov 6 Paul Hyland, Limerick RSF 4
(For vacant European super-bantamweight title)
2011
Mar 19 Guillermo Rigondeaux, Dublin L-RSF 1
(Interim WBA super-bantamweight title challenge)
Sep 17 Daniel Kodjo Sassou, Belfast RSF 8
2012

Feb 25 David Kanalas, Belfast RSF 1
Apr 21 Andreas Evensen, Frederikshavn, Denmark L-PTS 12
(For vacant WBA International featherweight title)
July 16 Jason Booth, Sunderland PTS 12
(For vacant WBO Inter-Continental super-bantamweight title)
2013
Oct 19 Marco McCullough, Belfast L-RSF 9
(For vacant Irish featherweight title)
2014
June 20 Krzysztof Rogowski, Belfast PTS 6
Sep 14 George Gachechiladze, Belfast PTS 6
2015
Inactive to date
FIGHTS: 19 WON: 16 DREW: 0 LOST: 3

STEVE COLLINS Jnr
Cruiserweight - Born: Dublin, 27 March, 1990
2013
July 12 Tommy Tolan, Dundalk PTS 4
July 20 Paul Morris, London PTS 4
Sep 20 Rolandas Cesna, London PTS 4
2014
Feb 15 Tommy Gifford, London DREW 4
Nov 29 Mareks Kovalevskis, London PTS 4
2015
Feb 20 Viktor Szalai, Dublin RSF 2
FIGHTS: 6 WON: 5 DREW: 1 LOST: 0

JAMIE CONLAN
Super-flyweight - Born: Belfast, 11 October, 1986 - Four Nations Junior Championships light-flyweight gold medallist, Liverpool, 2003; Four Nations Championships light-flyweight silver medallist, Glasgow, 2004; Irish Under-21 flyweight champion 2006 (Gary McDonagh); Ulster flyweight champion 2008 (Ruairi Dalton); Ulster flyweight runner-up 2009 (conceded walkover to his brother, Michael)
2009
Nov 6 Anwar Alfadi, Belfast PTS 4
2010

Feb 13 Itsko Vaselinov, Dublin RSF 5
June 11 Delroy Spencer, Belfast PTS 4
Sep 18 Hyusein Hyuseinov, Belfast RSF 3
Dec 3 Francis Croes, Belfast RTD 3
2011
May 13 Kyle King, Gillingham KO 3
June 25 Delroy Spencer, Craigavon PTS 6
2012
Jan 21 Elemir Rafael, Liverpool PTS 6
2013
Feb 9 Mike Robinson, Belfast RSF 10
Oct 19 Walter Rojas, Belfast RSF 1
2014
Apr 4 Benjamin Smoes, Belfast RSF 7
(For vacant WBO European super flyweight title)
June 20 Gabor Molnar, Belfast RSF 3
(WBO European super flyweight title defence)
Sep 6 Jose Estrella, Belfast PTS 10
(For vacant WBO Inter-Continental super-flyweight title)
2015
July 4 Junior Granados, Dublin PTS 10
(WBO Inter-Continental super-flyweight title defence)
FIGHTS: 14 WON: 14 DREW: 0 LOST: 0

DARREN CRUISE

Light-heavyweight - Born: Castlerea, 26 January, 1990 - European Schoolboys Championships silver medallist, Siofok, 2004; Irish Under-19 super-heavyweight champion 2008 (John Stokes)
2010
Aug 7 James Tucker, Dublin PTS 4
Nov 20 Zahir Mutafchiev, Castlebar PTS 4
2011
Jan 30 Mickey Doherty, Dublin PTS 4
Aug 12 Lee Murtagh, Castlebar L-PTS 4
2012
May 5 JJ McDonagh, Belfast L-PTS 3
(Quarter-final of Prizefighter tournament)

Aug 17 John Hutchinson, Castlebar L-PTS 6
2013
Inactive
2014
Feb 15 Robbie Long, Dublin NO-CON 2
Oct 4 Harry Matthews, Belfast PTS 4
Nov 22 Damian Taggart, Belfast PTS 4
2015
Feb 7 Iain Jackson, Belfast PTS 4
FIGHTS: 10 WON: 6 DREW: 0 NO-CON: 1 LOST: 3

CONRAD CUMMINGS
Middleweight - Born: Coalisland, 24 May, 1991
2014
Feb 22 Andrejs Loginovs, London PTS 4
Apr 4 Zahari Mutafchiev, Belfast RSF 3
June 20 Lajos Munkacsi, Belfast RSF 2
Sep 6 Robert Talarek, Belfast PTS 6
Nov 29 Norbert Szekeres, Frederiksberg, Denmark PTS 6
2015
Feb 28 Roberto Palenzuela, Belfast PTS 6
FIGHTS: 6 WON: 6 DREW: 0 LOST: 0

TJ (TERRY) DOHENY
Super-bantamweight - Born: Portlaoise, 2 November, 1986 - Based in Sydney - Four Nations Junior Championships flyweight gold medallist, Liverpool 2003; Irish Junior flyweight champion 2003 (Barry McCafferty); Six Nations Junior Tournament flyweight gold medallist, Rome, 2004; Four Nations Junior Championships, flyweight silver medallist, Aberavon, 2004; Irish flyweight runner-up 2006 (Conor Ahern); Irish bantamweight runner-up 2008 (John Joe Nevin)
2012
Apr 27 Pichit Sithkruwin, Hurtsville RSF 1
June 22 Chris Potter, Hurstville KO 1
Sep 14 Robert Oyan, Brisbane PTS 6
2013
Feb 22 Kongfah Signwancha, Hurstville RSF 3
Aug 17 James Mokoginta, Sawtell KO 9

(For vacant Pan-Asian super bantamweight title)
Dec 13 Dianever Orcales, Homebush PTS 12
(Pan-Asian super bantamweight title defence)
2014
Mar 15 Kaenpetch Manoprungroj, Kensington KO 3
(Pan-Asian super bantamweight title defence)
Sep 19 Roman Canto, Denham House RSF 9
(Pan-Asian super bantamweight title defence)
Nov 15 Egy Rozten, Moore Park RTD 3
2015
Feb 20 Khunkhiri Wor Wisaruth, Hurstville PTS 8
May 15 Marco Demecillo, Punchbowl PTS 12
(Pan-Asian super bantamweight title defence)
July 4 Mongkolchai Lookmuangkanch, Punchbowl RSF 1
FIGHTS: 12 WON: 12 DREW: 0 LOST: 0

ALAN DONNELLAN

Light-middleweight - Born: Athenry, 28 November, 1987
2010
May 15 Ryan Clark, Limerick PTS 4
Aug 7 Lester Walsh, Dublin PTS 4
Nov 6 Zahari Mutafchiev, Limerick PTS 4
2011
Inactive
2012
Mar 31 Vladimir Tazik, Seilles, Belgium RSF 1
July 21 Ciaran Healy, Belfast L-PTS 4
Oct 13 Marijan Markovic, Andenne, Belgium RSF 2
2013
May 11 Antoine Manuel, Saint Servais, Belgium L-PTS 4
Nov 2 Vitalie Mirza, Dublin L-PTS 4
2014
Oct 4 Iain Jackson, Belfast PTS 4
2015
Feb 7 Damian Taggart, Belfast PTS 4
May 2 Jozsef Racz, Derry PTS 4
FIGHTS: 11 WON: 8 DREW: 0 LOST: 3

ANTHONY FITZGERALD
Middleweight - Born: Dublin, 8 June, 1985
2008
Oct 26 Kirill Pshonko, Killarney PTS 4
2009
Jan 30 Robert Long, Dublin L-PTS 6
Mar 21 Janis Chernouskis, Dublin L-RSF 3
May 23 Denis Sirjatovs, Castlebar KO 2
July 25 Peter Cannon, Dublin RSF 3
Sep 26 Tadas Jonkus, Dublin PTS 4
Oct 24 Robert Long, Dublin PTS 8
Dec 5 Matt Scriven, Dublin PTS 8
2010
Feb 13 Ciaran Healy, Dublin PTS 10
(For vacant Irish super-middleweight title)
Aug 7 Phillip Townley, Dublin PTS 6
Sep 11 Robert Long, Dublin PTS 10
(Irish super-middleweight title defence)
Nov 6 Lee Murtagh, Limerick NO-CON 2
(Irish super-middleweight title defence)
Dec 10 Kevin Hammond, Dublin PTS 12
(For vacant WBF Inter-Continental middleweight title)
2011
Jan 30 Lee Murtagh, Dublin RSF 7
(Irish super-middleweight title defence)
Mar 19 Affif Belghecham, Dublin RSF 4
(For vacant EBA middleweight title)
2012
Feb 25 Alexey Ribchev, Hove PTS 8
May 5 Eamonn O'Kane, Belfast L-PTS 3
(Quarter-final of Prizefighter tournament)
2013
Feb 9 Andy Lee, Belfast L-PTS 10
Mar 9 Lazlo Haaz, Dundalk PTS 6
July 12 Eamonn O'Kane, Dundalk L-PTS 10
(For vacant Irish middleweight title)
Dec 14 Hassan N'Dam N'Jikam, Barcelona L-PTS 10

2014
June 14 Dan Blackwell, Belfast PTS 6
July 12 Harry Matthews, Birmingham PTS 4
Nov 15 Gary O'Sullivan, Dublin L-RSF 1
2015
Mar 28 John Brennan, Preston PTS 6
July 4 Kieron Gray, Dublin PTS 8
FIGHTS: 26 WON: 18 DREW: 0 NO-CON: 1 LOST: 7

CARL FRAMPTON

Super-bantamweight - Born: Belfast, 21 February, 1987 - European Schoolboys Championships silver medallist, Rome, 2003; Four Nations Junior Championships flyweight gold medallist, Aberavon, 2004; Irish flyweight champion 2005 (Derek Thorpe); Four Nations Championships flyweight bronze medallist, Liverpool, 2005; Commonwealth Championships flyweight bronze medallist, Glasgow, 2005; IABA multi-nations tournament flyweight gold medallist, Ballybunion, 2005; Gee-Bee tournament flyweight silver medallist, Helsinki, 2006; European Union Championships featherweight silver medallist, Dublin, 2007; Ulster featherweight champion 2008 (Eamon Finnegan); Irish featherweight champion 2009 (David Oliver Joyce); Ahmet Comert tournament featherweight gold medallist, Istanbul, 2009; Grand Prix tournament featherweight bronze medallist, Usti, 2009
2009
June 12 Sandor Szinavel, Liverpool RSF 2
Sep 4 Yannis Lakrout, Middlesbrough PTS 4
Nov 6 Ignac Kassai, Magherafelt RSF 3
2010
Feb 12 Yoan Boyeaux, London PTS 4
Mar 5 Istvan Szabo, Huddersfield RSF 1
June 11 Ian Bailey, Belfast PTS 6
Sep 18 Yuriy Voronin, Belfast RSF 3
Dec 3 Gavin Reid, Belfast RSF 2
(For vacant Celtic super-bantamweight title)
2011
Mar 5 Oscar Chacin, Huddersfield RSF 4
June 4 Robbie Turley, Cardiff PTS 10
(Celtic super-bantamweight title defence)
Sep 10 Mark Quon, Belfast RSF 4

(For vacant Commonwealth super-bantamweight title)
2012
Jan 28 Kris Hughes, London RSF 7
(Commonwealth super-bantamweight title defence)
Mar 17 Prosper Ankrah, Sheffied RSF 2
(Commonwealth super-bantamweight title defence)
May 26 Raul Hirales, Nottingham PTS 12
(For vacant IBF Inter-Continental super-bantamweight title)
Sep 22 Steve Molitor, Belfast RSF 6
(Commonwealth and IBF Inter-Continental super-bantamweight titles)
2013
Feb 9 Kiko Martinez, Belfast RSF 9
(European super-bantamweight title challenge)
Oct 19 Jeremy Parodi, Belfast KO 6
(European super-bantamweight title defence)
2014
Apr 4 Hugo Fidel Cazares, Belfast KO 2
Sep 6 Kiko Martinez, Belfast PTS 12
(IBF super-bantamweight title challenge)
2015
Feb 28 Chris Avalos, Belfast RSF 5
(IBF super-bantamweight title defence)
FIGHTS: 20 WON: 20 DREW: 0 LOST: 0

JAMES FRYERS
Light-welterweight - Born: Belfast, 21 October, 1992 - HSK Cadet Box Cup
bantamweight gold medallist, Hillerod, 2007; Irish Youth featherweight
champion 2009 (John O'Neill); Irish featherweight runner-up 2010 (Tyrone
McCullough); Ulster lightweight champion 2012 (James Tennyson, staged
in December 2011)
2012
Nov 27 Kristian Laight, London PTS 4
2013
Feb 9 Billy Smith, Belfast PTS 4
2014
Mar 15 Michael Mooney, Reading PTS 4
May 10 Alec Bazza, Belfast PTS 4

Oct 4 Lewis O'Mara, Belfast PTS 4
Nov 22 Sandor Horvath, Belfast RSF 2
2015
Mar 28 Mark Morris, Belfast RTD 5
(For vacant Boxing Union of Ireland Celtic Nations lightweight title)
May 2 Zoltan Horvath, Derry PTS 4
June 6 Sergejs Logins, Belfast RSF 1
FIGHTS: 9 WON: 9 DREW: 0 LOST: 0

PADDY GALLAGHER

Welterweight - Born: Belfast, 9 April, 1989 - Ulster light-welterweight runner-up 2008 (Paddy Murphy); Ulster light-welterweight runner-up 2009 (Stephen Donnelly); Irish Under-21 light-welterweight champion (Sonny Upton); Commonwealth Games welterweight gold medallist, New Delhi, 2010
2012
Sep 22 William Warburton, Belfast PTS 4
Nov 27 Andrew Patterson, London RSF 1
2013
Sep 14 Jozsef Garai, Belfast RSF 1
Nov 18 Aleksas Vaseris, London RSF 1
2014
Apr 5 Erick Ochieng, London L-PTS 3
(Quarter-final of Prizefighter tournament; Gallagher was reinstated when Ochieng was ruled unfit to fight again on the night)
Apr 5 Mark Douglas, London RSF 1
(Semi-final of Prizefighter tournament)
Apr 5 Johnny Coyle, London L-PTS 3
(Final of Prizefighter tournament)
Nov 22 Liam Griffiths, Belfast PTS 4
2015
Feb 28 Miguel Aguilar, Belfast PTS 4
FIGHTS: 9 WON: 7 DREW: 0 LOST: 2

DECLAN GERAGHTY

Lightweight - Born: Dublin, 11 May, 1990 - Irish cadet 46k champion 2007 (Liam McGuinness); Irish Under-19 flyweight champion 2008 (Gary Molloy); Irish flyweight champion 2009 (Conor Ahern); Grand Prix flyweight bronze medallist, Usti, 2009;

Gee-Bee tournament flyweight silver medallist, Helsinki, 2010; Tammer tournament flyweight bronze medallist, Tampere, 2010; Irish Under-23 featherweight champion 2012 (John Meli); Irish bantamweight champion 2013 (Gary McKenna)
2014
May 9 Sid Razak, Sheffield PTS 6
June 14 Renato Toth, Belfast RSF 1
July 12 Youssef Al Hamidi, Birmingham PTS 4
July 26 Kristian Laight, Manchester PTS 4
Sep 6 Simas Volosinas, Birmingham PTS 4
Sep 12 Ignac Kassai, Dublin PTS 4
Nov 15 Jono Carroll, Dublin L-DSQ 4
2015
Feb 20 Ibrar Riyaz, Birmingham PTS 6
July 4 Dinars Skripkins, Dublin RSF 3
FIGHTS: 9 WON: 8 DREW: 0 LOST: 1

RAY GINLEY
Light-heavyweight - Born: Belfast, 16 June, 1993 - European Schoolboy Championships bronze medallist, Portsmouth, 2007
2012
Feb 25 Stuart Maddox, Belfast RSF 1
Apr 7 James Tucker, Newark PTS 4
July 21 Jody Meikle, Belfast PTS 4
Nov 3 John Waldron, Dublin RSF 3
2013
Oct 12 Marlin Washington, Philadelphia RSF 3
2014
Oct 11 Quincy Miner, Winston-Salem RSF 2
2015
Inactive to date
FIGHTS: 6 WON: 6 DREW: 0 LOST: 0

GERARD HEALY
Light-middleweight - Born: Belfast, 29 September, 1983
2011
May 28 Aaron Fox, Belfast PTS 4
Sep 17 Dee Walsh, Belfast L-PTS 4

Oct 15 Liam Smith, Liverpool L-KO 1
2012
Feb 25 Oleksiy Chukov, Belfast PTS 4
Oct 13 William Warburton, Belfast L-PTS 4
Dec 1 John Hutchinson, Belfast L-PTS 4
2013
May 14 John Hutchinson, Belfast T-DRAW 3
2014
Oct 4 Liam Griffiths, Belfast PTS 4
Nov 22 Yanko Marinov, Belfast PTS 4
2015
June 6 Piotr Tomaszek, Belfast PTS 4
FIGHTS: 10 WON: 5 DREW: 1 LOST: 4

JOE HILLERBY
Middleweight - Born: Belfast, 19 December, 1987
2010
Oct 16 Gavin Putney, Northampton RSF 1
2011
Jan 21 Ryan Clark, London PTS 4
May 7 Bheki Moyo, London PTS 4
July 31 Iain Jackson, Luton PTS 4
Sep 17 Tommy Tolan, Belfast PTS 4
2012
Feb 25 Aleksandrs Radjuks, Belfast RSF 1
Apr 14 Willie Thompson, Belfast PTS 10
(For vacant Northern Irish light-middleweight title)
July 21 Lee Murtagh, Belfast L-RTD 6
(For vacant Irish super-middleweight title)
Nov 3 Robert Long, Dublin PTS 8
(For vacant Celtic Warrior light-middleweight title)
Dec 1 Phill Fury, Belfast L-PTS 8
2013
Sep 14 Vaclav Polak, Belfast PTS 6
2014
Inactive
2015

Mar 28 Damien Taggart, Belfast PTS 4
Apr 4 Hosea Burton, Newcastle L-RSF 4
FIGHTS: 13 WON: 10 DREW: 0 LOST: 3

DENNIS HOGAN
Middleweight - Born: Kilcullen, 1 March 1985 - Based in Brisbane
2011
Apr 1 Marlon Toby, Fortitude Valley RTD 2
May 13 Ben Dyer, Fortitude Valley RSF 3
June 17 Edmund Eramiha, Altona North DREW 5
Aug 6 Moses Ioelu, Fortitude Valley PTS 4
Sep 30 Tass Tsitsiras, Fortitude Valley PTS 4
Oct 21 Glen Fitzpatrick, Red Hill RSF 4
(For vacant Queensland super-middleweight title)
Oct 29 Robert Clarke, Hervey Bay PTS 4
2012
Feb 24 David Galvin, Hurstville PTS 6
Mar 23 Nathan Carroll, Mansfield RSF 7
(For vacant Queensland middleweight title)
June 22 Aswin Cabuy, Hurstville PTS 6
July 28 Arnel Tinampay, Broadbeach PTS 8
Sep 14 Singdet Sithsaithong, Brisbane PTS 10
2013
June 15 Khomkeaw Sithsaithong, Fortitude Valley RSF 2
Aug 3 Petchsuriya Looksaikongdin, Fortitude Valley KO 1
Sep 20 Gavin Prunty, Brisbane PTS 8
(For vacant Celtic light-middleweight title)
Nov 7 Nathan Carroll, Brisbane PTS 10
(Australian middleweight title challenge)
Dec 7 Robbie Bryant, Madeley PTS 10
(Australian middleweight title defence)
2014
Mar 16 Leroy Brown, Brisbane PTS 10
(Australian middleweight title defence)
May 21 David Galvin, Eatons Hill KO 6
July 6 Steve Moxon, Altona North PTS 12
Nov 13 Jose Miguel Rodriguez Berrio, New Yoek DSQ 3

2015
Apr 17 Tyrone Brunson, Hinckley, Minnesota PTS 10
(For vacant WBA North American light-middleweight title)
June 26 Kenny Abril, Niagara Falls PTS 10
(WBA North American light-middleweight title defence)
FIGHTS: 23 WON: 22 DREW: 1 LOST: 0

JOHN HUTCHINSON
Middleweight - Born: Buncrana, 28 May, 1986
2012
Aug 17 Darren Cruise, Castlebar PTS 4
Dec 1 Gerard Healy, Belfast PTS 4
2013
Feb 24 Mantas Bakstinas, Birmingham RSF 1
May 14 Gerard Healy, Belfast T-DRAW 3
July 27 Robert Brando-Hunt, Boston T-DRAW 2
Sep 14 Deividas Sajauka,Belfast PTS 4
Oct 26 Robert Brando-Hunt, Canton, Massachusetts PTS 4
2014
Mar 15 Peter McDonagh, Reading L-PTS 10
(For vacant Irish light-middleweight title)
Sep 6 Danny Shannon, Birmingham L-PTS 4
2015
Inactive to date
FIGHTS: 9 WON: 5 DREW: 2 LOST: 2

PATRICK HYLAND
Featherweight - Born: Dublin, 16 September, 1983
2004
Sep 24 Dean Ward, Dublin PTS 4
2005
Feb 13 Steve Gethin, Brentwood PTS 4
June 4 Peter Buckley, Dublin PTS 4
Sep 17 Imrich Parlagi, Dublin PTS 4
Nov 18 Craig Morgan, Dagenham PTS 4
2006
Mar 11 Tibor Besze, Dublin KO 1

June 23 Lajos Beller, Dublin RSF 1
July 14 Roman Rafael, Dublin RSF 1
2008
Jan 26 Gheorghe Ghiompirica, Cork PTS 8
Mar 15 Mike Dobbs, Boston RSF 1
Apr 19 Paul Griffin, Dublin RSF 3
(For vacant Irish featherweight title)
May 31 Robin Deakin, Belfast RSF 5
July 5 Geoffrey Munika, Dublin PTS 8
Sep 6 John Gicharu, Dublin RSF 1
Oct 4 Elvis Luciano Martinez, Philadelphia RSF 2
2009
Mar 14 Carlos Guevara, Dorchester, Massachusetts PTS 10
(For vacant IBA Inter-continental super-featherweight title)
July 25 Abdu Tebazalwa, Dublin PTS 12
(For vacant IBF International featherweight title)
Sep 26 Manuel Sequera, Dublin RSF 6
2010
Feb 13 Mickey Coveney, Dublin RSF 7
(Irish featherweight title defence)
Oct 2 Yordan Vasilev, Letterkenny PTS 6
Nov 20 Saut Laze, Castlebar PTS 8
2011
Apr 30 Daniel Kodjo Sassou, London PTS 6
June 25 Phillippe Fernois, Dublin PTS 12
(For vacant WBF featherweight title)
Aug 12 Fabrizio Trotta, Castlebar RSF 4
2012
Jan 28 Emmanuel Lucero, Atlantic City PTS 8
May 12 Frankie Archuleta, Poughkeepsie RSF 4
Aug 8 Carlos Fulgencio, New York PTS 8
Dec 8 Javier Fortuna, Las Vegas L-PTS 12
(For vacant interim WBA super-featherweight title)
2013
Inactive
2014
July 23 Noel Echevarria, New York RSF 4

Nov 15 Oszkar Fiko, Dublin PTS 8
2015
Mar 14 Manuel de los Reyes Herrera, New York Ko 4
FIGHTS: 31 WON: 30 DREW: 0 LOST: 1

PAUL HYLAND Jnr
Lightweight - Born; Belfast, 17 June, 1990
2014
May 10 Zoltan Horvath, Belfast PTS 4
June 6 Joe Beedon, Belfast PTS 4
Oct 4 Andy Harris, Belfast PTS 4
Nov 22 Pep1 Pirov, Belfast PTS 4
2015
Feb 7 Yordan Vasilev, Belfast PTS 6
Mar 28 Imre Nagy, Belfast RSF 5
June 6 Ivans Levickis, Belfast RSF 4
FIGHTS: 7 WON: 7 DREW: 0 LOST: O

JAMIE KAVANAGH
Light-welterweight - Born: Dublin, 28 May, 1990 - Based in Los Angeles - Irish Under-21 lightweight runner-up 2007 (Anthony Cacace); World Junior Championships light-welterweight silver medallist, Gaudalajara, 2008; Irish Under-19 light-welterweight champion 2008 (Patrick Ward); Irish light-welterweight runner-up 2008 (John Joe Joyce)
2010
May 15 William Ware, New York RSF 2
June 24 Luis Sanchez, Los Angeles PTS 4
Sep 30 Ricardo Malfavon, Los Angeles PTS 4
Dec 11 Jacob Thornton, Las Vegas RSF 1
2011
Feb 24 Ramon Flores, Los Angeles PTS 6
Apr 16 Sid Razak, Manchester PTS 6
June 23 John Willoughby, Los Angeles RSF 3
July 22 Marcos Herrera, Las Vegas PTS 6
Dec 10 Ramesis Gil, Washington DREW 6
2012
Mar 24 Cesar Cisneros, Houston RSF 5

May 26 Jorge Ibarra, Cancun, Mexico RSF 2
July 14 Paul Velarde, Las Vegas PTS 8
Nov 3 Ramon Valadez, Anaheim PTS 8
2013
Mar 8 Salvador Garcia, Indion T-PTS 5
June 8 Adolfo Landeros, Carson RSF 4
Aug 9 Antonio Meza, Indio KO 1
Dec 14 Daniel Ruiz, Playa del Carmen, Mexico L-RSF 6
2014
Mar 17 Andres Navarro, Boston PTS 8
June 5 Michael Clark, Boston RSF 5
2015
Mar 20 Miguel Zamudio, Indio RTD 5
FIGHTS: 20 WON: 18 DREW: 1 LOST: 1

LUKE KEELER
Middleweight - Born: Dublin, 27 April, 1987
2013
May 3 Renato Toth, Dublin RTD 1
July 12 Tommy Tolan, Dundalk PTS 4
Nov 2 Janos Lakatos, Dublin RSF 1
2014
Feb 15 Edgars Sniedze, Dublin RSF 2
June 6 Festim Lama, Belfast RSF 4
Sep 12 Laszlo Kovacs, Dublin PTS 6
Nov 15 Gary Boulden, Dublin RSF 1
2015
Feb 14 Luke Crowcroft, Blackpool PTS 3
(Quarter-final of Prizefighter tournament)
Feb 14 Tom Doran, Blackpool L-PTS 3
(Semi-final of Prizefighter tournament)
FIGHTS: 9 WON: 8 DREW: 0 LOST: 1

ANDY LEE
Middleweight - Born: London, 11 June, 1984 - World Junior Championships light-middleweight silver medallist, Santiago de Cuba, 2002; Irish middleweight champion 2003 (Eamonn O'Kane); Gee-Bee tournament middleweight silver medallist, Helsinki,

2003; Four Nations Championships middleweight gold medallist, Cardiff, 2003; Irish middleweight champion 2004 (Patrick Murray); European Union Championships middleweight silver medallist, Madrid, 2004; European Championships middleweight bronze medallist, Pula, 2004; Irish middleweight champion 2005 (Eamonn O'Kane); Four Nations Championships middleweight gold medallist, Liverpool, 2005

2006

Mar 10 Anthony Cannon, Detroit PTS 6

Apr 22 Wassim Khalil, Mannheim RSF 5

June 16 Rodney Freeman, Memphis RSF 1

Aug 10 Carl Cockerham, Las Vegas PTS 6

Sep 14 Jess Salway, Las Vegas KO 1

Nov 11 Dennis Sharpe, New York PTS 6

2007

Jan 25 Arturo Ortega, Las Vegas RSF 6

Mar 16 Carl Daniels, New York KO 3

May 18 Clinton Bonds, Memphis RSF 1

July 7 Thomas Hengstberger, Cologne KO 2

Aug 25 Ciaran Healy, Dublin RTD 4

Oct 2 James Morrow, Chicago RSF 1

Nov 15 Marcus Thomas, Plymouth, Michigan KO 1

Dec 15 Jason McKay, Dublin RTD 6

2008

Feb 2 Alejandro Gustavo Falliga, Limerick KO 5

Mar 21 Brian Vera, Uncasville, Connecticut L-RSF 7

July 19 Willie Gibbs, Limerick RSF 10

2009

Mar 21 Alexander Sipos, Dublin PTS 10

June 20 Olegs Fedotovs, Gelsenkirchen, Germany PTS 6

Aug 21 Anthony Schuler, Hammond, Indiana RSF 8

Nov 14 Affif Belghecham, Limerick PTS 10

2010

May 15 Mamadou Thiam, Limerick RTD 2

July 30 James Cook, Miami, Oklahoma KO 5

Sep 17 Michael Walker, Chicago RSF 8

Oct 2 Troy Lowry, Hammond, Indiana RSF 4

2011

Mar 12 Craig McEwan, Mashantucket RSF 10

May 18 Alex Bunema, Rosemont PTS 10
(For vacant North American middleweight title)
Oct 1 Bryan Vera, Atlantic City PTS 10
2012
Mar 10 Saul Duran, Novi KO 2
(North American middleweight title defence)
June 16 Julio Cesar Chavez Jnr, El Paso L-RSF 7
(WBC middleweight title challenge)
2013
Feb 9 Anthony Fitzgerald, Belfast PTS 10
May 15 Darryl Cunningham, New York RSF 1
Nov 23 Ferenc Hafner, Manchestr RSF 2
2014
Apr 12 Frank Haroche Horta, Esbjerg, Denmark PTS 8
June 7 John Jackson, New York KO 5
Dec 13 Matt Korobov, Las Vegas RSF 6
(For vacant WBO middleweight title)
2015
Apr 11 Peter Quillin, New York DREW 12
FIGHTS: 37 WON: 34 DREW: 1 LOST: 2

MARTIN LINDSAY

Featherweight - Born: Belfast, 10 May, 1982 - Istvan Dobo Junior Tournament bantamweight gold medallist, Eger, 2000; Irish bantamweight champion 2002 (Damien McKenna); Irish bantamweight runner-up 2003 (Brian Gillen); Commonwealth Championships featherweight silver medallist, Kuala Lumpur, 2003; Irish featherweight champion 2004 (Eamonn Touhey)

2004
Dec 2 Dai Davies, London RSF 1
2005
Apr 24 Rakhim Mingaleev, London PTS 4
July 2 Henry Janes, Dundalk RSF 2
Sep 17 Peter Feher, Dublin PTS 4
2006
Apr 21 Chris Hooper, Belfast KO 1
Oct 13 Nikita Lukin, Port Talbot PTS 6
2007

Mar 30 Buster Dennis, Crawley PTS 6
July 14 Jose Silveira, Rama, Ontario PTS 6
Oct 27 Uriel Barrera, Rama, Ontario PTS 10
(For vacant IBF Youth featherweight title)
Dec 8 Edison Torres, Belfast PTS 8
2008
Jan 19 Jason Hayward, Rama, Ontario RSF 1
May 16 Marc Callaghan, Turin PTS 8
Sep 20 Derry Matthews, Sheffield KO 9
(British featherweight title eliminator)
2009
Apr 25 Paul Appleby, Belfast RSF 6
(British featherweight title challenge)
Nov 6 Alfred Tetteh, Magherafelt PTS 8
2010
Mar 19 Jamie Arthur, Leigh PTS 12
(British featherweight title defence)
Sep 11 Yauheni Kruhlik, Houghton-le-Spring PTS 6
Dec 15 John Simpson, Belfast L-PTS 12
(British featherweight title defence)
2011
Inactive
2012
Mar 23 Maurycy Gojko, London PTS 6
May 5 Mickey Coveney, Belfast RSF 4
Sep 22 Renald Garrido, Belfast PTS 8
2013
Feb 9 Lee Selby, Belfast L-PTS 12
(British and Commonwealth featherweight titles challenge)
2014
May 10 Krzysztof Rogowski, Belfast RSF 3
May 21 Josh Warrington, Leeds L-PTS 12
(Commonwealth featherweight title challenge, also for vacant British title)
FIGHTS: 24 WON: 21 DREW: 0 LOST: 3

ROBBIE LONG

Middleweight - Born: Dublin, 26 February, 1983 - Irish Under-21 middleweight

champion 2003 (Sean Shevlin)
2008
Sep 6 Florin Bogdan, Dublin PTS 4
Oct 26 Sandris Tomsons, Killarney RTD 3
2009
Jan 30 Anthony Fitzgerald, Dublin PTS 6
July 25 Deniss Sirjatovs, Dublin PTS 4
Oct 24 Anthony Fitzgerald, Dublin L-PTS 8
Sep 11 Anthony Fitzgerald, Dublin L-PTS 10
(Irish super-middleweight title challenge)
2010
Dec 10 Andrejs Suliko, Dublin PTS 4
2011
Jan 30 James Tucker, Dublin PTS 4
June 25 Gary O'Sullivan, Dublin L-RSF 1
(Irish middleweight title challenge)
2012
Nov 3 Joe Hillerby, Dublin L-PTS 8
(For vacant Celtic Warrior light-middleweight title)
2013
Inactive
2014
Feb 15 Darren Cruise, Dublin NO-CON 2
FIGHTS: 11 WON: 6 DREW: 0 NO-CON: 1 LOST: 4

MATTHEW MACKLIN
Middleweight - Born: Birmingham, 14 May, 1982 - Istvan Dobo Junior Tournament light-middleweight gold medallist, Eger, 2000; Italia Junior Cup light-middleweight silver medallist, Cagliari, 2000; English welterweight champion 2001 (Justin Turley); Acropolis Cup light-middleweight silver medallist, Athens, 2001
2001
Nov 17 Ram Singh, Glasgow RSF 1
Dec 15 Cristian Hodorogea London KO 1
2002
Feb 9 Dmitri Protkunas, Manchester RTD 3
Mar 11 David Kirk, Glasgow PTS 4
Apr 20 Ilia Spassov, Cardiff KO 3

June 1 Guy Alton, Manchester RSF 3
Sep 28 Leonti Voronchuk, Manchester RSF 5
2003
Feb 15 Ruslan Yakupov, London PTS 6
May 24 Paul Denton, London PTS 6
Nov 6 Andrew Facey, Dagenham L-PTS 10
2004
Feb 21 Dean Walker, Cardiff KO 1
Apr 24 Scott Dixon, Reading RTD 6
June 12 Ojay Abrahams, Manchester PTS 4
2005
May 14 Michael Monaghan, Dublin KO 5
(For vacant Irish middleweight title)
Aug 4 Leo Laudat, Atlantic City RSF 3
Oct 28 Anthony Little, Philadelphia RSF 2
Nov 26 Alexey Chirkov, Sheffield KO 1
2006
June 1 Marcin Piatkowski, Birmingham RSF 4
Sep 29 Jamie Moore, Manchester L-KO 10
(British light-middleweight title challenge)
2007
July 20 Anatoliy Udalov, Wolverhampton KO 1
Aug 26 Darren Rhodes, Dublin RSF 4
Oct 20 Alessandro Furlan, Dublin RSF 8
2008
Mar 22 Luis Ramon 'Yory Boy' Campas, Dublin PTS 10
Sep 6 Francis Cheka, Manchester PTS 10
Oct 31 Geard Ajetovic, Birmingham PTS 10
2009
Mar 14 Wayne Elcock, Birmingham RSF 3
(British middleweight title challenge)
Sep 25 Amin Asikainen, Manchester RSF 1
(For vacant European middleweight title)
Dec 5 Rafael Sosa Pintos, Dublin PTS 10
2010
Vacated European title on March 24
Sep 18 Shalva Jomardashvili, Birmingham RTD 6

(For vacant European middleweight title)
Dec 11 Ruben Varon, Liverpool PTS 12
(European middleweight title defence)
2011
June 25 Felix Sturm, Cologne L-PTS 12
(WBA middleweight title challenge)
2012
Mar 17 Sergio Martinez, New York L-RTD 11
Sep 15 Joachim Alcine, Las Vegas RSF 1
2013
June 28 Gennandy Golovkin, Mashantucket L-KO 3
(WBA middleweight title challenge)
Dec 7 Lamar Russ, Atlantic City PTS 10
2014
Sep 27 Jose Yebes, Kiel PTS 8
Nov 15 Jorge Sebastian Heiland, Dublin L-KO 10
2015
May 9 Sandor Micsko, Birmingham KO 2
FIGHTS: 38 WON: 32 DREW: 0 LOST: 6

EAMONN MAGEE Jnr
Light-welterweight - Born: Belfast, 7 April, 1993 - Died: Belfast, 30 May, 2015 - Son of former Commonwealth light-welterweight champion Eamonn Magee
2014
June 6 Zoltan Horvath, Belfast RSF 2
2015
Mar 14 Dinars Skripkins, Belfast RSF 1
FIGHTS: 2 WON: 2 DREW: 0 LOST: 0

DAVID MAGUIRE
Cruiserweight - Born: Dublin, 8 March, 1977
2014
Feb 15 Moses Matovu, Dublin PTS 4
Sep 6 Igoris Borucha, Birmingham PTS 4
Nov 15 Paul Morris, Dublin RSF 2
2015
Inactive to date

FIGHTS: 3 WON: 3 DREW: 0 LOST: 0

MOSES MATOVU
Cruiserweight - Born: Uganda, 20 September, 1976 - Based in Bangor
2004
May 13 Shane Johnston, San Diego DREW 4
May 28 Gilbert Zaragoza, Oroville, California L-PTS 4
June 24 Carlos Raul Ibarra, Chula Vista, California L-RSF 3
Oct 16 James Sundin, Salt Lake City L-PTS 6
Dec 28 Shane Johnston, El Cajon, California PTS 4
2005
Feb 25 Shawn Hawk, Boise, Idaho L-RSF 3
Apr 16 Dave Foley, Ogden, Utah PTS 4
May 27 Otis Griffin, Sacramento DREW 4
June 7 Curtis Jones, El Cajon, California DREW 4
June 11 Viktor Zynoviyev, Las Vegas L-PTS 6
July 14 Ramiro ReducindO, Las Vegas L-PTS 4
Sep 10 Valente Tinajero, Ogden, Utah L-PTS 6
Sep 30 Otis Griffin, Brooks, California L-PTS 6
2006
Jan 28 Pharaoh Turner, Manistee, Michigan L-PTS 6
Feb 10 Max Alexander, Philadelphia L-PTS 6
Apr 20 Billy Drywater, Worley, Idaho L-PTS 4
2007
Inactive
2008
Apr 19 Jonathan O'Brien, Dublin L-PTS 6
2009
Inactive
2010
Inactive
2011
Inactive
2012
Jan 28 Wadi Camacho, London L-PTS 4
Mar 2 Irv Pascal, London PTS 4
Apr 14 Conall Carmichael, Belfast L-PTS 4

Apr 27 Courtney Owen, Belfast PTS 4
June 2 Danny Price, Manchester L-PTS 6
June 30 Nathan Owens, Halifax L-PTS 4
July 21 Stephen Reynolds, Belfast L-PTS 4
Sep 21 Barry Connell, Glasgow L-PTS 4
Oct 22 Gary Cornish, Glasgow L-PTS 6
Nov 30 Chris Keane, Wolverhampton L-PTS 6
Dec 8 Louis Cuddy, Liverpool L-PTS 6
Dec 15 David Howe, Sheffield L-PTS 4
Dec 23 Paul Drago, Manchester L-PTS 4
2013
Feb 22 Kash Ali, Rotherham L-PTS 4
Mar 2 Paul Butlin, North Hykeham L-PTS 4
Mar 9 Davie Drummond, Dundee L-RSF 2
May 14 Hughie Fury, Belfast L-PTS 4
May 24 Wayne Adeniyi, Liverpool L-PTS 4
June 29 Micky Steeds, Grays DREW 4
July 21 Hughie Fury, Milton Keynes L-PTS 4
Sep 20 Simon Vallily, London L-PTS 4
Sep 27 China Clarke, Leeds L-PTS 4
Oct 5 AJ Carter, Watford L-PTS 4
Nov 14 Ben Ileyemi, London L-PTS 4
Dec 14 Andy Jones, Liverpool L-PTS 4
Dec 22 Louis Cuddy, Manchester L-PTS 4
2014
Feb 15 David Maguire, Dublin L-PTS 4
Feb 22 Hosea Burton, Hull L-PTS 4
Mar 2 David Allen, Sheffield L-PTS 4
Mar 14 Craig Kennedy, Newport L-PTS 8
Mar 24 Kevin Reynolds, Glasgow PTS 4
Apr 12 Eddie Chambers, London L-RSF 1
May 21 Simon Vallily, Leeds L-PTS 4
June 6 Kenneth Odeke, Belfast L-PTS 4
June 20 Conall Carmichael, Belfast L-PTS 4
Aug 1 Simon Barclay, Wolverhampton L-PTS 4
Sep 6 D.L. Jones, London L-PTS 4
Sep 13 Jack Massey, Manchester L-PTS 4

Sep 28 Karl Wheeler, Whitwick L-PTS 6
Oct 11 Jose Lopes, London L-PTS 4
Nov 1 Sean Turner, Downpatrick L-PTS 4
Nov 14 Russ Henshaw, Sheffield L-RSF 2
2015
Jan 31 Isaac Chamberlain, London L-PTS 4
Feb 13 Shane Steward, Norwich L-PTS 4
Mar 14 Louie Darlin, London L-PTS 4
Mar 21 David Abraham, London L-PTS 4
May 1 Niall Kennedy, Dublin L-PTS 4
May 15 Russ Henshaw, Sheffield L-RSF 3
June 26 Tony Cruise, Barnsley L-PTS 6
July 4 Biola Kudus, London L-PTS 4
FIGHTS: 59 WON: 5 DREW: 4 LOST: 58

TOMMY McCARTHY

Heavyweight - Born: Belfast, 4 November, 1990 - European Schoolboys Championships 68k bronze medallist, Tver, 2005; HSK Junior Box Cup light-heavyweight gold medallist, Hillerod, 2007; Irish Cadet middleweight champion 2007 (Michael McDonagh); HSK Junior Box Cup light-heavyweight gold medallist, Hillerod, 2007; World Youth Championships light-heavyweight bronze medallist, Guadalajara, 2008; Ulster light-heavyweight champion 2008 (Paul Moffett); Irish Under-19 light-heavyweight champion 2008 (Stephen Ward); Ulster light-heavyweight runner-up 2009 (Stephen Ward, W/O); Irish light-heavyweight runner-up 2009 (Kenny Egan); Shkodra Memorial tournament light-heavyweight gold medallist, Albania, 2009; Irish light-heavyweight runner-up 2010 (Kenny Egan); Gee-Bee tournament light-heavyweight bronze medallist, Helsinki, 2010; Commonwealth Games light-heavyweight silver medallist, New Delhi, 2010; Gee-Bee tournamentheavyweight gold medallist, Helsinki, 2011; Irish Under-21 heavyweight champion 2011 (Thomas Farrell); Irish heavyweight champion 2012 (Christy Joyce); Irish heavyweight champion 2013 (Jimmy Sweeney); Grand Prix tournament heavyweight bronze medallist, Usti, 2013; European Championships heavyweight quarter-finalist, Minsk, 2013; World Championships heavyweight quarter-finalist, Almaty, 2013
2014
May 24 Rolandas Cesna, Dewsbury RSF 3
June 21 Imantas Davidaitis, Manchester RSF 2
Oct 4 Dimitar Spaiyski, Belfast RSF 1

Nov 15 Martin Horak, Dublin RSF 2
2015
Feb 20 Jakub Wojcik, Dublin RSF 6
FIGHTS: 5 WON: 5 DREW: 0 LOST: 0

MARCO McCULLOUGH
Featherweight - Born: Belfast, 22 November, 1989 - Dan Pozniak Junior Cup, bantamweight gold medallist, Vilnius, 2007; Irish Under-19 bantamweight champion 2007 (Sean Kilroy); Ulster featherweight champion 2009 (Carl Frampton, walkover)
2011
June 25 Eddie Nesbitt, Craigavon RSF 2
Sep 10 Dai Davies, Belfast L-PTS 4
2012
Apr 14 Sean Watson, Belfast RSF 1
Sep 8 Hyusein Hyuseinov, Belfast PTS 4
Oct 13 Valentin Marinov, Belfast RSF 1
Dec 1 Michael Kelly, Belfast PTS 4
2013
Feb 9 Ibrar Riyaz, Belfast PTS 4
May 14 Noel O'Brien, Belfast RSF 3
Oct 19 Willie Casey, Belfast RSF 9
(For vacant Irish featherweight title)
2014
Apr 4 Elemir Rafael, Belfast RSF 3
June 20 Martin Parlagi, Belfast PTS 10
(For vacant WBO European featherweight title)
Sep 6 Dmitry Kirillov, Belfast RTD 8
(WBO European featherweight title defence)
2015
Feb 28 Malkhaz Tatrishvili, Belfast RSF 1
FIGHTS: 13 WON: 12 DREW: 0 LOST: 1

JJ McDONAGH
Super-middleweight - Born: Mullingar, 2 December, 1985
2009
Nov 20 Jevgenijs Kiselevs, Belfast RSF 1
Dec 5 Mario Lupp, Dublin RSF 1

2010
Aug 7 Tommy Tolan, Dublin L-KO 3
Dec 10 Deniss Sirjatovs, Dublin RSF 4
2011
Jan 30 Phillip Townley, Dublin PTS 8
Dec 4 Stuart Maddox, Barnsley PTS 4
2012
Feb 25 Lee Murtagh, Hove KO 7
(For vacant Irish super-middleweight title)
May 5 Darren Cruise, Belfast PTS 3
(Quarter-final of Prizefighter tournament)
May 5 Joe Rea, Belfast PTS 3
(Semi-final of Prizefighter tournament)
May 5 Eamonn O'Kane, Belfast L-PTS 3
(Final of Prizefighter tournament)
2013
Nov 21 Tzvetozar Iliev, London PTS 4
2014
Feb 21 Michal Nieroda, London RSF 4
Aug 14 Schiller Hyppolite, Quebec City L-PTS 10
2015
Apr 17 Mark Till, Bournemouth PTS 4
May 29 Martins Kukulis, London RSF 4
FIGHTS: 15 WON: 12 DREW: 0 LOST: 3

PADDY McDONAGH

Super-middleweight - Born: Mullingar, 29 August, 1991 - Irish Youth light-heavyweight champion 2009 (Patrick Ward); Irish Under-21 light-heavyweight champion 2009 (Gerard McDonagh)
2009
Nov 20 Grigor Sarohanian, Belfast PTS 4
Dec 4 Mariusz Radziszewski, Cork PTS 4
2010
May 15 Ciaran Healy, Limerick PTS 4
Dec 10 Martins Kukulis, Dublin PTS 8
2011
Jan 30 Titusz Szabo, Dublin PTS 6

Mar 19 Jevgenijs Andrejevs PTS 6
Dec 4 James Tucker, Barnsley PTS 4
2012
Jan 21 John Waldron, Liverpool PTS 10
(For vacant Irish light-heavyweight title)
Apr 28 John Anthony, Hove L-PTS 6
2013
Dec 6 John Anthony, Doncaster PTS 6
2014
Mar 1 Lewis Patterson, London L-PTS 4
2015
May 29 Richard Horton, London PTS 4
FIGHTS: 12 WON: 10 DREW: 0 LOST: 2

PETER McDONAGH
Lightweight - Born: Galway, 21 December, 1977 - Based in London
2002
Apr 28 Aev Mittoo, London PTS 6
June 23 Dave Hinds, London PTS 6
Sep 14 Peter Buckley, London PTS 4
Oct 27 Ben Hudson, London L-PTS
2003
Feb 18 Dafydd Carlin, London L-PTS 4
Apr 8 Ben Hudson, London PTS 4
Nov 8 Ceri Hall, Bridgend L-PTS 4
Nov 22 James Gorman, Belfast L-PTS 4
2004
Feb 21 Chill John, Hove RSF 2
Mar 6 Barry Hughes, Glasgow L-PTS 6
Apr 7 Jon Honney, London PTS 10
(For vacant Southern Area lightweight title)
Nov 19 David Burke, London L-PTS 8
2005
Jan 21 Ryan Barrett, London L-PTS 8
Mar 4 Scott Lawton, Rotherham L-PTS 6
Apr 30 Rob Jeffries, Dagenham L-PTS 10
(Southern Area lightweight title defence)

May 14 Robert Murray, Dublin L-PTS 10
(For vacant Irish light-welterweight title)
Aug 7 Brunet Zamora, Rimini L-PTS 6
Nov 4 Anthony Christopher, London PTS 4
2006
Jan 28 Michael Gomez, Dublin RSF 5
(For vacant Irish lightweight title)
Sep 24 Jason Nesbitt, London PTS 4
Dec 1 Karl Taylor, London PTS 4
2007
Oct 5 Duncan Cottier, London PTS 4
2008
Feb 29 Giuseppe Lauri, Milan L-RSF 6
(European Union light-welterweight title challenge)
July 12 Andy Murray, Dublin, Ireland L-PTS 10
(For vacant Irish lightweight title)
Sep 27 Constantin Florescu, Brampton, Canada PTS 6
Dec 13 Lee Purdy, Brentwood PTS 10
(For vacant Southern Area light-welterweight title)
2009
Apr 11 Lenny Daws, London L-PTS 10
(For vacant English light-welterweight title)
June 12 Jimmy Briggs, London PTS 4
Sep 5 Lee Purdy, Watford L-PTS 10
(For vacant Southern Area welterweight title)
2010
Feb 13 Frankie Gavin, London L-PTS 6
Apr 3 Christopher Sebire, Manchester PTS 8
June 4 Yvan Mendy, Pont-Sainte-Maxence, France L-PTS 12
(For vacant WBF Inter-Continental light-welterweight title)
July 24 Michele Di Rocco, Quartu Sant'Elena, Italy L-PTS 6
Sep 4 Alex Arthur, Glasgow L-PTS 8
Oct 23 Curtis Woodhouse, London PTS 8
2011
Mar 18 Darren Hamilton, London L-RSF 8
(For vacant Southern Area light-welterweight title)
June 7 Yassine El Maachi, London L-PTS 3

(Quarter-final of Prizefighter tournament)
Sep 30 Johnny Greaves, London PTS 4
Nov 25 Gary McMillan, Motherwell L-PTS 6
2012
Jan 13 Jason Nesbitt, London PTS 6
Mar 31 Chris Johnson, Blackpool L-PTS 6
July 14 Ronnie Heffron, London L-PTS 8
Sep 14 Bradley Skeete, London L-PTS 10
Nov 1 Ronnie Heffron, London L-PTS 8
Nov 30 Bradley Saunders, Manchester L-PTS 8
2013
Mar 21 Bradley Skeete, London L-PTS 10
(Southern Area welterweight title challenge)
June 8 Liam Griffiths, Bluewater PTS 4
July 12 Paddy Murphy, Dundalk DREW 8
Oct 10 Dan Blackwell, London PTS 4
Nov 16 Arek Malek, Greenhithe PTS 6
2014
Mar 15 John Hutchinson, Reading PTS 10
(For vacant Irish light-middleweight title)
Nov 8 Zoran Cvek, Greenhithe RSF 6
2015
Mar 28 Adam Grabiec, Birmingham PTS 8
FIGHTS: 53 WON: 24 DREW: 1 LOST: 28

TYRONE McKENNA
Light-welterweight - Born: Belfast, 3 March, 1990 - HSK Junior Box Cup bantamweight gold medallist, Hillerod, 2007; Dan Pozniak Junior Cup bantamweight bronze medallist, Vilnius, 2008; Irish Under-19 featherweight champion 2008 (Charlie Haggerty); Irish Under-21 lightweight runner-up 2009 (Mark O'Hara)
2012
Aug 17 Anthony Morrison, Atlantic City PTS 4
2013
Oct 12 Korey Sloane, Philadelphia PTS 4
Dec 11 Jeffrey Combs, Allentown PTS 4
2014
July 26 Christian Daniels, Winston-Salem RSF 1

Oct 11 Anthony Dave, Winston-Salem RSF 2
2015
Feb 7 Teodor Stefanov, Belfast PTS 4
Mar 28 Istvan Kiss, Belfast RSF 3
June 6 Sylwester Walczak, Belfast PTS 4
FIGHTS: 8 WON: 8 DREW: 0 LOST: O

MICHAEL McKINSON

Welterweight - Born: Belfast, 17 April, 1994
2014
Oct 4 Jan Salamacha, Belfast PTS 4
Nov 1 Pawel Seliga, Downpatrick PTS 4
Nov 22 Teodor Stefanov, Belfast PTS 4
2015
Feb 7 Aleksas Vaseris, Belfast PTS 4
Mar 28 Dan Carr, Portsmouth PTS 4
July 4 Jerome Samuels, Bournemouth RTD 3
FIGHTS: 6 WON: 6 DREW: 0 LOST: 0

MICHAEL McLAUGHLIN

Light-middleweight - Born: Carndonagh, 21 September, 1984 - Based in Boston - Irish Under-21 light-welterweight runner-up 2003 (John Joe McDonagh)
2010
Oct 2 Valentin Stoychev, Letterkenny DREW 4
2011
Sep 17 Mark Betts, Belfast RSF 4
2012
May 19 Noel Garcia, Boston DSQ 3
Sep 8 Antonio Chaves Fernandez, Dorchester L-PTS 4
Nov 10 Robert Brando-Hunt, Providence RSF 3
2013
Mar 10 Jimmy LeBlanc, Dorchester RTD 1
May 24 Antonio Chaves Fernandez, Dorchester PTS 6
Oct 26 Sergio Cabrera, Canton, Massachusetts PTS 6
2014
Mar 15 Paul Souza, Boston RSF 2
Apr 26 Pedro Gonzalez, Dorchester T-PTS 4

Oct 30 Paulo Souza, Plymouth, Massachusetts RSF 2
2015
Feb 26 Rafael Francis, Melrose DSQ 1
Feb 27 Roberto Valenzuela, Quincy T-PTS 4
FIGHTS: 13 WON: 11 DREW: 1 LOST: 1

CHRISTINA McMAHON
Bantamweight - Born: Carrickmacross, 18 June, 1974
2010
Aug 7 Ineta Lieknina, Dublin RSF 3
Dec 10 Polina Pencheva, Dublin PTS 4
2011
Mar 19 Julija Cvetkova, Dublin RSF 4
2012
Nov 3 Stephanie Ducastel, Dublin PTS 8
(For vacant Celtic Warrior bantamweight title)
2013
Mar 9 Karina Kopinska, Dundalk PTS 8
Sep 14 Lana Cooper, Belfast RSF 5
2014
Inactive
2015
May 2 Catherine Phiri, Lusaka PTS 10
(For vacant interim WBC bantamweight title)
FIGHTS: 7 WON: 7 DREW: 0 LOST: 0

DANIEL McSHANE
Lightweight - Born: Belfast, 9 November, 1993 - Pirkka Junior Tournament featherweight gold medallist, Tampere, 2009
2012
Oct 13 Evgeni Geshev, Belfast RSF 3
Dec 1 Janis Puksins PTS 4
2013
Feb 9 Pavels Senkovs, Belfast PTS 4
Mar 9 Ignac Kassai, Dundalk RSF 2
June 28 Ivans Levickis, Belfast RSF 3
Sep 14 Istvan Kovacs, Belfast PTS 8

Oct 19 Oszkar Fiko, Belfast DSQ 3
2014
Mar 8 Ignac Kassai, Kecskemet, Hungary PTS 4
Oct 4 Qasim Hussain, Belfast PTS 4
2015
Mar 28 Zoltan Horvath, Belfast L-RSF 2
FIGHTS: 10 WON: 9 DREW: 0 LOST: 1

CIARAN McVARNOCK

Lightweight - Born: Belfast, 11 April, 1992
2013
Dec 7 Ivan Ruiz Garrido, Liverpool PTS 4
2014
May 10 Harvey Hemsley, Liverpool PTS 4
2015
Feb 7 Aivaras Balsys, Belfast PTS 6
FIGHTS: 3 WON: 3 DREW: 0 LOST: 0

ALFREDO MELI

Middleweight - Born: Belfast, 6 June, 1990 - Irish Under-19 welterweight champion (Bernard Redmond); HSK Junior Box Cup middleweight silver medallist, Hillerod, 2007; Ulster middleweight champion 2012 (Walkover, staged in December 2011)
2012
Apr 27 Sergej Drob, Belfast RSF 1
June 2 Andrejs Loginovs, London RSF 3
Nov 27 Danny Brown, London PTS 4
2013
Nov 9 Kieron Gray, Belfast PTS 4
2014
Mar 21 Festim Lama, Belfast PTS 6
May 10 Samet Hyuseinov, Belfast PTS 4
June 6 Dan Blackwell, Belfast PTS 6
June 14 Damien Taggart, Belfast PTS 4
Nov 1 Iain Jackson, Downpatrick PTS 4
2015
May 1 Valentin Stoychev, Dublin RSF 1
FIGHTS: 10 WON: 10 DREW: 0 LOST: 0

PAUL MOFFETT
Super-middleweight - Born: Belfast, 2 June, 1984 - Ulster light-heavyweight runner-up 2008 (Tommy McCarthy)
2012
Apr 14 Ciaran Healy, Belfast PTS 4
Apr 27 Jamie Boness, Belfast RSF 1
July 21 Tommy Tolan, Belfast DREW 4
Oct 13 Gavin Putney, Belfast RTD 2
2013
Inactive
2014
Feb 1 Kerry Hope, Cardiff L-PTS 6
2015
Inactive to date
FIGHTS: 5 WON: 3 DREW: 1 LOST: 1

MARK MORRIS
Lightweight - Born: Belfast, 8 November, 1988
2013
Nov 9 Andy Harris, Belfast PTS 4
2014
Mar 21 Ryan Corrigan, Belfast RSF 1
2015
Mar 28 James Fryers, Belfast L-RTD 5
(For vacant Boxing Union of Ireland Celtic Nations lightweight title)
FIGHTS: 3 WON: 2 DREW: 0 LOST: 1

BEN MULLIGAN
Light-welterweight - Born: Fivemiletown, 20 May, 1986
2012
Sep 22 Mariusz Bak, Belfast L-PTS 4
2013
Nov 25 Ryan McNicol, Glasgow L-PTS 4
2014
May 10 Derek Potter, Belfast L-PTS 4
Oct 6 David Savage, Glasgow L-PTS 6
Nov 29 Sean Davis, Walsall L-PTS 4

2015
Mar 8 Jordan Ellison, Houghton-le-Spring, L-PTS 4
Mar 19 Richard Barclay, Glasgow L-PTS 6
FIGHTS: 7 WON: 0 DREW: 0 LOST: 7

PADDY MURPHY

Welterweight - Born: Newry, 28 September, 1987 - Based in Brisbane, Australia - Ulster light-welterweight champion 2008 (Paddy Gallagher)
2011
May 13 David Bainbridge, Fortitude Valley RSF 1
Sep 30 Mick Shaw, Fortitude Valley PTS 4
Oct 28 Kurt Finlayson, Mansfield PTS 4
Dec 15 Brett John Smith, Brisbane RSF 4
(For vacant Queensland welterweight title)
2012
Mar 2 Robert Clarke, Mansfield RSF 1
July 27 Daniel Roy Maxwell, Maroochydore PTS 6
Sep 14 Harrison Gardner, Brisbane RSF 2
Dec 11 Yang Xing Xin, Hong Kong DREW 6
2013
Apr 20 Alex Ahtong, Brisbane PTS 10
(For vacant WBF Asia Pacific welterweight title)
July 12 Peter McDonagh, Dundalk DREW 8
Nov 16 Adrian Campbell, Brisbane PTS 8
Dec 11 Alex Ah Tong, Flemington PTS 8
2014
Sep 3 Mark Ramirez, Eatons Hill RSF 2
Nov 8 Rivan Cesaire, Chandler, Queensland L-PTS 10
(Australian welterweight title challenge)
2015
Inactive to date
FIGHTS: 14 WON: 11 DREW: 2 LOST: 1

JOHN JOE NEVIN

Super-featherweight - Born: Mullingar, 7 June, 1989 - Four Nations junior light-flyweight gold medallist, Liverpool, 2006; Irish Under-21 light-flyweight champion 2006 (walkover); Irish Under-19 flyweight champion 2007 (Prabjoj Singh); Dan Pozniak

Junior Cup flyweight gold medallist, Vilnius, 2007; Irish bantamweight champion 2008 (TJ Doheny); Olympic qualifying tournament bantamweight gold medallist, Pescara, 2008; European Union Championships bantamweight gold medallist, Cetwieno, 2008; Reached second series in Olympic Games, losing to gold medallist Enkhbat Badar-Uugan (Mongolia); Irish bantamweight champion 2009 (Ryan Lindberg); European Union Championships bantamweight silver medallist, Odense, 2009; World Championships bantamweight bronze medallist, Milan, 2009; President's Cup bantamweight silver medallist, Baku, 2009; Irish bantamweight champion 2010 (Derek Thorpe); Grand Prix bantamweight gold medallist, Ostrava, 2010; Irish bantamweight champion 2011 (Tyrone McCullagh); Feliks Stamm Memorial bantamweight gold medallist, Warsaw, 2011; World Championships bantamweight bronze medallist, Baku, 2011; Irish bantamweight champion 2012 (Michael Nevin); Olympic Games bantamweight silver medallist, London, 2012; European Championships bantamweight gold medallist, Minsk, 2013

2014
Mar 17 Alberto Candelaria, Boston PTS 6
Oct 11 Calvin Stifford, Winston-Salem RSF 1
Nov 15 Jack Heath, Dublin RSF 1
2015
Inactive to date
FIGHTS: 3 WON: 3 DREW: 0 LOST: 0

CRAIG O'BRIEN
Light-middleweight - Born: Dublin
2015
Feb 20 Jakub Czaprowicz, Dublin PTS 4
May 1 Asen Vasilev, Dublin PTS 4
FIGHTS: 2 WON: 2 DREW: 0 LOST: 0

JOHN O'DONNELL
Welterweight - Born: Galway, 13 November, 1985
2004
Apr 16 Jason Nesbitt, Bradford PTS 4
June 2 Dave Hinds, Nottingham PTS 4
Sep 24 Chris Long, Nottingham RSF 4
Nov 12 Ernie Smith, London PTS 6
2005

Apr 10 Duncan Cotter, Brentwood PTS 4
July 9 Ben Hudson, Nottingham RSF 3
Oct 21 Ben Hudson, London PTS 4
2006
Jan 20 Matt Scriven, London RSF 4
Jan 28 Zaid Bediouri, Dublin PTS 6
Feb 17 Karl Taylor, London PTS 4
May 12 Duncan Cottier, London RTD 3
July 12 Darren Gethin, London PTS 8
Sep 15 Silence Saheed, London PTS 6
Dec 8 Ernie Smith, Dagenham KO 2
2007
Mar 23 Stuart Elwell, Nottingham PTS 10
(For vacant English welterweight title)
May 5 Christian Solano, Las Vegas L-RSF 2
2008
May 10 Billy Smith, Nottingham PTS 4
June 27 Jay Morris, London RSF 6
July 19 Sergejs Volodins, Limerick RSF 5
Oct 4 Sergejs Savrinovics, Norwich RTD 3
Nov 15 Suleyman Dag, Castlebar RSF 3
2009
Apr 11 Craig Watson, London PTS 12
(Commonwealth welterweight title challenge)
Sep 5 Tom Glover, Watford RSF 6
2010
May 7 Laszlo Robert Balogh, Widnes RSF 5
Sep 10 Terrance Cauthen, London PTS 12
2011
Feb 19 Craig Watson, London L-PTS 12
(For vacant British welterweight title)
2012
Apr 14 Martin Welsh, Belfast PTS 8
Oct 12 Tomas Mendez, Montreal PTS 8
Dec 1 Stephen Haughian, Belfast PTS 8
2013
July 6 Jay Morris, London PTS 4

2014
Inactive
2015
May 2 Laszlo Fazekas, Derry PTS 8
FIGHTS: 31 WON: 29 DREW: 0 LOST: 2

EAMONN O'KANE

Middleweight - Born: Dungiven, 18 March, 1982 - Irish middleweight runner-up 2003 (Andy Lee); Commonwealth Championships middleweight runner-up, Kuala Lumpur, 2003; Four Nations Championships middleweight gold medallist, Glasgow, 2004; Tammer tournament middleweight bronze medallist, Tampere, 2004; Irish middleweight runner-up 2005 (Andy Lee); Irish middleweight runner-up 2007 (Darren Sutherland); Commonwealth Championships middleweight gold medallist, Liverpool, 2007; Ulster middleweight champion 2008 (Martin Lynch); European Championships middleweight bronze medallist, Liverpool, 2008; Ulster middleweight runner-up 2009 (Stephen O'Reilly); Commonwealth Games middleweight gold medallist, New Delhi, 2010; Gee-Bee tournament middleweight silver medallist, Helsinki, 2010; Algirdas Socikas tournament middleweight silver medallist, Kaunas, 2010
2011
June 4 Dmitrijus Kalinovskis, Cardiff RSF 1
June 25 Tommy Tolan, Craigavon RTD 5
Sep 10 Joe Rea, Belfast PTS 8
2012
Mar 17 Wayne Reed, Sheffield PTS 6
May 5 Anthony Fitzgerald, Belfast PTS 3
(Quarter-final of Prizefighter tournament)
May 5 Ryan Greene, Belfast RSF 1
(Semi-final of Prizefighter tournament)
May 5 JJ McDonagh, Belfast PTS 3
(Final of Prizefighter tournament)
Sep 22 Terry Carruthers, Belfast PTS 6
Dec 8 John Ryder, London L-RSF 8
(British middleweight title eliminator)
2013
Feb 9 Gary Boulden, Belfast PTS 6
July 12 Anthony Fitzgerald, Dundalk PTS 10
(For vacant Irish middleweight title)

Oct 19 Kerry Hope, Belfast PTS 12
(For vacant IBF Inter-Continental middleweight title)
2014
Apr 4 Alvaro Gaona, Belfast KO 1
(For vacant WBC International Silver middleweight title)
Sep 6 Virgilijus Stapulionis, Belfast T-DREW 4
(IBF Inter-Continental middleweight title defence)
2015
Feb 13 Ferenc Hafner, Swindon RSF 4
May 2 Lewis Taylor, Derry PTS 12
(IBF Inter-Continental middleweight title defence)
FIGHTS: 16 WON: 14 DREW: 1 LOST: 1

STEPHEN ORMOND

Lightweight - Born: Dublin, 18 April, 1983 - Irish featherweight champion 2002 (Gavin Brown); Box-Am Tournament featherweight silver medallist, Tenerife, 2002; Irish featherweight champion 2003 (Eamonn Touhey); Four Nations Championships featherweight silver medallist, Cardiff, 2003; Irish lightweight champion 2005 (Dean Murphy)
2008
Oct 26 Juris Ivanovs, Killarney PTS 4
2009
Jan 30 Jevgenijs Kirillovs, Dublin PTS 4
Mar 19 Jonathan Ocassio, Worcester, Massachusetts RTD 1
June 5 Sergi Ganjelashvili, New York PTS 6
July 18 Israel Suarez, New York PTS 6
Nov 21 Andrew Costa, Crossville, Tennessee RSF 1
2010
Sep 4 Johnny Greaves, Glasgow PTS 4
Dec 4 Sebastien Cornu, Glasgow RSF 6
2011
Mar 12 Mickey Coveney, Glasgow RSF 7
June 25 Valentin Stoychev, Dublin RSF 5
Sep 9 Ibrar Riyaz, London PTS 8
2012
Mar 10 Paul Appleby, Glasgow L-PTS 10
(For vacant Celtic super-featherweight title)

July 5 Mickey Coveney, London PTS 10
2013
May 3 Laszlo Robert Balogh, Dublin RSF 2
(For vacant World Boxing Union lightweight title)
Sep 20 Adam Mate, London
(For vacant WBO European lightweight title) RSF 1
Oct 7 Adam Dingsdale, London PTS 10
(WBO European lightweight title defence)
Dec 7 Derry Matthews, Liverpool PTS 10
(WBO European lightweight title defence)
2014
Apr 4 Karim El Ouazghari, Belfast RSF 5
(WBO European lightweight title defence)
2015
Feb 14 Terry Flanagan, Wolverhampton L-DSQ 10
(WBO European lightweight title defence)
July 4 Jacek Wylezol, Dublin RSF 2
FIGHTS: 20 WON: 18 DREW: 0 LOST: 2

GARY O'SULLIVAN

Middleweight - Born: Cork, 14 July, 1984
2008
Jan 26 Peter Dunn, Cork RSF 6
Mar 15 Robert Harris, Boston RSF 1
Apr 19 Tye Williams, Dublin RSF 1
July 5 Eugen Stan, Dublin PTS 6
Sep 13 Sergejs Volodins, Cork RTD 1
Oct 26 Idiozan Matos, Killarney RSF 3
2009
Mar 14 Jimmy LeBlanc, Dorchester, Massachusetts DSQ 4
Apr 25 Marcin Piatkowski, Cork KO 1
July 25 Arturs Jaskuls, Dublin PTS 6
Dec 4 Ciaran Healy, Cork PTS 10
(For vacant Irish middleweight title)
2010
June 26 Sylvain Touzet, Cork RSF 3
2011

May 21 Ryan Clark, London KO 1
June 25 Robbie Long, Dublin RSF 1
(Irish middleweight title defence)
2012
Mar 10 Paul Morby, Glasgow PTS 6
July 14 Matthew Hall, London PTS 12
(For vacant WBO International middleweight title)
2013
May 3 Tadas Jonkus, Dublin RSF 3
July 20 Billy Joe Saunders, London L-PTS 12
(WBO International middleweight title defence)
2014
June 5 Jose Medina, Boston PTS 6
Nov 15 Anthony Fitzgerald, Dublin RSF 1
2015
Feb 26 Larry Smith, Melrose, Massachusetts RSF 2
Mar 14 Milton Nunez, New York RSF 3
May 23 Melvin Betancourt, Boston KO 2
FIGHTS: 22 WON: 21 DREW: 0 LOST: 1

DEREK POTTER

Super-featherweight - Born: Belfast, 20 September, 1994
2014
May 10 Ben Mulligan, Belfast PTS 4
2015
Inactive to date
FIGHTS: 1 WON: 1 DREW: 0 LOST: 0

JASON QUIGLEY

Middleweight - Born: Ballybofey, 19 May, 1991 - Irish Under-21 champion, 2008;
Irish Intermediate champions, 2008; Dan Pozniak Junior Cup silver medallist,
Vilnius, 2008; Dan Pozniak Youth Cup gold medallist, Vilnius, 2009; European
Youth Championships gold medallist, Szczecin, 2009; Irish Youth welterweight
champion, 2009 (Gary Molloy); International Round Robin (v England, Germany and
Italy), Dublin, 2009; Irish middleweight runner-up 2010 (Darren O'Neill); Grand
Prix tournament middleweight gold medallist, Ostrava, 2010; Irish middleweight
runner-up 2011 (Darren O'Neill); Gee-Bee tournament middleweight gold medallist,

Helsinki, 2011; Algirdas Socikas tournament - gold medallist, Kaunas, 2012; Irish Under-23 middleweight champion 2012 (Michael Reilly); European Under-22 Championships middleweight gold medallist, Kaliningrad, 2012; Irish middleweight champion 2013 (Roy Sheahan); Grand Prix tournament middleweight gold medallist, Usti, 2013; European Championships middleweight gold medallist, Minsk, 2013; Three Nations tournament middleweight gold medallist, Berck-sur-Mer, 2013; World Championships middleweight silver medallist, Almaty, 2013

2014
July 12 Howard Reece, Las Vegas RSF 1
Aug 16 Fernando Najera, Carson RTD 2
Oct 30 Greg McCoy, Plymouth, Massachusetts KO 1
2015
Mar 6 Lanny Dardar, Los Angeles KO 1
Mar 20 Tolutomi Agunbiade, Indio KO 2
Apr 30 Joshua Snyder, Indio RSF 2
July 11 Tom Howard, Los Angeles RSF 2
FIGHTS: 7 WON: 7 DREW: 0 LOST: 0

PAUL QUINN
Featherweight - Born: Annalong, 7 December, 1990
2012
Oct 13 Ignac Kassai, Belfast PTS 4
Dec 1 Tibor Meszaros, Belfast PTS 4
2013
Apr 27 David Kis, Belfast RSF 1
Nov 9 Sajid Khan, Belfast RSF 1
2014
Mar 21 Joe Beedon, Belfast PTS 4
Nov 1 Dawid Knade, Downpatrick RSF 6
2015
Inactive to date
FIGHTS: 6 WON: 6 DREW: 0 LOST: 0

STEVIE QUINN JNR
Bantamweight - Born: Belfast, 3 February, 1993
2011
May 28 Delroy Spencer, Belfast PTS 6

2012
Mar 15 Fernando Arenas, Panama City PTS 4
May 31 David Paz, Panama City PTS 4
June 16 Anastacio Zurdo, Panama City PTS 4
Oct 13 Ryan McNichol, Belfast PTS 4
2013
Nov 30 Roris Samudio, Colon City, Panama RSF 3
2014
July 19 Ivan Trejos, Boquete L-PTS 6
Aug 23 Daniel Moreno, Panama City L-PTS 4
2015
Mar 14 Stephon McIntyre, Jersey City PTS 6
FIGHTS: 9 WON: 7 DREW: 0 LOST: 2

JOE REA
Middleweight - Born: Ballymena, 24 July, 1983 - Based in Sydney
2004
June 11 Devin Womack, Plymouth, Massachusetts RSF 1
Aug 10 Henry Dukes, Hyannis, Massachusetts NO-CON 2
Oct 1 Robert Muhammad, Boston PTS 4
2005
Mar 25 Jerald Lowe, Boston RSF 3
Apr 1 Cory Phelps, New Haven, Connecticut RSF 2
Nov 19 Michael Rayner, Boston RSF 1
2006
July 7 Valentino Jalomo, Hyannis, Massachusetts DREW 4
2007
Inactive
2008
Apr 13 Jamie Ambler, Birmingham PTS 4
Nov 22 Martin Murray, London L-PTS 3
(Quarter-Final of Prizefighter tournament)
2009
Nov 6 Phillip Townley, Belfast PTS 4
2010
Inactive
2011

Feb 12 Dominik Britsch, Muelheim, Germany L-PTS 8

Mar 5 Grzegorz Proksa, Huddersfield L-KO 4

June 4 Patrick Nielsen, Copenhagen L-RSF 3

July 10 Kenny Anderson, Colne L-RTD 4

Sep 10 Eamonn O'Kane, Belfst L-PTS 8

Sep 17 Levan Ghvamichava, Belfast L-RTD 1

2012

May 5 Simon O'Donnell, Belfast PTS 3

(Quarter-final of Prizefighter tournament)

May 5 JJ McDonagh, Belfast L-PTS 3

(Semi-final of Prizefighter tournament)

Aug 25 Florian Wildenhof, Prembroke, Malta L-DSQ 6

Sep 14 Frank Buglioni, London L-RSF 2

Nov 3 Brendan Fitzpatrick, Dublin L-PTS 8

(For vacant Celtic Warrior super-middleweight title)

2013

Mar 9 Myles Cash, London L-PTS 4

June 14 Eddie Lenart, Hurstville, New South Wales PTS 6

2014

Apr 25 Rocky Jerkic, Hurstville L-RSF 1

June 27 Michael Zerafa, Malvern L-PTS 8

Aug 29 Dane Mulival, Hurstville PTS 6

Sep 19 Steven Ma, Denham Court DREW 6

Sep 27 Leroy Brown, St Marys DREW 8

Nov 14 Peter Georgiou, Hurstville L-PTS 4

Dec 16 Zhou Yun Fei, Shanghai L-PTS 6

2015

Jan 31 Bilal Akkawy, Sydney DREW 4

Mar 7 Trent Broadhurst, Surfers Paradise L-KO 1

Apr 10 Luke Sharp, Northbridge DREW 6

Apr 17 Jake Carr, Hurstville L-PTS 6

May 8 Dwight Ritchie, Somerton L-PTS 6

June 13 Faris Chevalier, Newstead L-RTD 3

July 11 David Toussaint, Woden L-KO 1

(For vacant New South Wales super-middleweight title)

FIGHTS: 37 WON: 10 DREW: 5 NO-CON: 1 LOST 21

MARTIN ROGAN
Heavyweight - Born: Belfast, 1 May, 1974 - Irish super-heavyweight runner-up 2003 (Thomas Crampton); Irish super-heavyweight champion 2004 (Jimmy Upton)
2004
Oct 28 Lee Mountford, Belfast RSF 1
2005
Mar 18 Billy Bessey, Belfast PTS 4
June 4 Tony Booth, Manchester RSF 2
2006
May 20 Darren Morgan, Belfast PTS 4
Oct 7 Paul King, Belfast PTS 6
Oct 26 Jevgenijs Stamburskis, Belfast RSF 3
2007
Oct 13 Radcliffe Green, Belfast RSF 2
2008
Apr 11 Alex Tibbs, London RSF 2
(Quarter-final of Prizefighter tournament)
Apr 11 Dave Ferguson, London PTS 3
(Semi-final of Prizefighter topurnament)
Apr 11 David Dolan, London PTS 3
(Final of Prizefighter tournament)
Dec 6 Audley Harrison, London PTS 10
2009
Feb 28 Matt Skelton, Birmingham RSF 11
(Commonwealth heavyweight title challenge)
May 15 Sam Sexton, Belfast L-RSF 8
(Commonwealth heavyweight title defence)
Nov 6 Sam Sexton, Belfast L-RTD 6
(Commonwealth heavyweight title challenge)
2010
Nov 6 Yavor Marinchev, Limerick RSF 1
Nov 20 Werner Kreiskott, Castlebar PTS 6
2011
Inactive
2012
Apr 14 Tyson Fury, Belfast L-RSF 5
(For vacant Irish heavyweight title)

2013
Feb 9 Ladislav Kovarik, Belfast PTS 4
Feb 23 Albert Sosnowski, London RSF 3
(Quarter-final of Prizefighter tournament)
Feb 23 Audley Harrison, London L-PTS 3
(Semi-final of Prizefighter tournament)
Nov 16 Erkan Teper, Ludwigsburg L-RSF 1
2014
June 4 Michael Sprott, Auckland L-PTS 3
(Quarter-final of Super 8 tournament)
2015
Inactive to date
FIGHTS: 22 WON: 16 DREW: 0 LOST: 6

LEON SENIOR
Light-heavyweight - Born: Dublin, 1 April, 1980
2007
Nov 18 Michael Banbula, London PTS 4
2008
Jan 31 David Gentles, London L-PTS 6
Mar 22 Sandris Tomsons, Dublin PTS 4
May 16 Ricky Strike, London PTS 4
2009
Inactive
2010
Inactive
2011
Inactive
2012
May 26 Paul Morris, Brentwood PTS 4
July 7 Vygaudas Laurinkus, London PTS 4
Sep 15 Jevgenijs Andrejevs, London PTS 4
Dec 8 Bartlomiej Grafka, Brentwood PTS 6
2013
Mar 9 Danny Couzens, London PTS 10
(For vacant Southern Area light-heavyweight title)
July 5 Egidijus Kakstys, London PTS 6

Sep 20 Dan Woodgate, Gillingham PTS 10
(Southern Area light-heavyweight title defence)
Nov 16 Arfan Iqbal, Greenhithe L-RSF 6
2014
Mar 15 Tony Hill, Reading T-DRAW 2
(Southern Area light-heavyweight title defence)
May 17 Bob Ajisafe, London L-RSF 5
2015
Inactive to date
FIGHTS: 14 WON: 10 DREW: 1 LOST: 3

TONY SENIOR
Middleweight - Born: London, 11 January, 1984 - Based in Australia - Brother of Leon Senior
2013
Oct 12 Amir Ghasemi Tabar, Lakemba RSF 1
Nov 29 Alireza Imani, Hurstville RSF 1
Dec 7 Tuathong Singmanasak, Madeley RSF 1
2014
Feb 21 Aswin Cabuy, Hurstville PTS 4
May 31 Reza Taher Abadi, Bankstown RTD 1
Dec 6 Rickson Yamo, Hurstville RSF 4
2015
July 4 Pramool Boonpok, Punchbowl PTS 4
FIGHTS: 7 WON: 7 DREW: 0 LOST: 0

PHILIP SUTCLIFFE JNR
Light-welterweight - Born: Dublin, 27 June, 1989 - Irish light-welterweight champion 2009 (John Joe Joyce); European Union Championships light-welterweight bronze medallist, Odense, 2009; Grand Prix multi-nations welterweight silver medallist, Usti, 2009; Algirdas Socikas tournament light-welterweight gold medallist, Kaunas, 2010; Irish light-welterweight runner-up 2011 (Ross Hickey); Algirdas Socikas tournament light-welterweight bronze medallist, Kaunas, 2012
2013
Mar 9 Zoltan Kovacs, Dundalk RSF 1
May 14 Liam Finn, Belfast RSF 2
July 12 Radoslav Mitev, Dundalk RSF 1

Oct 19 Lubos Priehradnik, Belfast RSF 4
Nov 2 Karoly Lakatos, Dublin RSF 4
2014
Sep 12 Martin McCord, Dublin PTS 4
2015
Feb 20 Terry Needham, Dublin RSF 1
May 1 Yoann Portailler, Dublin PTS 8
FIGHTS: 8 WON: 8 DREW: 0 LOST: 0

DAMIAN TAGGART

Welterweight - Born: Omagh, 24 November, 1982
2007
Dec 8 Peter Dunn, Belfast PTS 4
2008
Mar 29 Janis Chernouskis, Letterkenny L-RSF 1
Nov 15 Jevgenijs Fjodorovs, Castlebar RSF 3
2009
Nov 6 Johnny Greaves, Magherafelt PTS 4
Dec 5 Wladimir Borov, Dublin PTS 6
2010
Inactive
2011
June 25 Giuseppe Deprato, Craigavon PTS 4
Sep 10 Sid Razak, Belfast L-RSF 2
2012
Inactive
2013
Inactive
2014
June 14 Alfredo Meli, Belfast L-PTS 4
July 12 Max Maxwell, Birmingham L-PTS 8
Sep 12 Dave Fidler, Sheffield L-RSF 2
Nov 1 Dee Walsh, Downpatrick L-PTS 4
Nov 22 Darren Cruise, Belfast L-PTS 4
2015
Feb 7 Alan Donnellan, Belfast L-PTS 4
Mar 28 Joe Hillerby, Belfast L-PTS 4

FIGHTS: 14 WON: 5 DREW: 0 LOST: 9

JAMES TENNYSON
Super-featherweight - Born: Belfast, 6 August, 1993 - Irish Under-21 lightweight runner-up 2011 (Mark O'Hara); Ulster lightweight runner-up 2012 (James Fryers, staged in December 2011)
2012
Sep 8 Fikret Remziev, Belfast RSF 4
Oct 13 Tibor Meszaros, Belfast RSF 1
Nov 3 Ignac Kassai, Dublin RSF 1
Dec 7 Mickey Coveney, Wishaw PTS 6
2013
Mar 9 David Kis, Dundalk RSF 1
Apr 27 Mickey Coveney, Belfast RSF 2
(For vacant Irish super-featherweight title)
May 24 David Kanalas, Liverpool KO 2
June 28 Andrei Hramyka, Belfast RSF 1
Oct 19 Pavel Senkovs, Belfast L-RSF 2
2014
Apr 18 Ignac Kassai, Budapest RSF 3
May 10 Ian Bailey, Belfast PTS 8
2015
Feb 7 Simas Volosinas, Belfast RSF 2
Mar 28 Kris Hughes, Belfast DSQ 7
(Celtic featherweight title challebge)
June 6 Krzysztof Rogowski, Belfast RSF 3
FIGHTS: 14 WON: 13 DREW: 0 LOST: 1

WILLIE THOMPSON
Welterweight - Born: Ballyclare, 2 January, 1980
2007
June 30 Paul Royston, Belfast PTS 4
Aug 25 Artur Jashkul, Dublin PTS 4
Oct 13 Peter Dunn, Belfast PTS 6
Dec 8 Duncan Cottier, Belfast PTS 4
2008
Mar 22 Semjons Morosheks, Dublin PTS 4

May 31 Janis Chernouskis, Belfast PTS 6
Dec 18 Karl Chiverton, Dublin DREW 4
2009
May 15 Michael Jennings, Belfast L-RSF 4
Oct 10 Ashley Theophane, London L-PTS 6
Nov 19 Paul Burns, Wilshaw L-PTS 6
2011
Mar 5 Kris Carslaw, Scotstoun L-PTS 10
(British Masters light-middleweight title challenge)
2012
Apr 14 Joe Hillerby, Belfast L-PTS 10
(For vacant Northern Ireland light-middleweight title)
Sep 8 Liam Griffiths, Belfast PTS 4
Oct 13 Lee Murtagh, Belfast L-PTS 10
(Irish light-middleweight title challenge)
2013
Inactive
2014
June 6 Liam Griffiths, Belfast PTS 4
2015
Inactive to date
FIGHTS: 15 WON: 8 DREW: 1 LOST: 6

IAN TIMS

Light-heavyweight - Born: Dublin, 4 December, 1979 - Irish middleweight runner-up 1999 (Conal Carmichael); Irish light-heavyweight champion 2002 (Michael McDonagh); Box-Am Tournament light-heavyweight silver medallist, Tenerife, 2002; Irish heavyweight champion 2005 (Alan Reynolds); Irish heavyweight runner-up 2006 (Alan Reynolds); Four Nations Championships heavyweight silver medallist, Dublin, 2006; Irish heavyweight champion 2007 (John Sweeney)
2008
Mar 22 Klaids Kristapsons, Dublin PTS 4
Apr 19 Mirica Edvardo, Dublin PTS 4
July 12 Jevgenijs Andrejevs, Dublin PTS 4
Sep 13 Alexander Ignatov, Cork RTD 1
Oct 26 Remigijus Ziausys, Killarney PTS 6
2009

Jan 30 Jevgenijs Stamburskis, Dublin PTS 6
Dec 4 Radoslaw Musial, Cork RSF 2
2010
Inactive
2011
Jan 30 Viktor Szalai, Dublin RSC 3
Mar 19 Michael Sweeney, Dublin PTS 10
(For vacant Irish cruiserweight title)
2012
Jan 21 Juho Haapoja, Seinajoki L-PTS 12
(European Union cruiserweight title challenge)
Sep 7 Tony Conquest, London L-RTD 7
(For vacant WBO International cruiserweight title)
2013
Inactive
2014
Sep 12 Tamas Danko, Dublin PTS 4
Nov 15 Paul Drago, Dublin L-RTD 1
2015
Inactive to date
FIGHTS: 13 WON: 10 DREW: 0 LOST: 3

TOMMY TOLAN
Middleweight - Born: Belfast, 4 November, 1973
2001
Nov 16 Tomas Da Silva, Dublin L-RSF 6
2002
Inactive
2003
Apr 5 Ray Atherton, Belfast RSF 2
Oct 4 George Robshaw, Belfast L-PTS 4
Nov 22 Wes Flemming, Belfast RSF 1
2004
Inactive
2005
May 14 Michael Banbula, Dublin PTS 4
2006

Inactive
2007
Inactive
2008
Inactive
2009
Inactive
2010
May 15 Michael Sweeney, Limerick L-PTS 4
Aug 7 JJ McDonagh, Dublin KO 3
Dec 15 Tony Jeffries, Belfast L-RSF 2
2011
June 25 Eamonn O'Kane, Craigavon L-RTD 5
Sep 17 Joe Hillerby, Belfast L-PTS 4
Oct 15 Rocky Fielding, Liverpool L-PTS 6
Dec 14 Billy Joe Saunders, London L-RSF 1
2012
Feb 25 Liam Williams, Cardiff L-PTS 4
Mar 10 Callum Johnson, Glasgow L-RSF 1
Apr 14 Dee Walsh, Belfast L-RSF 4
July 21 Paul Moffett, Belfast DREW 4
Sep 21 David Brophy, Glasgow L-PTS 4
Nov 9 Paul Smith, Liverpool L-RTD 4
2013
Feb 9 Callum Smith, Belfast L-RSF 1
July 12 Steve Collins Jnr, Dundalk L-PTS 4
2014
Aug 2 George Hillyard, London L-PTS 6
Nov 30 Matt Scriven, Leeds PTS 4
2015
Feb 6 Rastislav Frano, Leeds PTS 4
Mar 14 Phillip Townley, Belfast RSF 3
June 7 Matt Scriven, Leeds PTS 4
FIGHTS: 25 WON: 8 DREW: 1 LOST: 16

SEAN TURNER
Heavyweight - Born: Dublin, 2 April, 1991

2014
June 14 Zoltan Elekes, Belfast RSF 1
Sep 12 Istvan Ruzsinszky, Dublin KO 4
Nov 1 Moses Matovu, Downpatrick PTS 4
2015
Feb 20 Peter Erdos, Dublin RSF 1
July 4 Janis Ginters, Dublin RTD 1
FIGHTS: 5 WON: 5 DREW: 0 LOST: 0

ANTHONY UPTON
Light-welterweight - Born: London, 15 January, 1992 - Raised in Dublin and Belfast - Based in Romford
2013
Oct 18 Dan Carr, London PTS 4
2014
Mar 21 Alec Bazza, Belfast RSF 4
Apr 26 Kristian Laight, London PTS 4
July 19 Arek Malek, London PTS 4
Sep 10 Siarhei Afonin, Minsk, Belarus PTS 4
Oct 11 Radoslav Mitev, London RSF 2
Dec 13 Janos Vass, London RSF 1
2015
Mar 7 Lubos Priehradnik, London PTS 6
May 16 Istvan Kiss, London KO 3
FIGHTS: 9 WON: 9 DREW: 0 LOST: 0

PAUL UPTON
Light-middleweight - Born: London, 12 July, 1989 - Raised in Dublin and Belfast - Based in Romford
2013
July 27 Dee Mitchell, London PTS 4
Oct 18 Duane Green, London PTS 4
2014
Mar 8 Kevin McCauley, Peterborough PTS 4
Apr 26 Jason McArdle, London PTS 4
Oct 11 Ashley Howard, London RSF 1
2015

Feb 5 Aaron Robinson, London PTS 4
Mar 7 Zoran Cvek, London DSQ 4
Apr 18 Chris Jenkinson, Oldham PTS 6
FIGHTS: 8 WON: 8 DREW: 0 LOST: 0

SONNY UPTON
Light-welterweight - Born: London, 27 June, 1989
2013
Nov 16 Nabil Krissi, Vratsa, Bulgaria L-PTS 6
Dec 6 Traian Dimitrov, Pavia, Italy RSF 2
2014
Feb 15 Kevin McCauley, London PTS 4
May 31 Zoltan Bali, Teguise, Canary Islands KO 1
Sep 10 Vadzim Astapuk, Minsk, Belarus RSF 5
Oct 11 Gary Cooper, London L-RSF 1
2015
Feb 5 Gareth Piper, London PTS 4
Mar 7 Ivan Duvancic, London RSF 4
May 16 Dmitrijs Ovsjannikovs, London PTS 6
FIGHT: 9 WON: 7 DREW: 0 LOST: 2

DEE WALSH
Light-middleweight - Born: Belfast, 4 January, 1990
2011
Sep 17 Gerard Healy, Belfast PTS 4
2012
Feb 18 Lee Noble, Rotherham PTS 4
Apr 14 Tommy Tolan, Belfast RSF 4
June 30 Julio Sanchez, Malaga PTS 4
Sep 22 Robert Studzinski, Belfast PTS 6
2013
Inactive
2014
May 10 Krisztian Duka, Belfast RSF 1
June 14 Jozsef Kormany, Belfast RSF 1
(For vacant International Masters Bronze title)
Oct 4 Adam Grabiec, Belfast PTS 4

Nov 1 Damian Taggart, Downpatrick PTS 4
Nov 22 Terry Maughan, Belfast RSF 2
(For vacant Irish light-middleweight title)
2015
Mar 28 Peter Orlik, Belfast RSF 1
June 6 Patryk Litkiewicz, Belfast PTS 8
FIGHTS: 12 WON: 12 DREW: 0 LOST: 0

GERARD WHITEHOUSE
Welterweight - Born: Balbriggan, 9 August, 1995
2014
Nov 1 Jakub Czaprowicz, Downpatrick RSF 1
2015
Feb 20 Karoly Lakatos, Dublin PTS 4
May 1 Teodor Stefanov, Dublin PTS 4
FIGHTS: 3 WON: 3 DREW: 0 LOST: O

LUKE WILTON
Bantamweight - Born: Barking, 12 May, 1988 – Based in Belfast
2008
Mar 29 Istvan Ajtai, Letterkenny RSF 1
Apr 19 Delroy Spencer, Dublin PTS 4
May 31 Kemal Plavci, Belfast PTS 4
Dec 18 Usman Ahmed, Dublin L-PTS 4
2009
Apr 25 Delroy Spencer, Belfast PTS 4
May 15 Anwar Alfadi, Belfast DREW 6
June 28 Delroy Spencer, Luton L-PTs 4
Nov 6 Kevin Coglan, Belfast PTS 4
Nov 20 Muharen Osmanov, Belfast RSF 1
2010
May 8 Sali Mustafov, Belfast RSF 1
Dec 15 Usman Ahmed, Belfast PTS 6
2011
May 28 Salim Salimov, Belfast RSF 3
Sep 10 Arpad Vass, Belfast PTS 6
2012

Apr 27 Francis Miyeyusho, Belfast RSF 1
(For vacant International Masters super-flyweight title)
Sep 8 Galin Paunov, Belfast RSF 3
Nov 3 Stefan Slavchev, Dublin RSF 2
2013
Feb 23 Kevin Satchell, Liverpool L-PTS 12
(British flyweight title challenge)
June 28 Kallum De'Ath, Belfast PTS 6
Nov 9 Valentin Marinov, Belfast PTS 6
2014
Mar 1 Lee Haskins, Bristol L-RSF 2
May 10 Stefan Slavchev, Belfast PTS 6
2015
Inactive to date
FIGHTS: 21 WON: 16 DREW: 1 LOST: 4

MATTHEW WILTON
Middleweight - Born: Belfast, 20 May, 1990
2012
Apr 27 James Smith, Belfast RTD 1
Sep 8 Gavin Putney, Belfast PTS 4
Oct 13 Liam Griffiths, Belfast PTS 4
Dec 1 Jozsef Garai, Belfast PTS 4
2013
Mar 9 Milos Baraz, Dundalk RSF 1
Apr 27 Johnny Greaves, Belfast RSF 4
June 28 Ideh Ochuko, Belfast PTS 8
Nov 9 Matt Seawright, Belfast PTS 4
2014
Mar 21 Lewie O'Mara, Belfast PTS 6
Sep 6 Adam Cieslak, Belfast PTS 4
2015
Inactive to date
FIGHTS: 10 WON: 10 DREW: 0 LOST: 0

Thanks again for your support.

For more info, visit:

www.irishboxingreview.com

info@irishboxingreview.com

On Twitter: @irishboxreview

Facebook.com/irishboxingreview

Made in the USA
Lexington, KY
22 November 2015